Josette Baer

Alexander Dubček Unknown
(1921–1992)

The Life of a Political Icon

With a foreword by Jan Pešek
and
oral history interviews
with Pavol Dubček and Ivan Laluha

Josette Baer

Alexander Dubček Unknown
(1921–1992)

The Life of a Political Icon

With a foreword by Jan Pešek
and
oral history interviews
with Pavol Dubček and Ivan Laluha

ibidem-Verlag
Stuttgart

Bibliografische Information der Deutschen Nationalbibliothek
Die Deutsche Nationalbibliothek verzeichnet diese Publikation in der
Deutschen Nationalbibliografie; detaillierte bibliografische Daten sind im
Internet über http://dnb.d-nb.de abrufbar.

Bibliographic information published by the Deutsche Nationalbibliothek
Die Deutsche Nationalbibliothek lists this publication in the Deutsche Nationalbibliografie;
detailed bibliographic data are available in the Internet at http://dnb.d-nb.de.

Cover picture: Portrait of the politician and statesman Alexander Dubček, undated, SNK Martin, Slovakia. Reprint with kind permission.

∞
Gedruckt auf alterungsbeständigem, säurefreien Papier
Printed on acid-free paper

ISBN-13: 978-3-8382-1126-8

© *ibidem*-Verlag
Stuttgart 2018

Alle Rechte vorbehalten

Das Werk einschließlich aller seiner Teile ist urheberrechtlich geschützt. Jede Verwertung außerhalb der engen Grenzen des Urheberrechtsgesetzes ist ohne Zustimmung des Verlages unzulässig und strafbar. Dies gilt insbesondere für Vervielfältigungen, Übersetzungen, Mikroverfilmungen und elektronische Speicherformen sowie die Einspeicherung und Verarbeitung in elektronischen Systemen.

All rights reserved. No part of this publication may be reproduced, stored in or introduced into a retrieval system, or transmitted, in any form, or by any means (electronic, mechanical, photocopying, recording or otherwise) without the prior written permission of the publisher. Any person who does any unauthorized act in relation to this publication may be liable to criminal prosecution and civil claims for damages.

Printed in the EU

This study is dedicated to my husband Peter who has been supporting my research for years, in academic and psychological terms. One could not wish for a better friend.

Table of Contents

Foreword by Jan Pešek XI
Abbreviations XIII
Acknowledgements XVII

X.   Introduction 1
    X. 1   Alexander Dubček – Naïve Apparatchik,
           Independent Thinker, Courageous Reformer,
           or Political Dreamer? 1
    X. 2   Analytical Framework and Conceptual Matrix 12
         X. 2. 1   Analytical Framework 12
         X. 2. 2   Conceptual Matrix 14
    X. 3   Method, Key Issues, Research Interest 15
         X. 3. 1   Method: Contextual Biography 15
         X. 3. 2   Key Issues 17
                X. 3. 2. 1 Czechoslovakism and the Czechoslovak
                          Nation 17
                X. 3. 2. 2 *Rovný s Rovným* – The Three Prague
                          Agreements (1945–1946) 30
                X. 3. 2. 3 The Relationship between the KSČ
                          and the KSS (1948–1967) 43
         X. 3. 3   Research Questions 47

I.   Childhood, Early Years and Education (1921–1939) . 51
    I. 1   Childhood in Soviet Kyrgyzia and Gorky
         (1925–1938) 51
    I. 2   The Soviet Purges of the 1930s and Return to
         Czechoslovakia (1938) 56

II.   Dear Sasha – A Career in the Communist Party
      (1939–1968) 63
    II. 1   The Slovak National Uprising (1944) 63
    II. 2   Political Training in Moscow (1955–1958) 68
    II. 3   The Slovak *predjarie* (Pre-Spring) (1963–1967) 73

	II. 3. 1	Currency Reform and the Consumer Goods Industry (1953–1958) 75
	II. 3. 2	The Scientific-Technical Revolution (early 1960s) 78
	II. 3. 3	The Rehabilitation Commissions (1955–1968) ... 80
II. 4	First Secretary of the KSS (1963–1968) 85	
	II. 4. 1	A Soviet Cosmonaut (1963) 88
	II. 4. 2	A Rebellious Party Member (1964) 94
	II. 4. 3	Ideological Unity and Party Discipline à la Novotný (1964) 98
	II. 4. 4	'Electing' the President and the Tasks of Loyal Journalists (1964) 105
	II. 4. 5	Comrade Cvik (1965) 110
	II. 4. 6	A Failed Intrigue: The Dubčeks in the SNP (1965–1967) 113
	II. 4. 7	The Affair of the Bear (1966) 124
	II. 4. 8	Anonymous Letters (1963, 1966) 132
II. 5	The Eight Months of the Czechoslovak Spring (1968) 141	

III. Oblivion? Dubček's Dissent and Return to Politics (1969–1992) **159**

- III. 1 Soviet Salami Tactics 160
- III. 2 The Politics of Normalization 171
  - III. 2. 1 The Purges at Charles University (1969) 173
  - III. 2. 2 Travel Restrictions 179
- III. 3 Everyday Life in Czechoslovakia 181
  - III. 3. 1 Fear 181
  - III. 3. 2 The Weekend, Socialization and Humour 184
  - III. 3. 3 The Underground 188
- III. 4 Dissent and Return to Politics (1970–1989) 191
  - III. 4. 1 Dubček's Protest Letters 191
  - III. 4. 2 The StB's Psychological Terror 199
  - III. 4. 3 November 1989 and the Transition to Democracy 204

Conclusion **211**

Oral History Interview with Pavol Dubček, MD **219**

Oral History Interview with Professor Ivan Laluha **222**

Oral History Interview with Mr Miloslav Liška **227**

Appendix **231**
    Dubček in Data 231
    Chronology... 233
    Bibliography... 253
    Index.. 273

Foreword by Jan Pešek

This year in August, the Slovaks and Czechs remember what happened fifty years ago: the Czechoslovak Spring of 1968 and its brutal end by Warsaw Pact troops. The Czechoslovak Spring has been well researched, or so the knowledgeable Western reader might think. This latest biography of Alexander Dubček by the Swiss political scientist and historian Josette Baer, a renowned specialist on Czechoslovak and Slovak history and political thought, presents a new approach to the political history of Slovakia and Czechoslovakia. As the first non-Slovak historian, Baer investigates two crucially important chapters of Slovak history that so far have been under-researched: the years of the Pre-Spring from 1963 to 1968 and the years of the so-called Normalization (1969–1989).

The liberalization of the Czechoslovak Communist regime began in 1963 with Dubček's election as First Secretary of the Slovak Communist Party KSS; the Czechoslovak Spring originated in Bratislava and, with Dubček's election to First Secretary of the Czechoslovak Communist Party KSČ in January 1968, the way for the reformers was free. Baer focuses on Dubček's career in the KSS in the 1960s and his dissent in the 1970s. After the Communist Party had relieved him from all functions in Party and state, Dubček, the former most powerful politician of Czechoslovakia, found employment at the State Forestry in Bratislava. The State Security Service StB monitored him and his family every day, exerting psychological terror to the maximum. The Normalization regime under General Secretary KSČ and President in personal union Gustáv Husák wanted to delete Dubček and his reform course from Czechoslovak collective memory – an endeavour that was not only unsuccessful but would backfire in November 1989: the Communist Party was brought down in 10 days by the people, who had not forgotten Dubček and his attempt at Socialism with a Human Face.

Baer's biography closes important gaps in international and interdisciplinary scholarship about the Czechoslovak Spring. Her book is a must-read for everybody interested in the history of Central Europe in the 20th Century and the history of European Communism alike.

Jan Pešek, Bratislava, August 2018

Abbreviations

Archives and libraries

ABS ÚSTRČR Archiv Bezpečnostných Složek – Ústav pro Studium Totalitních Režimů České Republiky – Archives of the State Security Services at the Institute for the Study of Totalitarian Regimes of the Czech Republic, Prague.

AMSNP Archív Múzeum Slovenského Národného Povstania – Archives of the Museum of the Slovak National Uprising, Banská Bystrica, Slovak Republic.

HÚ SAV Historický Ústav Slovenskej Akadémie Vied – Institute of History at the Slovak Academy of Sciences, Bratislava, Slovak Republic.

SNA Slovenský Národný Archív, Bratislava – The Slovak National Archives, Bratislava, Slovak Republic.

SNK Slovenská Národná Knižnica, Martin – The Slovak National Library, Martin, Slovak Republic.

Political parties, associations and organizations; media

CC KSČ Central Committee of the Czechoslovak Communist Party

CC KSS Central Committee of the Slovak Communist Party

COMECON Council for Mutual Economic Assistance; see RVHP

CP Communist Party

ČSNB Československá Národní Banka – Czechoslovak State Bank

ČSSD	Česká Strana Sociálně Demokratická – Czech Social Democratic Party
ČSTK	Československá Tlačová Kancelária – Czechoslovak Press Chancellery
ČT	Česká Televize – Czech National TV
DS	Demokratická Strana – Slovak Democratic Party
FZ	Federálne Zhromaždenie – Federal Assembly
HG	Hlinkova Garda – Hlinka Guards
HSĽS	Hlinkova Slovenská Ľudová Strana – Hlinka's Slovak People's Party
HZDS	Hnutie Za Demokratické Slovensko – Movement for a Democratic Slovakia
IMF	International Monetary Fund
KPSS	Komunističeskaia Partiia Sovetskogo Soiuza – Communist Party of the Soviet Union
ÚKRK KSČ	Ústřední Kontrolní a Revízni Komise KSČ – Central Control and Revision Commission of the Communist Party of Czechoslovakia
ÚKRK KSS	Ústředná Kontrolná a Revízná Komisia KSS – Central Control and Revision Commission of the Slovak Communist Party
KSČ	Komunistická Strana Československa – Communist Party of Czechoslovakia
KSS	Komunistická Strana Slovenska – Slovak Communist Party
MP	Member of Parliament
MV	Ministerstvo Vnútra – Ministry of Interior, Slovakia
MZV	Ministerstvo Zahraničních Věcí – Czechoslovak Ministry of Foreign Affairs

NAM	Non-Aligned Movement
NATO	North Atlantic Treaty Organisation
NF	Národní Fronta – National Front
NKVD	Narodnii Kommissariat Vnutrënnikh Del – The People's Commissariat for Internal Affairs
ODS	Občanská Demokratická Strana – Czech Civic Democratic Party
OF	Občánské Forum – Czech Civic Forum
RVHP	Rada vzájomnej hospodárskej pomoci – Council for Mutual Economic Assistance
SDSS	Sociálnodemokratická strana Slovenska – Social Democratic Party of Slovakia
SPS	Slovenský Poslanecký Klub – Slovak Parliamentarians Club
SĽS	Slovenská Ľudová Strana – Slovak People's Party
SNP	Slovenské Národnie Povstanie – Slovak National Uprising
SNR	Slovenská Národná Ráda – Slovak National Council
SNS	Slovenská Národná Strana – Slovak National Party
SSl	Strana Slobody – Slovak Party of Freedom
SSSR	Soiuz Sovietskich Socialističeskich Respublik – Union of the Soviet Socialist Republics
StB	Státní Bezpečnost – Czechoslovak State Security Service
STV	Slovenská Televízia – Slovak National TV
TASR	Tľačová Agentura Slovenskej Republiky – Slovak Press Agency

ÚV KSČ	Ústředný Výbor Komunistická Strana Československa – Central Committee of the Communist Party of Czechoslovakia
ÚV KSS	Ústředný Výbor Komunistická Strana Slovenska – Central Committee of the Slovak Communist Party
VPN	Verejnosť proti násiliu – Slovak Public Against Violence
ZNB	Zbor Národnej Bezpečnosti – Corps of National Security, Slovakia

Acknowledgements

Not another biography of Alexander Dubček! Surely, – all there is to say about the Prague Spring of 1968 has already been said – or so the historically informed reader might think. True, Dubček's reform programme (*akční program*) and the military invasion by Warsaw Pact troops on 21 August 1968 have been widely researched and analysed. Therefore, the eight months of the Czechoslovak Spring are not the focus of this political biography, but Czechoslovakia and Slovakia's political history prior to and after the invasion of 1968, embodied in the life of Alexander Dubček. The archive material I found in Slovak and Czech archives is available to the English reader for the first time.

Two main aspects of Dubček's life are unknown to the Western reader; these are the gaps I aim to fill with this book. First, Dubček's career in the Slovak Communist Party KSS in the 1960s that culminated with his election as First Secretary of the Czechoslovak Communist Party KSČ in January 1968, providing him with the legislative, executive and judicial power to embark on his reform course. Second, his life after June 1969, when, back home after some months as Czechoslovak ambassador to Turkey, he was ousted from all functions in state and Party.

A principal goal of the Normalization regime (1969–1989) was to efface Dubček from the collective memory of the Czechoslovak people. The almighty StB (State Security Service) had him and his family under constant surveillance, but they could not silence him. After 1969, Dubček was a dissident in the truest sense of the Latin *dissidere*, which means 'sitting apart': a former insider who became an outsider, a fellow believer who dared to protest against the powers that be, among them, Gustáv Husák.

In this volume, I have tried to convey to the reader how the Cold War and the Soviet Union's role in it affected the political history of Central Europe – and with that, the life of a leading Czechoslovak Communist who believed in Marxism-Leninism and the rightfulness of his political reforms. I have tried to probe into Dubček's thought and activities with a dispassionate, rational and fair approach.

My thanks: The Stiftung zur Förderung der wissenschaftlichen Forschung of the University of Zurich UZH granted me a generous stipend, which allowed me to do research in Slovak and Czech archives. I am greatly indebted to my colleagues and friends for their interest in my research and willingness to discuss specific issues with me. In alphabetical order: Jozef Banáš, Mária Banášová, Juraj Benko, Vladimír Handl, Michael Hässig, Karen Henderson, Vlasta Jaksicsová, Lukas Joos, Marina Jozef, Juraj Kalina, Ivan Kamenec, Miloslav Liška, Miroslav Londák, Anna Mazurkiewicz, Slavomír Michálek, Delia Popescu, Francis Raska, Jaroslava Roguľová, Marc Winter and my great friend XY, whose wish for anonymity I respect.

I would like to thank Dušan Čabrak, deputy major of Uhrovec, and the lovely guide Mrs Mikušová for taking the time to show me the birthplace of Alexander Dubček in Uhrovec, now a museum, in July 2017. The ladies at the SNK Martin were, as always, professional, friendly, swift and uncomplicated: Ľudmila Šimková, Karin Šišmišová, Miroslava Pražková and everybody else who helped me with the material – thank you. Deputy director Augustin Matovčik SNK went to great lengths to help me with pressing copyright problems. Mária Zsigmondová and Marek Púčik at the Slovak National Archives SNA in Bratislava were very helpful, friendly and professional. My thanks go also to Jitka Bílková, Veronika Chroma, Juraj Kalina and Michal Kurej at the Archives of the State Security Forces at the Institute for the Study of Totalitarian Regimes (ABS ÚSTRČR) in Prague. Lisa Brun at the Institute of Philosophy at UZH took care of the financial management of this project.

The ladies at the housing office of the Slovak Academy of Sciences SAV have made my annual research stays since 2008 such a joyful and uncomplicated matter: Maria Vallová, Božena and Ľubica Konečná, thank you. Valerie Lange at ***ibidem*** publishers is an exceptionally patient, effective and supportive editor. I thank Peter Thomas Hill for proofreading my manuscript and teaching me how to express myself in elegant and scholarly English.

This study could not have been written without Stanislav Sikora and Jan Pešek's expertise. Stanislav was my supervisor, teaching me how the liberalization of the regime began in Slovakia, from where it spread to the Czech part. From his publications, I learnt about the Slovak Pre-Spring (*predjarie*). Jan Pešek, a specialist on the history of the KSS, was also extremely helpful, explaining to me the complicated relationship between the KSS and the KSČ, and the non-existent balance of power between the two political parties. Thanks to Stanislav and Jan, I was able to understand how the *predjarie* changed Czechoslovak society, and the citizens' support of Dubček's Reform Communism.

My very special thanks go to Pavol Dubček, Ivan Laluha and Miloslav Liška, who answered all my questions, thereby contributing to our Western knowledge about politics and daily life under Communism, the aftermath of the Velvet Revolution of 1989, the Velvet Divorce of 1992 and sports under the Communist regime.

Needless to say, any errors and shortcomings in this volume are my own.

Josette Baer
Zurich, Bratislava and Prague, August 2018

X. Introduction[1]

X. 1 Alexander Dubček – Naïve Apparatchik, Independent Thinker, Courageous Reformer, or Political Dreamer?

> "From him radiated what one calls the magic of charisma. He conquered people by taking a genuine interest in them and with a pure and direct smile. From his eyes sprang kindness and benevolence. He was not ashamed to admit that he did not know a thing. He was not a convincing speaker, rather the opposite, but it was wonderful that people believed him. For the first time, a Communist leader stood before the people who, they felt, had a human heart."[2]

The former most powerful politician of Czechoslovakia was a pensioner, living quietly in Bratislava, when the Velvet Revolution of November 1989 started in Prague and immediately spread to Slovakia. The mass protests of Czech and Slovak citizens, the foundation of the OF in the Czech part and the VPN in Slovakia and the country-wide general strike, in which the state media participated, led to the abdication of the KSČ. The events catapulted the 68-year-old Dubček onto the political scene of a

---

[1] All translations from Slovak and Czech into English are by me, if not otherwise referred to. I shall be using the concept "Marxism-Leninism" as the official ideology of the Soviet bloc after 1945 since I focus on Dubček's political thought and his belief in Marxism-Leninism, not the theoretical details of Marxism and Marxism-Leninism.

[2] Jozef Banáš, *Zastavte Dubčeka! Príbeh človeka, ktorý prekážal mocným* (Bratislava: Ikar, 2009), 145. This popular biography is very well researched. Banáš is a historical witness: in 1968, he was 20 years old. Large parts of his book are fiction, that is, how Dubček could have acted and what he could have said. However, in the context of Slovak history and the Slovaks' way of thinking and acting, Banáš's extraordinarily talent for imagination renders his biography authentic. See: http://www.jozefbanas.sk/index.php/english; accessed 5 June 2017.

new Czechoslovakia, a country that was about to reconnect with its democratic traditions after 41 years of Communist rule.

I wondered how Dubček began his career in the KSS and KSČ. As a young Party member, he was too insignificant to raise suspicions of 'Slovak bourgeois nationalism' in the early 1950s, hence was not one of the accused in the 1954 trial of elder, prominent Slovak Party members born at the turn of the 20th century. Furthermore, young Dubček was from proper proletarian stock; he was raised in a Communist family and grew up in Soviet Kyrgyzia, where his family had moved in 1925 to support the building of Socialism – in the Party's ever watchful and powerful eyes, he was beyond suspicion.

I was curious about the origins of the idea of reforming the Socialist system: did Dubček have his own ideas about a reform course or did he follow the Soviet party line that embarked on a course of de-Stalinization, after General Secretary Nikita S. Krushchev (1894–1971) had criticized Stalin's crimes in his secret speech to the 20th Congress of the Soviet Communist Party on 25 February 1956? In 1956, Dubček was in Moscow, attending the Higher School of Politics of the Soviet Communist Party; because he spoke Russian fluently, he had a particular close insight into the significance of Krushchev's speech – and what consequences the revelations about Stalin's crimes could prompt for the states of the Soviet bloc.

Furthermore, I wanted to get a better understanding of the relationship between the Czechoslovak and Slovak Communist parties, which – to some extent – reflect the relationship between Czechs and Slovaks ever since the end of WWII. The Slovak Communist Party (KSS) was founded in 1939 as an illegal organization in the Slovak state, while the leaders of the Czech Communist Party (KSČ) fled to Moscow after the Munich Agreement in 1938. In June 1945, the KSČ, then completely under Stalin's control, allowed the KSS some autonomy in Slovakia, hoping that the Party would emerge victorious from the parliamentary elections of 1946. When this plan did not work out – the centre-right Democratic Party (DS) won in Slovakia – the KSČ changed its strategy: it subordinated the KSS under its leadership to gather strength and discipline for the assumption of power.

Alexander Dubček is so well known, nothing new can be written about him – or so one might think. Is this true? What do we really know about the father of Czechoslovakia's reform communism? Dubček is the symbol of *Socialism with a Human Face*.[3] The Western reader knows about Dubček's career in the Czechoslovak Communist Party (KSČ) only from his memoirs.[4] A study of his early years, that is, before he and his followers in the Party's top echelons launched the reform course in 1968, is more than due, especially in view of the 50th anniversary of the Czechoslovak Spring in 2018.

Up to date, there is no scholarly analysis available in an international language that informs the reader about Dubček's early career in the Slovak Communist Party (KSS) prior to his election as First Secretary[5] of the KSČ in January 1968. The

---

[3] The origin of the expression *Socialism with a Human Face* is unclear: According to Zdeněk Mlynář (1930–1997) and Ota Šik (1919–2004), the Czech sociologist Radovan Richta (1924–1983) coined the expression. The Czech journalist and translator Antonín J. Liehm (*1924) thinks that Western Communists invented the expression to give Czechoslovak Reform Communism a positive name; Vlasta Jaksicsová, "Spor o Dubčeka", in DUBČEK (Bratislava: Veda, 2018), 1–14, 3.

[4] Alexander Dubček, *Leben für die Freiheit* (München: Bertelsmann, 1993); *Hope Dies Last. The Autobiography of Alexander Dubcek* (London: HarperCollins, 1993).

[5] The KSČ changed the title of 'First Secretary' to 'General Secretary' in 1971, following slavishly the Soviet Communist Party under Brezhnev, while the KSS kept the title 'First Secretary'; Jan Pešek, *Centrum Moci. Aparát Ústredného výboru Komunistickej strany Slovenska 1948–1989* (Bratislava: AEP, 2006), 21. For a history of the KSS see Jan Pešek, *Komunistická*

Czechoslovak Spring has been subject to various historical analyses, but all studies, translations of documents and biographies[6] focus on Dubček's eight months as First Secretary, the famous action programme (*akční program*)[7] that his government launched in April 1968, the invasion[8] of the Warsaw Pact troops on the night of 21 August 1968, and his subsequent fall from Leonid I. Brezhnev's (1906–1982) grace.

Who was the person and politician Dubček? How could he gain power in the KSS, convincing the Stalinists to go along with a reform course in the early 1960s, while the Czech comrades were suffering under First Secretary Antonín Novotný's (1904–1975) Stalinist style of government? What were the ideological origins and intellectual inspiration of his reform course – the new Soviet thinking about the future of Socialism[9] or his own

---

Strana Slovenska. Dejiny politického subjektu I. (Bratislava: Veda, 2012). A planned second volume did not materialize.

[6] In chronological order: *Dubček's Blueprint for Freedom. His Documents on Czechoslovakia Leading to the Soviet Invasion* (London: William Kimber, 1969); Pavel Tigrid, *Why Dubcek Fell* (London: Macdonald, 1971); Gordon H. Skilling, *Czechoslovakia's Interrupted Revolution* (Princeton, NJ: Princeton University Press, 1976); *Sedm pražských dnů. 21–27. srpen 1968. Dokumentace* (Praha: Academia, 1990); William Shawcross, *Dubcek. Revised and Updated Edition* (New York: Touchstone, 1990); Kieran Williams, *The Prague Spring and its Aftermath. Czechoslovak Politics, 1968–1970* (Cambridge, New York: Cambridge University Press, 1997).

[7] An English translation of the *akční program* in *Hope Dies Last*, 287–335.

[8] *Strategic Warning & the Role of Intelligence. Lessons learnt from the 1968 Soviet Invasion of Czechoslovakia* (CreateSpace Independent Publishing Platform, 2012); Matthew J. Ouimet, *The Rise and Fall of the Brezhnev Doctrine in Soviet Foreign Policy* (Chapel Hill, London: The University of North Carolina Press, 2003). For a Slovak analysis of the French media's coverage of the invasion see Pavol Petruf, "Vojenská intervencia krajín Varšavskej zmluvy v Československu v auguste 1968 na stránkach publikovaných francúzskych diplomatických dokumentov", in *Slovensko a Európa medzi Demokraciou a Totalitou. Kapitoly z dejín 20. Storočia k jubileu Bohumily Ferenčuhovej* (Bratislava: Veda, 2017), 213–229.

[9] Michail Gorbačov a Zdeněk Mlynář, *Reformátoři nebývají šťastni. Dialog o „perestrojce", Pražském jaru a socialismu* (Praha: Victoria Publishing, 1994), 21. The English translation is *Conversations with Gorbachev. On*

reform ideas that originated in the particularly complex environment of Czech and Slovak Communism?[10]

Slovak historians have published several excellent studies about the *predjarie*, the precursor or run-up to the Czechoslovak Spring that had begun in Slovakia in 1963 in the context of the lukewarm rehabilitation of the victims of the show trials of the 1950s, a rehabilitation that Dubček as First Secretary of the KSS had initiated and presided over.[11] Unfortunately, they are not available in an international language. The Institute of History of the Slovak Academy of Sciences HÚ SAV published a selection of Dubček's speeches, newspaper articles and

---

perestroika, socialism, the Prague Spring and the crossroads of socialism (New York: Columbia University Press, 2002). See also Zdeněk Mlynář's memoirs of the Prague Spring *Mraz přichází z Kremlu* (Köln: Index, 1979).

[10] The best reference book in English about Slovakia's history is Mikuláš Teich, Dušan Kováč and Martin D. Brown, eds., *Slovakia in History* (Cambridge: Cambridge University Press, 2011). See also the encyclopaedia of Slovak history by Vojtech Dangl, Valerián Bystrický a kol., *Chronológia Dejín Slovenska a Slovákov. Od najstarších čias po súčasnosť. Dejiny v dátumoch, dátumy v dejinách, vol I a II* (Bratislava: Veda, 2014). A superb account of Slovakia's economic and political development is Miroslav Londák, Slavomír Michálek, Peter Weiss et al., *Slovakia. A European Story* (Bratislava: Veda, 2016). Highly recommendable about the Communist era is Jan Kalous a Jiří Kocian, eds., *Český a slovenský komunismus (1921–2011)* (Praha: Ústav pro studium totalitních režimů, 2012). See also the chronology of Czechoslovakia's foreign policy by Pavol Petruf, *Československá zahraničná politika 1945-1992 (vybrané udalosti a fakty v dátumoch)* (Bratislava: Prodama, HÚ SAV, 2007).

[11] Miroslav Londák, Stanislav Sikora a Elena Londáková, *Predjarie. Politický, ekonomický a kultúrny vývoj na Slovensku v rokoch 1960–1967* (Bratislava: VEDA, 2002); Valerián Bystrický a kol., *Rok 1968 na Slovensku a v Československu* (Bratislava: HÚ SAV, 2008); Miroslav Londák, Stanislav Sikora a kol., *Rok 1968 a jeho miesto v našich dejinách* (Bratislava: Veda, 2009); Stanislav Sikora, *Po Jari krutá zima* (Bratislava: Veda, 2013); Miroslav Londák, Stanislav Sikora a Elena Londáková, *Od predjaria k normalizácii. Slovensko v Československu na rozhraní 60. a 70. rokov 20. storočia* (Bratislava: VEDA, 2016).

interviews that had appeared from 1963 to 1992.[12] A bibliography of Dubček's speeches, interviews and radio broadcasts and studies about him was published in 2007.[13] A compilation of memoirs of Dubček's relatives, friends and acquaintances was published in 1998; among the authors was the Soviet physicist and Nobel Peace Laureate Andreii D. Sakharov (1921–1989).[14]

In January 1968, Dubček convinced the majority of the CC of the KSČ that Novotný posed a serious threat to Czechoslovakia because he was alienating the Czechs from the Slovaks, risking the state's sovereignty by driving a wedge between the Slovaks and Czechs, whose relations had been more than difficult since WWII. On his official visit to Slovakia in August 1967, Novotný offended the Slovak people and the KSS leadership.[15] The almighty State Security Service StB wanted to get rid of Novotný too because he had ordered that they compose lists of persons to be arrested – one had to expect a new purge (*čistka*), a renaissance of the Stalinist terror of the 1950s. In January 1968, the CC of the KSČ elected Dubček First Secretary – and the atmosphere in the country swiftly changed: the citizens were optimistic that the times of brutal Stalinist terror were over. A new era of liberalization began. Hopes were high that

---

[12] Jozef Žatkuliak a Ivan Laluha, eds., *Alexander Dubček: Od totality k demokracii. Prejavy, články a rozhovory. Výber 1963–1992* (Bratislava: Veda, 2002).

[13] Soňa Šváčová, Michela Garaiová, Anna Klimová a Blanka Snopková, *Alexander Dubček v slovenskej a českej tlači* (Banská Bystrica: Štátna vedecká knižnica, 2007). The bibliography covers the years 1963 to 2004.

[14] Tereza Michálova, ed., *Dubček známy neznámy* (Bratislava: Prospero, 1989 (2)). The volume contains memoirs of Dubček's friends, relatives and Slovak politicians, among them statements of his sons, his granddaughter, his dentist, his Italian friend Vittorio Caffeo, former Slovak president Michal Kováč (1930–2016) and Russian physicist and nobel laureate Andreii Sakharov (1921–1989).

[15] Dušan Kováč, *Dejiny Slovenska* (Praha: Lidové Noviny, 2007 (2)), 283.

Communism could not only be reformed, but also made more human and less violent.

Jo Langer (1912–1990), whose husband Oscar Langer had been arrested in 1951 to serve as a 'witness' in the show trial[16] of the Zionist and Titoist conspiracy against the state in November 1952, described her mixed feelings at the advent of the reforms:

> "It is difficult if not impossible to explain to a westerner why we sat in front of the TV in a trance of gratitude [...] Total strangers exchanged smiles, listened to each other's transistor radios in the streetcar and discussed events. [...] I felt the charm of all this. I wanted to rejoice so much that there were times when I almost did. [...] I felt increasingly that this 'new socialism' was only skin deep. The Party remained infallible."[17]

My biography focuses on two under-researched aspects of or phases in Dubček's life: first, *his career in the KSS after the end of WWII,* which resulted in his election as First Secretary of the KSS in 1963 and First Secretary of the KSČ in 1968; and second, *his years in political oblivion* after the KSČ relieved him of all functions in Party and state in April 1969. Gustáv Husák (1913–1991), who had spent almost a decade in prison (1954–1963)

---

[16] On the 1952 show trial see Artur London, *On Trial* (London: Macdonald, 1970); Karel Kaplan, *Report on the Murder of the General Secretary* (Columbus: Ohio State University Press, 1990); Igor Lukes, *Rudolf Slansky. His Trial and Trials. Cold War International History Project Working Paper no. 50* (Washington, D.C.: Woodrow Wilson Center, 2008), on http://www.wilsoncenter.org/sites/default/files/WP50IL.pdf.Slánský; accessed 6 June 2017

[17] Jo Langer, *Convictions. My Life with a Good Communist* (London: Granta, 2011), 214. Langer's memoirs in Slovak: Jo Langerová, *Môj život s Oscarom L.* (Bratislava: Marenčin PT, 2007). Prominent members of the 1952 show trial were Rudolf Slánský (1901–1952) and Vladimír Clementis (1902–1952). The first biography of Vladimír Clementis in English is my *'Spirits that I've cited?' Vladimír Clementis (1902–1952). The Political Biography of a Czechoslovak Communist* (Stuttgart, New York: ibidem, Columbia University Press, 2017).

for his alleged 'Slovak bourgeois nationalism', followed him in office, establishing the course of Normalization on Moscow's diktat.[18] Note that I shall not deal with the invasion of the Warsaw Pact troops, since Pauer's superb study explains and analyses to the full the preparation, conduct and consequences of the military invasion of 21 August 1968.[19]

Dubček grew up in a Communist family and spent the crucially important years as a young child and teenager in the Soviet Union, hence in a strictly Communist environment. He did not experience the democratic system and civil liberties of the Czechoslovak Republic, which President Tomáš Garrigue Masaryk (1850–1937)[20] had established on 28 October 1918 after

---

[18] The first academic biography of Husák is Slavomír Michálek, Miroslav Londák a kol., *Gustáv Husák. Moc politiky. Politik moci* (Bratislava: Veda, 2013). For a review see my "A Man Motivated by Power", *New Eastern Europe 4*, no. 5 (2014): 156–160. See also my attempt at a psychological profile of Husák in "Vertrauen ist nichts, Macht ist alles. Gustáv Husák (1913–1991) und die tschechoslowakische Normalisierung. Versuch eines politischen Psychogramms", in *Vertrauen* (Basel: Schwabe, 2015), 161–179. For an excellent analysis of the trial of the 'Slovak bourgeois nationalists' and its connection with the Slánský trial see Jan Pešek, "Nepriateľ so stranickou legitimáciou. Proces s tzv. Slovenskými buržoáznymi nacionalistami", in *Storočie procesov. Súdy, politika a spoločnosť v moderných dejinách Slovenska* (Bratislava: Veda, 2013), 210–226.

[19] Jan Pauer, *Prag 1968. Der Einmarsch des Warschauer Paktes. Hintergründe – Planung – Durchführung* (Bremen: Edition Temmen, 1995).

[20] A selection of studies in chronological order: Otakar Funda, *Thomas Garrigue Masaryk. Sein philosophisches, religiöses und politisches Denken* (Bern: Peter Lang, 1978); Roland J. Hoffmann, *Thomas G. Masaryk und die tschechische Frage* (München: Oldenbourg, 1988); Jozef Novák, ed., *On Masaryk. Texts in English and German* (Amsterdam: Rodopi, 1988); Stanley B. Winters, ed., *T. G. Masaryk (1850–1937). Thinker and Politician* (Basingstoke: MacMillan, SSEES, University of London, 1989); Robert B. Pynsent, ed., *T. G. Masaryk (1850–1937). Thinker and Critic* (Basingstoke: MacMillan, SSEES, University of London, 1989, 1990); Harry Hanák, ed., *T. G. Masaryk (1850–1937). Statesman and Cultural Force* (Basingstoke: MacMillan, SSEES, University of London, 1990); Jaroslav Opat, *Filozof a politik T. G. Masaryk, 1882–1893* (Praha: Melantrich, 1990); *Masaryk a myšlenka evropské jednoty* (Praha: Filosofická Fakulta Univerzity Karlovy FFUK, 1992); Zwi Batscha, *Eine Philosophie der Demokratie. Thomas G.*

four tireless years of lobbying in France, Great Britain and the USA. To Dubček, democracy both as a theory of society and a political system was unknown, if not politically alien. Owing to the fact that young Alexander was from proper proletarian stock, hence had a perfect class background and spoke Russian fluently, the Party allowed him to embark on a political career after the Communist coup d'état of 1948. In the Party's eyes, he was the embodiment or role model of the future generation of Communists: young, loyal, modest, decent and disciplined. After the "victorious 25 February 1948" (*vítězní únor*)[21] had ended the three years of limited democracy of the National Front (NF) under President Edvard Beneš (1884–1948), Dubček received a position in a factory and would be sent to Moscow to the Party school.

Masaryks Begründung einer neuzeitlichen Demokratie (Frankfurt a. Main: Suhrkamp, 1994); Dalibor Truhlar, *Thomas G. Masaryk. Philosophie der Demokratie* (Frankfurt a. Main: Peter Lang, 1994); Josette Baer, *Politik als praktizierte Sittlichkeit. Zum Demokratiebegriff von Thomas G. Masaryk und Václav Havel* (Sinzheim: Pro Universitate, 1998) and Radan Hain, *Staatstheorie und Staatsrecht in T. G. Masaryks Ideenwelt* (Zürich: Schulthess, 1999). See also the Masaryk Institute and the Archive of the Academy of Sciences of the Czech Republic MÚA in Prague on https://www.mua.cas.cz; accessed 9 June 2017.

[21] Selected and recommended studies in chronological order: Karel Kaplan, *The Short March. The Communist Takeover in Czechoslovakia 1945–1948* (London: Hurst & Co, 1987); *1948. Únor 1948 v Československu: Nástup komunistické totality a proměny společnosti* (Praha: Ústav pro soudobé dějiny AV ČR, v.v.i., 2011); various authors, "Na cestě k moci a ovládnutí státu", in *Český a slovenský komunismus,* 70–116. For an analysis of the political persecutions after 1948 in Slovakia see Jan Pešek, "Najbrutálnejšie obdobie komunistického režimu (1948–1953)", in *Štátna moc a spoločnosť na Slovensku 1945 – 1948 – 1989* (Bratislava: HÚ SAV a Prodama, 2013), 193–311. For an analysis of media reports about the 'victorious 25 February 1948' see Stanislav Holubec, "Léta 1948–1949", in *Ještě nejsme za vodou. Obrazy druhých a historická paměť v období postkomunistické transformace* (Praha: Scriptorium, 2015), 124–136. I thank Francis Raska for recommending Holubec's study to me.

Krushchev's secret speech prompted the *thaw*, the short-term liberalization in domestic affairs of the bloc states and Soviet relations with the principal class enemy, the USA. In Marxist-Leninist terms, the Stalin cult and the crimes and purges committed under the reign of the *velikii vožd* (the Great Leader Stalin) had been a subjective aberration, a mistaken interpretation of the legacy of Marx and Lenin. In its perennial wisdom, the Soviet CP understood the objective signs of the times, the need for social, political and economic reforms – which prompted an immediate change of the political course in the bloc states. These changes in domestic and foreign policy are commonly referred to as *de-Stalinization*.

Communism in Czechoslovakia collapsed in November 1989 with the Velvet Revolution; the Cold War ceased to exist in 1991 with the dissolution of the Warsaw Pact. Finally, after twenty years being a *persona non grata* to the Party and the public, Alexander Dubček experienced reverence and respect at home and abroad. The Czechoslovak parliament elected him chairman of the Federal Assembly, a position he held until his untimely death: on 7 November 1992, when the separation of Czechoslovakia into two sovereign states was already fixed in the agreement of the peaceful separation[22] that would become known as the Velvet Divorce, he died of the injuries of a car

---

[22] Two recommendable Slovak studies are Jozef Žatkuliak and Peter Weiss, "The Slovak National Council's Role in the Constitutional Development from 1990 to 1992 and the Trouble Slovakia Encountered on Its Way towards Sovereignty", in *Slovakia. A European Story*, 71–114; Slavomír Michálek and Peter Weiss, "The Foreign Policy Context of the Break-Up of Czechoslovakia from 1989 to 1992 and the Relations of Prague and Bratislava with Washington", in *Slovakia. A European Story*, 117–158. A very detailed Czech analysis of the Velvet Divorce is Jan Rychlík, *Rozdělení Česko-Slovenska, 1989–1992*. (Praha: Vyšehrad, 2012).

accident that had happened on 1 September 1992.[23] On 1 January 1993, Slovakia became a sovereign state, in spite of the fact that the separation was a violation of the democratic Federal Constitution (ČSFR).[24] After some years of political difficulties – one could call them teething troubles of the new political system – the Slovak Republic joined NATO and the EU in 2004, finally firmly in the West.

Let me now present the contents of this study: In chapter I, I introduce the reader to Dubček's childhood, upbringing, and early political activities in the KSS (1921–1939). Chapter II deals with his political activities during WWII, the SNP, and his career in the Party that peaked with the Czechoslovak Spring (1939–1968). Chapter III focuses on his dissident activities in the years of the Normalization and his comeback to Czechoslovak politics during the Velvet Revolution (1969–1992). In the conclusion, I shall answer my research questions.

---

[23] https://www.washingtonpost.com/archive/local/1992/11/08/czech-le ader-alexander-dubcek-dies/6d214b3a-0224-4de1-b025-171d9d4fbc83 /?utm_term=.8b0539ebebdc; accessed 13 June 2017.

[24] After months of negotiations, Czech Prime Minister Václav Klaus (*1941) and Slovak Premier Vladimír Mečiar (*1942) could find no common course of economic privatization; they agreed in the summer of 1992 to divide the state. The agreement was a violation of the Czechoslovak Federal Constitution, since only a plebiscite could have rendered such a decision legitimate; Karel Vodička, "Wie der Koalitionsbeschluss zur Auflösung der ČSFR zustande kam", in *Osteuropa 45*, no. 2 (1994): 175-186, 182. In a survey in 1990, only 9.6% of Slovaks and 5.3% of Czechs were in favour of separation; in 1991, 11% of Slovaks and 6% of Czechs supported the separation. The agreement between Klaus and Mečiar prompted President Václav Havel (1936–2011) to resign in protest; Vodička, 181. Because of the different structures of the Slovak and Czech economies, the economic transformation hit the Slovaks much harder than the Czechs: the unemployment rate in the first half of 1992 was 2.7% in the Czech part and 11.3% in the Slovak part; Jiří Kosta, "Systemwandel in der Tschechoslowakei. Ökonomische und politische Aspekte", in *Osteuropa 41*, no. 9 (1990): 802–818, 993.

X. 2 Analytical Framework and Conceptual Matrix

X. 2. 1 Analytical Framework

The biography of a politician who had held executive functions in Party and state should include various aspects: negotiations and decision-making; relations to domestic politicians, parties and interest groups; foreign policy strategy; analysis of the international situation; personal allegiances, political friends and adversaries; relations to Czech and Slovak exile communities abroad; relations to the country's ethnic and political minorities; strategies on economic, education and social policy, to name but the most common ones. This biography cannot cover all these aspects.

I shall focus on two principal aspects of Dubček's thought and activities: first, an analysis of his *ideas about Slovakia's constitutional status in the common state*, and second, *his ideas about Czechoslovak domestic politics,* that is the country's reform course.

Note that I shall not deal with Dubček's thought about foreign policy issues, especially the relations with the Soviet Union, since the international aspects of the Czechoslovak Spring have been abundantly analysed in the studies dealing with the invasion and occupation mentioned above. Dubček was only ever interested in Czechoslovakia's domestic reform course; he had no intention of making his country a role model for the other bloc states to follow, let alone leave the bloc and have Czechoslovakia join NATO and the West. His position was clear: Czechoslovakia was a member of the bloc of Socialist states, loyally fulfilling her military and economic duties in the Warsaw Pact and the COMECON (RVHP) – but, as a sovereign state, she had the right to embark on a domestic reform course.

However, the Soviet leadership and all leaders of the bloc states, save for Romania's Nicolae Ceaușescu (1918–1989),[25] had quite a different perception of Dubček's reforms. Czechoslovakia's open borders and the free press posed a serious threat to the security of the entire bloc – the country bordering on West Germany and Austria was a gateway for Capitalist Imperialism to enter the Socialist bloc.

---

[25] My esteemed colleague Delia Popescu on Ceaușescu's Romania in an e-mail conversation of 9 June 2017: "Technically, Romania did not outright leave the Warsaw Pact, but it had limited participation (plus, Ceaușescu ended up using it as a forum to score political points against the Soviet Union but he hung in there symbolically). Romania was still part of at least one of its bodies, the Political Consultative Committee. But even before Ceaușescu took power, there were signs of Romania's non-alignment. In 1958, Romania demanded the withdrawal of all Soviet troops and military personnel, which did happen (the Soviet Union pretended it was a decision made in Moscow in order to save face). Also, importantly, the initial purpose of the Warsaw Pact was putatively to create a sort of East-West balance in foreign affairs (read: manipulating the West into thinking everything was great in Eastern Europe), and only later did the Soviet Union start focusing on creating an actual military alliance. Interestingly, the military alliance came on the heels of the 1956 events (Hungary etc.) and after Albania joined Yugoslavia in the non-aligned group as the Sino-Soviet crisis was ongoing. So, the Soviet Union had to let both Yugoslavia and Albania go first, but couldn't let Romania get out scot-free, yet the situation of the early 60s was not favorable enough for the Soviet Union to start an invasion over it (the Soviet-Chinese dispute diverted a lot of Soviet attention). Romania also took steps to reorganize its army and other army related services to make it costly for the Soviet Union to intervene. There was also the issue of the way the Pact was structured. The effective leadership (even in the way ranks were organized) was the Soviet military. Other countries also objected to the Soviet military leadership of the Warsaw Pact, which by the early 1960s was becoming more entrenched and publicly spelled out. Romania had early and strong objection to that. So, it wasn't surprising or unexpected for the Soviet Union to see Romania very cranky over the Pact."
A fascinating memoir of the Ceaușescu era is Ion Pacepa, *Red Horizons. The True Story of Nicolae and Elena Ceaușescus' Crimes, Lifestyle and Corruption* (Lanham, MD: Abebooks, 1990). Equally fascinating is Jaap Scholten, *Comrade Baron. A journey through the vanishing world of the Transylvanian aristocracy* (Reno, NV: Helena History Press, 2016). I am indebted to Katalin Kádár Lynn for giving me Scholten's book.

My analysis of Dubček's political ideas and decisions unfolds in the area of Czechoslovak domestic politics from 1945 to 1992, that is, the years of his political career in the Party, the years of his dissident activities and comeback. The analytical framework thus involves the following historical events and contexts: the immediate post-war years of limited democracy under the guidance of the NF (1945–1948); the Stalinization of Czechoslovakia (1948–1960) that ended with the Socialist Constitution adopted in 1960 and the new name ČSSR;[26] the beginning of the liberalization, the *predjarie* (Pre-Spring) that peaked in the Czechoslovak Spring; the Normalization under Husák (1969–1989) and the transition to democracy and rule-of-law state (1989–1992).

X. 2. 2 Conceptual Matrix

The following questions are to guide the reader through the analysis; they represent a conceptual matrix that is divided into two parts, the first focussing on *Dubček's political thought* and, the second, on his *political goals*.

Political thought, key concepts: national identity, political identity, Czechoslovakism, Federalism, Socialism with a Human Face. What political arguments did Dubček use to legitimate his political goals? Which thinkers, politicians or philosophers inspired him? Did he develop his own ideas about politics or follow the Soviet Party line?

Political goals, key concepts: What status of Slovakia within Czechoslovakia did he project? How did he justify political liberalization within the limits of Marxism-Leninism? What should a modern Socialist society look like, and what role did civil rights and liberties play in his reform course?

---

[26] H. Gordon Skilling, "The Czechoslovak Constitution of 1960 and the Transition to Communism", *The Journal of Politics 24*, no. 1 (1962): 142–166.

X. 3 Method, Key Issues, Research Interest

X. 3. 1 Method: Contextual Biography

This study has an interdisciplinary focus: it presents an analysis of political ideas against a background of established historical facts. The combination of political theory analysis with contextual biography[27] is particularly suitable for a biography of Dubček, because it is based on a specific approach to biographical and historical writing. The *contextual biography method* offers us a deeper insight into the historical context, presupposing that a person's activities, thoughts and personal impressions cannot be separated from the historical circumstances he or she was subject to. The British historian Sir Ian Kershaw, FBA (Fellow of the British Academy), on the method and its relevance:

> "Any attempt to incorporate such themes [technology, demography, prosperity, democratization, ecology, political violence, add. JB] in a history of twentieth-century Europe *would not by-pass the role of key individuals* who helped to shape the epoch. [...] *They are neither their prime cause nor their inevitable consequence.* New biographical approaches which recognize this are desirable, even necessary. Their value will be, however, *in using biography as a prism on wider issues of historical understanding and not in a narrow focus on private life and personality.*"[28]

The method of contextual biography and the analysis of political thought as a *dimension of biographical writing* affords a unique insight into Slovakia and Czechoslovakia's political environment: Dubček's personal views, perceptions of events and

---

[27] Simone Lässig, "Introduction: Biography in Modern History – Modern Historiography in Biography", in *Biography between structure and agency. Central European lives in international historiography* (New York: Berghahn, 2008), 1–26.

[28] Ian Kershaw, "Biography and the Historian", in *Biography between ...*, 27–39, 34, 38, italics by me.

ideas render vibrant the historical context in which he thought and acted. Through the prism of his ideas and thoughts the intellectual and political atmosphere of the second half of the 20th century in Czechoslovakia is more clearly revealed. Dubček adhered to the Leninist principle that a good Communist is allowed to think on his own, that the Party, naturally within the theoretical confines and principles of Marxism-Leninism, tolerates and appreciates different views and opinions.

Note that I shall present no summary of the ideology that had captivated so many minds at the turn of the 20th century; Marxism-Leninism has been subject to countless historical, philosophical and sociological studies. Marx, Engels, Lenin and Stalin's works can be found in libraries and on the Internet. For those willing to delve into the depths of Marxist-Leninist theory, I recommend Sir Isaiah Berlin's (1909–1997) biography of Marx,[29] the texts of Ernest Mandel (1923–1995),[30] Neil Harding's analysis of Leninism,[31] and Leszek Kołakowski's superb study of Marxist thought.[32] Edvard Radzinsky's biography of Stalin,[33] William Taubman's biographies of Khrushchev and Gorbachev,[34] *The Black Book of Communism,*[35] François Furet's superb historical study of Communism,[36] and Tony Judt and

---

[29] Isaiah Berlin, *Karl Marx* (Princeton, NJ: Princeton University Press, 2013, (5)).
[30] Ernest Mandel's texts on https://www.ernestmandel.org/en/; accessed 24 June 2017.
[31] Neil Harding, *Leninism* (London: MacMillan, 1996).
[32] Leszek Kołakowski, *Main Currents of Marxism. The Founders. The Golden Age. The Breakdown* (New York, London: Norton, 2005).
[33] Edvard Radzinsky, *Stalin* (New York, Toronto: Anchor books, 1996).
[34] William Taubman, *Khrushchev. The Man and His Era* (New York, London: Norton & Co., 2004); *Gorbachev. His Life and Times* (London; Simon & Schuster, 2017).
[35] Stéphane Courtois et al., *The Black Book of Communism. Crimes. Terror. Repression* (Cambridge, MA, London: Harvard University Press, 1999).
[36] François Furet, *The Passing of an Illusion. The Idea of Communism in the Twentieth Century* (Chicago, London: The University of Chicago Press,

Timothy Snyder's debate about intellectuals in the 20th century offer excellent information.³⁷ The series of the Cold War International History Project (CWIHP papers),³⁸ published at the Woodrow Wilson Center in Washington D.C., USA, offers outstanding research about the Soviet bloc, China and international politics during the Cold War.

X. 3. 2 Key Issues

X. 3. 2. 1 Czechoslovakism and the Czechoslovak Nation

Prior to the foundation of the First Czechoslovak Republic in 1918, Czech intellectuals in the Austrian and Slovak intellectuals in the Hungarian part of the Habsburg monarchy engaged in debates about their kinship, focussing on their close cultural and linguistic features.³⁹ For the purpose of a clear understanding of the different Slovak and Czech perceptions of the common state and each other after WWII and under the Communist regime, I shall briefly elaborate on Czechoslovakism as the principal political programme and philosophical basis of the state.

Czechoslovakism is a historical concept with two interpretations: first, it is the idea that Czechs and Slovaks form one

---

1999). I thank Vlasta Jaksicsová for recommending Furet's historical study to me.

[37] Tony Judt with Timothy Snyder, *Thinking The Twentieth Century* (New York: Penguin, 2012).

[38] Cold War International History Project at the Woodrow Wilson Center on https://www.wilsoncenter.org/program/cold-war-international-history-project; accessed 23 May 2016.

[39] For a detailed chronology of the beginnings of political Czechoslovakism see Jan Rychlík, *Češi a Slováci ve 20. století. Česko-slovenské vztahy 1914–1945* (Bratislava, Praha: AEP, Ústav T. G. Masaryka, 1997), 23–39, referred to as *Češi a Slováci I*. Jan Rychlík, *Češi a Slováci ve 20. století. Česko-slovenské vztahy 1945–1992* (Bratislava, Praga: AEP, ÚTGM, 1998), referred to as *Češi a Slováci II*.

nation, and second, it is the political programme of the state of the Czechs and Slovaks.[40]

On 28 October 1918, Czechoslovakia came into being as a new state in Central Europe – thanks to the efforts of the *exile troika* of Masaryk, Beneš and Milan Rastislav Štefánik (1880–1919).[41] In a pragmatic step, Masaryk had reformulated his Czech nation-building theory into his Czechoslovak state-building theory to convince the Allies of WWI that, on the grounds of natural law,[42] the *Czechoslovak nation* deserved sovereignty as much as Poland, whose reconstruction and sovereignty was a stipulation of US President Woodrow Wilson's famous plan of 14 points. Masaryk conceived of the Slovaks as kin of the Czechs who spoke an eastern Czech dialect. This was clearly not the case; Slovak had been a written language since 1843, albeit neither recognized by the Hungarian government nor the international community of states.[43] For reasons of political

---

[40] Dušan Kováč, *Slováci. Česi. Dejiny* (Bratislava: AEP, 1997), 118–119.
[41] The best biography of Milan Rastislav Štefánik known to me is Peter Macho, *Milan Rastislav Štefánik. V hlavach a v srdciach* (Bratislava: HÚ SAV a Prodama, 2011). For an analysis of Štefánik's activities in France see Fréderic Guelton, Emanuelle Braud a Michal Kšiňan, *Milan Rastislav Štefánik v archívnich dokumentov Historickej služby francúzskeho ministerstva obrany* (Paris, Bratislava: service historique de la Défense, Vojenský historický ústav, Ministerstvo obrany SR, 2008, 2009).
[42] About natural law and positive law in the context of the foundation of Czechoslovakia see my study "The Genesis of Czechoslovakism. An Interdisciplinary Inquiry into the Influence of Rousseau's Réligion Civile", in *East European Faces of Law and Society: Values and Practices* (Leiden: Brill Nijhoff, 2014), 307–345.
[43] The Slovak patriots (*národovci*) Ľudovít Štúr (1815–1856)), Michal Miloslav Hodža (1811–1870) and Jozef Miloslav Hurban (1817–1888) had coined the Slovak written language in 1843, based on the central Slovak dialect, which was a political decision. Masaryk wrote in the first volume of his study of Russian philosophy and thought in 1913: "The Slovaks lack a language of their own, and the political conditions [they are subject to in the Hungarian kingdom, add. JB] led to the fact that the Slovak dialect vanished as a literary language"; T. G. Masaryk, "Slavjanofilství. Mesianismus pravoslavné teokracie. Slavjanofilství a Panslavismus", in *Rusko a Evropa*.

pragmatism, Masaryk conveniently ignored the efforts of the Slovak patriots in the early 19th century to gain recognition for their language. By declaring the Czechs and Slovaks one nation, he was able to convince the Czech and Slovak exile communities in the USA of his plan of founding the Czechoslovak nation state; they supported him by signing the Pittsburgh Agreement on 31 May 1918. Masaryk thus created a historically incorrect yet politically successful portrait of the Czechs and Slovaks as one nation, thereby liberating it from the Habsburg monarchy's oppressive rule. In 1905, Masaryk had written:

> "Just think how we consider Bohemia, Moravia, Silesia and, finally, Slovakia as separate units! Two million Czechs [*dva miliony Čechů*] live in the Hungarian kingdom! [...] We won't give up *a third of our nation*."[44]

Studie o duchovních proudech v Rusku, vol. I (Praha: Ústav T. G. Masaryka, 1995), 181–246, 225. This was a pragmatic, clever, and, in terms of political strategy, very astute spin. Masaryk was familiar with the situation in Slovakia, since he was in constant contact with the Hlasists. One has to understand this quote not only with regard to his independence plans, but also in the context of his self-defence: he was fighting his Slovak enemies, the conservative Martinists led by Svetozár Hurban Vajanský, who were attacking him and his associates for their modern views. In the late 1890s, Masaryk and Vajanský's families befriended each other, since the Masaryks used to spend their summer holidays in Slovakia. About the end of their friendship see my "Thomas G. Masaryk and Svetozár Hurban Vajanský. A Czecho-Slovak friendship?", *KOSMAS. Czechoslovak and Central European Journal 26*, no. 2 (2013): 50–62. On Masaryk's role in the foundation of the Slovak *Hlas* movement see Zdeněk Urban, "K Masarykovu vztahu ke Slovensku před první světovou válkou", in *Masaryk a Slovensko (soubor statí)* (Praha: Masarykova společnost a Ústav T. G. Masaryka, 1992), 68–89; Dušan Kováč, *Slováci. Češi. Dějiny*, 59–63; and Tomas D. Marzík, "The Slovakophile Relationship of T. G. Masaryk and Karel Kálal prior to 1914", in *T. G. Masaryk (1850–1937), Thinker and Politician*, 191–209. Masaryk's political advice was crucial to the Slovak student association *Detvan;* the association was Masaryk's recruiting pool for his plans of modernization and future Czechoslovak independence.

[44] Tomáš G. Masaryk, "Proststředky národa malého", in *Ideály humanitní* (Praha: Melantrich, 1991), 85–88, 87, italics by me.

In the decade before the war, Masaryk had pragmatically blended the historic rights of the lands of the Bohemian Crown with the natural law justification for the Czechoslovak nation.[45] With natural law, he justified to the WWI Allies the Czechoslovak nation's right to a sovereign nation state; with the historic rights of the Bohemian Crown, he legitimated the sovereignty of the Czechoslovak nation over the territory of the Czech lands with a large German minority and Slovakia with a large Hungarian minority. Masaryk shared the view of the Czech journalist Karel Havlíček (1821–1856),[46] who had pursued the argument that the codification of the Slovak language in 1843 had been a breach of faith, similar to the breaking of a contract. This criticism is referred to in the literature as *odtrhati se:* to tear oneself away, to leave the union, or, to cut the umbilical cord. Such a union or contract, however, had never existed:

> "In the historical literature, in particular the Czech literature, the concepts of 'linguistic separation' [*jazykovej odluke*] or 'farewell' [*rozluke*] have been in use for years. These concepts, however, are incorrect. The concepts of 'separation' and 'farewell' implicate a former union [*jednota*] that did not exist. Not even the Slovaks were at one with themselves. And only a part of the Slovaks used Czech as their written language."[47]

From Masaryk's point of view, the Czechoslovak state had a threefold legitimacy: First, the state was legitimate in ethical terms, since the people would be sovereign in a democracy and

---

[45] Anton Štefánek, *Masaryk a Slovensko* (Praha: Náklad spisovatelový, 1931), 34.

[46] A selection of studies on Havlíček: Barbara K. Reinfeld, *Karel Havlíček (1821–1856). A National Liberation Leader of the Czech Renascence* (New York, NY, Boulder, CO: Columbia University Press, 1982); Ilona Bažantová, "Zapomenutý ekonom Karel Havlíček Borovský", *Politická Ekonomie 5*, no. 2 (1999): 621–629 and Marie L. Neudorflová, "Karel Havlíček, T. G. Masaryk a demokracie", in *Spisovatelé, společnost a noviny v promínách doby* (Praha: Literární Archiv Národného Písemnictví, 2006), 11–28.

[47] Kováč, *Slováci. Češi. Dejiny*, 36–37, emphasis by me.

rule-of-law state that embodied the values of liberty, equality and fraternity. An important factor was Masaryk's personal life; he was married to the American Protestant Charlotte Garrigue (1850–1923).⁴⁸ Thanks to his wife, Masaryk had an insight into how US democracy worked – and why Austrian imperial and Hungarian monarchical rule did not and should not.

Second, Czechoslovakia was legitimate in terms of public international law, since the victorious Allies would dictate the terms and conditions of the peace negotiations in St. Germain and Trianon, the latter being of crucial importance for Slovakia's independence from Hungary.

Third, the state was legitimate because of the consent of the Czech and Slovak expat communities in the USA who had emigrated from Austria-Hungary exactly because of the oppression of the feudalist and aristocratic regime. The distinguished Slovak historian Dušan Kováč about the building of the state:

> "Czech politicians often said that the Slovaks would get everything they wished for. The majority of the Slovaks accepted the idea that, in the first phase, in the interest of international recognition and a smooth separation from the Hungarian administration, the centralist model of the state would be the best solution. All forces concentrated on achieving that basic goal – a plan that not too long ago had been referred to as the crazy ideas of an ageing Prague professor."⁴⁹

---

⁴⁸ For a portrait of Masaryk's wife Charlotte and eldest daughter Alice see my *Seven Czech Women. Portraits of Courage, Humanism and Enlightenment* (Stuttgart, New York: ibidem, Columbia University Press, 2015), 35–85. See also Marie L. Neudorflová, ed., *Charlotta G. Masaryková. Sborník příspěvků z konference ke 150. výročí jejího narození, konané 10. listopadu 2000* (Praha: Masarykův ústav Akademie věd ČR, 2001).

⁴⁹ Kováč, *Slováci. Česi. Dejiny*, 66–67. Quoting "the crazy ideas of an ageing Prague professor", Kováč refers to the Czech journalist Ferdinand Peroutka (1895–1978), a close confidant of Masaryk's who published a book about the foundation of the state in 1927. Peroutka criticized the Prague politicians who, during WWI, conceived of Masaryk as a "dangerous nut", since he planned to break up Austria-Hungary; Ferdinand

The distinguished Czech historian Jan Rychlík about Czechoslovakism:

> "To pretend that the Czechs and Slovaks were one nation was generally accepted. While many Czechs truly believed that Czechs and Slovaks formed one nation, the Slovaks considered the Czechoslovak nation as a strategic construct that should be given up once the goal [the international recognition of the Czechoslovak Republic, add. JB] had been achieved. From a Czech perspective, the idea of one nation should form the basis of the state. [...] Yet in that phase of development one should not understand the concept of Czechoslovakism in a negative fashion, since, without it, there would have been no Czechoslovakia at all."[50]

Was the foundation of Czechoslovakia on 28 October 1918 legitimate in democratic terms? I think yes, for three reasons: first, on 30 October 1918, the Slovak National Council (SNR) independently expressed its wish to form a state with the Czechs;[51] second, Beneš's negotiations with Czech politicians in

---

Peroutka, "O účasti na revoluci" (1924), in *Kdo nás osvobodil?* (Praha: Náklad Svazu národního osvobození, Tisk 'Pokrok', 1927), 5–25.

[50] Rychlík, *Češi a Slováci I,* 54–55.

[51] The Martin Declaration signed on 30 October 1918 was the Slovak National Council's (SNR) independent expression of the desire to leave the Hungarian kingdom and form a common state with the Czechs, while the Prague Declaration of 28 October included Slovakia as a part of the common state. Because of war censorship, the signatories in Martin did not know about the events in Prague when they agreed on the contents and formulation of the declaration. Milan Hodža (1878–1944) informed them when he reached Martin during the evening of 30 October. Vavro Šrobár signed the Prague Declaration as representative of the SNR in Prague; Márian Hronský a Miroslav Pekník, *Martinská deklarácia. Cesta slovenskej politiky k vzniku Česko-Slovenska* (Bratislava: Veda, 2008), 264. See also Jörg K. Hoensch, *Geschichte der Tschechoslowakei* (Stuttgart, Berlin, Köln: Kohlhammer, 1992 (3)), 39, and Jan B. Kozák, *T. G. Masaryk a vznik Washingtonské deklarace v říjnu 1918* (Praha: Melantrich, 1968), 27. Hoensch and Kozák consider the Slovak radicals' claims for autonomy in the 1920s and 1930s as unsubstantial; their questioning of the legitimacy of the Pittsburgh Agreement and the Prague Declaration had no legal grounds, as no government of the nations at war had officially recognized the SNR. The council emerged as a result of a pragmatic *ad hoc* decision of the patriots convening in Martin to validate their subsequent declaration. The

Geneva in October 1918;⁵² and third, the consent of the Czechs and Slovaks in the USA who had signed the Pittsburgh Agreement.

A crucially important factor for Czechoslovakia's international recognition was the *legia*, the Czechoslovak army that Slovak and Czech soldiers who had deserted from the Austro-Hungarian army had formed during the war. The *legia*, fighting at the side of the Allies on all fronts, had proved the Czechs and Slovaks' wish for independence in a common state. The Allies perceived the *legia* as the army of a state in the making. A third reason for the Allies' recognition of Czechoslovakia's new territorial borders was the politically astute and clever *fait accompli* in Slovakia: By November 1918, Czechoslovak troops had secured Slovakia's borders at the Danube, and Masaryk's associate Vavro Šrobár (1867–1950)⁵³ had set up the Czechoslovak government in Slovakia. Šrobár and his handful of men, dedicated to implementing the common state and bringing about

---

foundation of the SNR and the Martin declaration should be understood as an immediate reaction to Austro-Hungarian foreign minister Gyula Andrassy's (1823–1890) receipt of President Wilson's (1856–1924) note on the conditions for signing a peace agreement on 27 October 1918. Hronský and Pekník stress that the Martin Declaration did not create a "new nation, but a new state", 281.

52 In mid-October, Beneš met with delegates from the Czech National Council in Geneva: they agreed on the political system of a Republic and the composition of the first provisional government with Masaryk as president. Karel Kramář (1860–1937) was the first Prime Minister, Beneš kept the Ministry of Foreign Affairs, Antonín Švehla (1873–1933) led the Ministry of Internal Affairs, Alois Rašin (1867–1923) the Ministry of Finance, and František Soukup (1871–1940) the Ministry of Justice. Václav Klofáč (1868–1942) was the Minister of Defence, and Štefánik the Minister of War. On 28 October, the Revolutionary National Assembly (*Revoluční Národní Shromáždění*) declared the independence of the sovereign Czechoslovak Republic in Prague; the first Czechoslovak government was established the same day.

53 Josette Baer, *A Life Dedicated to the Republic. Vavro Šrobár's Slovak Czechoslovakism* (Stuttgart, New York: ibidem, Columbia University Press, 2014).

regime change, immediately began to replace the Hungarian administration in early November, and by the summer of 1920, when the Trianon peace negotiations with Hungary started, Czechoslovak rule was firmly established on Slovak territory.

Thanks to Masaryk's conception of the Czechoslovak state and the continuous efforts of Štefánik and Beneš in exile and Šrobár in Slovakia, the Republic came into being. According to Masaryk's thinking, the last phase of the historical democratization process had begun with the foundation of the sovereign state. From now on, there was only one goal the Czechoslovaks had to concentrate on: to secure the state and its institutions through the citizens' continuous improvement of the social, economic and political conditions – their nations' new lives in a democracy and sovereign state.

Masaryk achieved what no philosopher before him had achieved – he had created a state, his Platonic dream of the *polis*, yet without Plato's authoritarian order. In the Czechoslovak Republic, the people, not a king or emperor, were the sovereign, realizing Rousseau's sovereignty of the people. Masaryk was the *spiritus rector* of Czechoslovak sovereignty, following Plato's imperative he so admired that philosophers should be kings, *viz.*, in the 20th century, presidents and moral leaders.

The First Republic's inherent problem that Hitler would use to carve up Czechoslovakia was Masaryk's *constitutional construct of the Czechoslovak nation*, a concept Czechs and Slovaks were divided about. The Czechs conceived of the state as a unitarist one,[54] a realization of the Czech programme of independence, with Slovakia as a territorial attachment and enlargement. The Slovaks, on the other hand, rejected the idea of the political nation, because they had only the worst memories

---

[54] Kováč, *Slováci. Česi. Dejiny*, 122.

of the idea and concept of 'political nation': the Magyar interpretation of a united Hungarian political nation had resulted in the harsh Magyarization, the cultural and linguistic assimilation of non-Magyar citizens in the Hungarian kingdom.[55] Masaryk, however, did not understand the Slovak viewpoint:

> "Masaryk's personal origins made it difficult for him to understand an issue that was no problem to him. [...] He felt a Czechoslovak in the truest sense of the word, that is, as Czech and Slovak in one person."[56]

At the turn of the 20th century, intellectuals of the two nations had begun to promote *cultural Czechoslovakism*, the idea of the kinship of Slovaks and Czechs that originated in the closeness of their languages. In 1908, the annual meeting of the association *Československá jednota* (Czechoslovak union) in the Moravian spa town of Luhačovice[57] had become a tradition of Czechoslovakism and its adherents; the meetings improved relations, since the members not only discussed themes of cultural exchange and education, but also economic and political issues.

In a survey the Slovak journal *Prúdy (Currents)*, edited by former Hlasists,[58] undertook in 1914, 39 Czech and 37 Slovak

---

[55] Kováč, *Slováci. Češi. Dejiny*, 123.
[56] Hain, 225. Masaryk's father was a Slovak coachman, his mother a Moravian cook who spoke German; Masaryk grew up in the eastern Moravian village of Hodonín, close to the Slovak border.
[57] Rychlík, *Češi a Slováci I*, 38.
[58] The Hlasists derived their name from the journal *Hlas (The Voice)*, which they published from 1898 to 1904; they were inspired by the progressive and modern political thought of Masaryk. Masaryk's Realism was his method of thinking about politics and society; his approach was based on the empiricism and positivism applied in the natural sciences. Vajanský, on the other hand, was preaching passivity, endurance, instilling fantasies of liberation by the Russian Tsar. In general, the Catholic faction was preaching very much the same – save for the hope of liberation by Russia, since they were loyal to the Vatican. Both camps, the Lutherans and the Catholics alike, were neither capable of nor willing to offer the citizens a feasible political programme that would fight the assimilation and the concomitant discrimination of the Slovak patriots. The Hlasists were a tiny group, struggling to survive, but after the *prevrat*, they were representing

intellectuals addressed issues of political unity in terms of agriculture, politics, economy and culture; because of the war, the survey's results were published only in 1919. But they illustrated that progressive Czech and Slovak intellectuals truly believed in the existence of a Czechoslovak nation.[59] But, prior to WWI, the majority of Czech politicians considered the monarchy as a fact and could not imagine the Czech lands outside of Austria, let alone the end of the Habsburg monarchy.

The activities of cultural Czechoslovakism formed the intellectual basis of *political Czechoslovakism*, the programme of and demand for a common independent state. For both Slovaks and Czechs, Czechoslovakia was a perfect political solution. The Slovaks would benefit from the political experience and economic support of the Czechs. The Czechs on their own, that is, without the argument of the Czechoslovak nation and its right to sovereignty over her territory that included Slovakia, could not have convinced the Allies to recognize the new state. The plan of a Czechoslovak state, carved out of the Habsburg

---

the young Republic and its democracy in Slovakia. As the new political elite, they governed Slovakia according to the democratic principles of Czechoslovak state theory. Two former Hlasists crucially determined Czechoslovak history: the astronomer and general of the French Army Štefaník and the physician Šrobár. An attempt in the 1930s to renew the Hlasist movement with the journal *Nový hlas* (*New Voice*) failed owing to major changes in the Slovak political landscape; Ivan Kamenec, "Novohlasistická skupina a Robotnická academia na Slovensku v rokoch 1933–1937", in *Slovensko v labyrinte moderných európskych dejín. Pocta historikov Milanovi Zemkovi* (Bratislava: HÚ SAV, 2014), 211–222.

[59] *Prúdy V*, no. 9–10 (1919): 399–567. The journal *Prúdy* was a re-edition or follow up of *Hlas*: it offered the readers a secular political perspective, a focus on scientific methods in politics and the promotion of the political union and kinship of Czechs and Slovaks. For a superb summary of the history and significance of *Prúdy* see Milan Zemko, "Prúdisti v čase, ktorý trhol oponou", in *Kapitoly z histórie stredoeurópskeho priestoru v 19. a 20. Storočí. Pocta k 70-ročnému jubileu Dušana Kováča* (Bratislava: HÚ SAV, 2012), 269–280.

Empire, attacked the essential pillar of Austro-Hungarian power: dualism, established in the *Ausgleich* (compromise) of 1867.

Slovak and Czech politicians conceived of Czechoslovakism as the state's ethical legitimation. Some had a Czechoslovak political identity, considering themselves members of the Czech or Slovak nation, respectively. Others embodied a Czechoslovak national and political identity, thus believing that Czechs and Slovaks formed one nation. National and political identities were also formed along confessional lines. In general, it can be said that Czech Protestants, Catholics and Jews welcomed the common state. Slovak Lutherans and Jews were generally supportive of the common state, as it meant liberation and democratization, while, on the other hand, radical circles among the Slovak Catholics conceived of the ruling Czech liberalism as atheistic. They also felt that Czech leadership in the common state was centralistic, discriminating against their religious beliefs and way of life.

Central planning from Prague was necessary because of the different economic conditions in the Czech lands and Slovakia. While the Czech lands had experienced an industrial boom in the 19th century, Slovakia's industrialization was protracted because Hungary's socio-economic system had been largely based on agriculture. Industrialization in Slovakia began only in the 1920s. Czechoslovak institution building began immediately after the Prague declaration of independence on 28 October 1918; it replaced the Austrian and Hungarian administrations with the institutions of a modern representative democracy that included minority rights.[60]

---

[60] The Germans and the Hungarians formed the two largest minorities; the delegates of their parties enjoyed political participation and representation in the Czechoslovak parliament; for the legal aspects of minority

This process of co-ordination and centralization provoked resistance mainly from Slovak Catholic circles. The new administrative institutions, schools, universities, hospitals and factories required trained personnel, which only the Czechs could provide, since the Magyar personnel refused to serve Czechoslovakia or left for Hungary after 1918. Some Slovaks, led by the Catholic priest Andrej Hlinka (1864–1938), who became a radical autonomist in the mid-1920s, felt overruled by the 'atheist and Hussite Czechs' in their own homeland.

From the text of the Pittsburgh Agreement, American Slovaks and autonomists at home deduced an alleged promise by Masaryk to establish Slovak autonomy. They protested against "Czech centralism", equating Masaryk's statements "Slovakia will have her own administration, her parliament and her courts" and "Slovak will be the administrative language in schools, in the administration and overall in public life" with a constitutionally granted autonomy, that is, self-government.[61]

Czechoslovakia ceased to exist with the Munich Agreement of 30 September 1938. Great Britain, Italy and France sacrificed the only democracy in Central Europe for a fickle peace in Europe. This policy of appeasement spectacularly failed; Munich only encouraged Hitler to go ahead with his megalomaniac plans of *Lebensraum im Osten*:

---

rights in the Czechoslovak constitution see Hain, 217–229. For a historiography of identity-formation see Jiří Kořalka, "Nationsbildung und nationale Identität der Deutschen, Österreicher, Tschechen und Slovaken um die Mitte des 19. Jahrhunderts", in *Ungleiche Nachbarn. Demokratische und nationale Emanzipation bei Deutschen, Tschechen und Slovaken (1815–1914)* (Essen: Klartext, 1993), 33–48.

[61] The text of the Pittsburgh Agreement, document no. 14, in Jan Galandauer, *Vznik Československé Republiky 1918* (Praha: Svoboda, 1988), 299–300.

"'Our enemies are small worms', he would tell his generals in August 1939. 'I saw them in Munich'".⁶²

The majority of the Sudeten Germans had been rallying against the Republic, supporting the *Sudetendeutsche Partei* led by Konrad Henlein (1898–1945). Czechoslovak politicians were trying to save what could be saved of the Republic, but the radicals of the HSĽS (Hlinka's Slovak People's Party) used Munich as a platform to push forward the issue of Slovak autonomy. Munich prompted the Žilina Agreement (*Žilinská dohoda*) in October 1938, which led to Slovakia's autonomy; the Vienna Arbitration (*Viedenská arbitráž*) in November 1938 consigned southern and eastern parts of Slovakia to Hungary and, on 15 March 1939, the Republic ceased to exist: Nazi Germany invaded the Czech lands and established the protectorate of Bohemia and Moravia. On 14 March, Slovakia had to proclaim independence; she was a pseudo-sovereign state at Hitler's beck and call.

The majority of the Slovaks had accepted the declaration of Slovak autonomy on 6 October 1938. A prominent signatory of the Žilina Agreement was Jozef Tiso,⁶³ a former MP for the HSĽS in the First Republic. The Czechoslovak government, betrayed by its former allies and in a state of disorientation because of the resignation of President Beneš and his government, accepted the Žilina Agreement. Czechoslovakia's status changed to a federation with a new official name for Slovakia, *Slovenska krajina*; the country's new official name was the hyphenated *Czecho-Slovakia*. The government in Prague was responsible for international affairs, defence, currency, the state budget and customs, public traffic and the post.⁶⁴

---

62 Ian Kershaw, *Hitler* (London: Penguin, 2008), 445.
63 The best biography of Tiso known to me is Ivan Kamenec, *Tragédia politika, kňaza a človeka. Dr. Jozef Tiso, 1887–1947* (Bratislava: Premedia, 2013).
64 Kováč, *Dejiny Slovenska*, 210.

The Žilina Agreement's rationale was that of *loyalty to the Republic in exchange for autonomy*. Slovak self-government would only strengthen the Republic. From the viewpoint of a Slovak citizen, the Žilina Agreement made sense: why would they want to support 'Prague centralism' if Prague did not acknowledge their demands for self-government within the common state? From a Czech perspective, 'Slovak autonomism' unnecessarily burdened the Republic at the time the state had lost the substantial territories of the Sudetenland to Germany. But in the municipal elections of May 1938, the HSĽS was no longer the strongest party in Slovakia:

> "1,452 communities held elections. Slovenska Jednota [an electoral association of Agrarians, Social Democrats, the Slovak National Party and other small parties, add. JB] received the majority of the votes with 43.93%, followed by HSĽS with 26.93% and KSČ with 7.4%. [...] The results of these elections were never published, but they confirm that the Slovak citizens were aware of the threat against the Republic and supported its preservation."[65]

X. 3. 2. 2 *Rovný s Rovným* – The Three Prague Agreements (1945–1946)

To understand the impact and depth of the reform course of the Dubček government in 1968, a brief summary of the two nations' constitutional status after WWII is required. In this subchapter, I also present the KSČ's assumption of power on the so-

---

[65] Kováč, *Dejiny Slovenska*, 209. Slovenská Jednota won the majority because the SNS left the autonomist bloc and joined the former centralist parties. In the parliamentary elections of 1935, the autonomist bloc of HSĽS and SNS had won 30.1% of the vote; the parties of the Rusinian and Polish minorities had supported them, because they also pursued autonomy. The ruling Agrarians had achieved 17.6% and their coalition partner, the Social Democrats 11.3%; Alena Bartlová, "Posledné parlamentné voľby v máj 1935", in *V medzivojnovom Československu 1918–1939* (Bratislava: Veda, 2012), 439–440, 439.

called 'victorious 25 February 1948', the origins of the two CP's different viewpoints and political agendas.

During WWII and after the victory, which the Czechs and Slovaks celebrated at the side of the Allies, *rovný s rovným* (equal among equals) was the fundamental basis of negotiations between Slovaks and Czechs: *rovný s rovným* was the principle and goal that expressed the Slovaks' wish for a constitutional amendment, changing their status within the Republic. Represented by the SNR, they were pursuing constitutional equality with the Czechs in the common state. During the war, the Slovak National Council (SNR), composed of the Communists and several centre-right parties, hence reflecting the Slovak people's political pluralism, had pushed forward *rovný s rovným* as a blueprint for the negotiations with the London exile government under President Beneš. Their common goal was the resistance against Tiso's Slovak State on the one hand, and Nazi occupation in the Czech lands, on the other. The principal goal was the restoration of Czechoslovakia.

The agreement had been concluded in December 1943 in Moscow, under the auspices of the watchful eyes of the *velikii vozhd*. The so-called Christmas Agreement foresaw two political goals, once the war was won: First, constitutional equality of the Slovaks with the Czechs in the common state, and, second, the expulsion of the Sudeten Germans from the Czech lands and the Hungarians from southern Slovakia. Initially, the SNR had planned to drive a hard bargain, to get a reward for their support of the exile government and a reward for the Slovaks who had fought and died in the SNP, alongside the Red Army. Clearly, all Slovak political parties wanted the common state back, but in a different constitutional form. The SNR wanted self-government in Slovakia, true autonomy; Slovak administrators who were familiar with the nation's customs and economic and political situation should govern Slovakia, not Czech civil servants like in the First Republic.

In general, it can be said that to the Slovaks, regardless of their party affiliation, *rovný s rovným* was an issue of democratization; to the Czechs, it was a threat to the rebuilding of the common state in the politically sensitive years after WWII. The majority of the Slovaks thought that the nation did not fight in the SNP and against Tiso to have the old Prague centralism back. The majority of the Czechs, following Beneš's 'stab in the back' myth,[66] thought that one could not trust the Slovaks; they had betrayed Czechoslovakia with the Žilina Agreement of 1938 and were prone to Catholic authoritarianism anyway.

With the liberation in May 1945, Czechoslovakism was again the theoretical fundament of the common state, the state-building theory of Czechoslovakia's reconstruction, but now with a different interpretation: Czechoslovakia was formally declared as the *common state of two brotherly nations*, which meant that the idea of the Czechoslovak nation *de jure* ceased to exist and the Slovaks were recognized as a nation – yet not *de facto*. In practice, the old centralism was back with the NF, and the Slovaks' attempts to achieve self-government failed, also because they were not united enough to push through one principal goal – *rovný s rovným*.

---

[66] Kováč, *Slováci. Ceši. Dejiny*, 78. Beneš adhered to the idea of a Czechoslovak nation and created the absurd myth of the Slovak betrayal in October 1939 in London exile in a conversation with Milan Hodža: "It is impossible that the Slovaks are not aware of what they have done. No Czech will ever forget this. For twenty years, we have done everything for the Slovaks and when we were in the worst possible situation, the Slovaks stabbed us in the back;" Dokumenty z historie československej politiky, c. d. dok. č. 28, quoted from Kováč, *Slováci. Ceši. Dejiny*, 78. Beneš did not mention his remark in his autobiography, portraying his conversation with Hodža as amicable and founded on the basic agreement that Czechs and Slovaks would reconstruct their common state after the war; Edvard Beneš, *Paměti II. Od Mnichova k nové válce a k novému vítězství* (Praha: Academia, 2008), 98.

The KSS pressed forward, representing the demands of the SNR, which foresaw the constitutional recognition of the Slovaks as a nation on an equal footing with the Czechs; the common Slovak viewpoint was that the SNR as the nation's representative had the right to demand a post-war political reward in the form of a legal guarantee, a recognition of the SNR's executive and legislative power on Slovak territory and its authority to supervise the Slovak government trustees (*poveréniky,* ministers with executive power limited by the government). Had these demands been granted, Czechoslovakia would have turned into a federation,[67] with Prague in charge of defence, diplomacy, international trade and commerce – a political system similar to the Austro-Hungarian *Ausgleich* of 1867, yet without the absolutist rule of the Habsburg Dynasty and the Catholic clergy.

The Moscow negotiations from 22 to 29 March 1945 resulted in the Košice Agreement (*Košický vládny program*), named after the eastern Slovak town, where the government announced it to the people. The Košice Agreement had a provisional character: it recognized the Slovaks as a nation and the SNR as the ruling organ in Slovakia, responsible for the supervision of the government trustees, but without a precise definition of its range of responsibility.[68] President Beneš and the government in Prague had full authority over the entire territory of Czechoslovakia – which contested the authority of the SNR on Slovak territory. The Košice agreement did not resolve the constitutional status of Slovakia.

Further negotiations could take two directions: either towards the strengthening of the SNR and the building of parallel

---

[67] Kováč, *Dejiny Slovenska*, 250.
[68] Kováč, *Dejiny Slovenska*, 252.

organs in the Czech lands, which would result in a symmetrical federative model, or towards the strengthening of the authority of the Prague government, which would lead to a centrally ruled unitary state.[69] In the years leading up to the Communist coup d'état in February 1948, the position of the SNR would weaken and the centralist position strengthen.

At the end of March 1945, the first post-war Czechoslovak government was established. Beneš and the members of the exile government arrived in Košice on 3 April, and on 5 April the president appointed the new government. The Red Army liberated Prague on 9 May 1945, and on 10 May, the Czechoslovak government moved to the capital. The negotiations about Slovakia's constitutional status began. They became known as the *Three Prague Agreements* (*první, druhá a třetí Pražská dohoda*).

The fact that the negotiations went into three rounds and were held in Prague, and not one round of negotiations in the Slovak capital Bratislava, reflects the changing balance of power between the parties, the disunity of the SNR, the reluctance of the NF dominated government to acknowledge in principle Slovak equality, and the Communist control of the NF; the KSČ's switching of positions would eventually tip the scales in favour of centralism. Every political party, either Czech or Slovak would lose – only the Communists would gain. Czech and Slovak historians analysed the Three Prague Agreements in detail.[70] I shall present only a brief summary.

After the government had arrived in liberated Prague, the years of "guided democracy [*roky riadenej demokracie*]" began.[71] The issues of the *odsun*, the expulsion of the Germans from the Czech lands and the war retributions were quickly

---

[69] Kováč, *Dejiny Slovenska*, 252.
[70] Rychlík, *Češi a Slováci II*, 27–51; Kováč, *Dejiny Slovenska*, 250–254.
[71] Kováč, *Dejiny Slovenska*, 245.

resolved; the SNR issued the order for the establishment of the courts of retribution on Slovak territory on 15 May, while a presidential decree established courts of retribution in June 1945 in the Czech lands. The presidential decree of 2 August annulled the Czechoslovak citizenship of the Germans and Magyars.[72] The government declared itself "the government of the People's Democracy [*vláda ľudovej demokracie*]" – which demonstrated already the Communists' influence in linguistic terms – and announced the transformation of the political system and the establishment of national councils.[73]

An important decision had been made in the Moscow negotiations in March 1945: the National Front was composed of members of all political parties, holding executive, judicial and legislative power. It served as a recruiting base for government positions, representing a union of all political parties in charge of the reconstruction of the state, industry and agriculture. Among the 25 members were nine Slovaks.[74] In the months prior to the end of WWII, the majority of Czechoslovak politicians had shared the view that the multi-party system of the First Republic had got out of control. Masaryk's Republic had been too generous with the minorities, the Sudeten Germans, the Carpathian Germans and the Hungarians in the south of Slovakia – what had been the result? They had thanked the Republic's democratic generosity by weakening it prior to its destruction by Hitler. Therefore, a slimming-down of the party system was required. It was widely believed that Czechoslovakia's future security would be guaranteed with the expulsion of the Germans from the Czech lands and the Hungarians from southern Slovakia.

---

[72] Kováč, *Dejiny Slovenska*, 245, 370.
[73] Kováč, *Dejiny Slovenska*, 245.
[74] Kováč, *Dejiny Slovenska*, 245.

Post-war Czechoslovakia from 1945 to 1948 was neither a Republic nor a parliamentary democracy, but it was no totalitarian state either – not yet. In constitutional terms, the political system was a hybrid, a democracy limited by the stipulations of the Košice Agreement that had, under the psychological and political authority of Beneš and Stalin, secured the NF's dominant position:

> "This fact was of key significance, and worked to the disadvantage of the non-Communist parties. These parties jointly shared in building up the new system, and they accepted the political conception of a regulated democracy. Beneš was the prominent advocate of the latter as a defensive measure taken to prevent a repetition of Munich. A regulated democracy was a limited democracy and was conditional on the fact that if one or more government parties were to try to take full power, it would limit the forces of democracy to acting in its own self-defence. A regulated democracy can be justified only when there is co-operation between democratic parties with equal representation in the coalition."[75]

Limited democracy is legitimate in terms of political morality, if all involved parties agree on fair play and keep to the rules of democratic procedure – which the KSČ blatantly did not. The post-war atmosphere was not conducive to democratic procedure or fair play; the people were exhausted after five years of Nazi occupation in the Czech lands and clerical-fascist propaganda and rule in Slovakia:

> "The war had radicalized the population, and a large part considered fundamental political and social reforms a solution for the difficult situation. That was why a critical part of the population supported the nationalization of the key industries, banks and insurances, pushed forward by the Communists, the Social Democrats and the trade unions. The presidential decrees of October 1945 realized the nationalizations. The Communists also pushed forward a radical land reform [*radikálnu pozemkovú reformu*], which the poor farmers and the agricultural workers welcomed. In general, radical and apparently simple

---

[75] Kaplan, *The Short March*, 189.

measures seemed attractive to improve the difficult post-war situation."⁷⁶

The KSČ had the full support of Stalin – it was ready to assume power. It had demonstrated its strength already in the Moscow negotiations in March 1945. When Soviet troops occupied Sub-carpathian Ruthenia (*Podkarpatksá Rus*) and joined it to the Ukrainian Soviet Republic on 29 June 1945, the Czechoslovak government caved in to the Soviet annexation.⁷⁷ The pre-Munich borders were restored in the Czech lands and Slovakia, but the parliamentary democracy of the First Republic was not fully established. A crucial change occurred in the party landscape: the NF banned the Agrarians who had been a powerful party in both parts of the state in the First Republic. Since the HSĽS had been banned already during the SNP, the KSS and the DS were the only parties that could run in the parliamentary elections in Slovakia.⁷⁸

The first post-war parliamentary elections were scheduled for 26 May 1946; in the months running up to the elections, the parties started negotiations in May 1945, which led to the first Prague Agreement, signed on 2 June 1945.⁷⁹ The basis for the negotiations was the proposal by the SNR of 26 May: the Slovaks wanted a federation and clear definitions of the authority of the Czecho-Slovak parliament and the Prague government on Slovak territory. The first Prague Agreement did not adopt a federation, but extended the authority of the central institutions and the president to common areas such as inner security, basic reforms of the school system, the system of public healthcare and social welfare. The agreement's stipulation

---

76 Kováč, *Dejiny Slovenska*, 246.
77 On Sub-Carpathian Ruthenia see http://www.carpatho-rusyn.org/fame/pod.htm; accessed 10 June 2017.
78 Kováč, *Dejiny Slovenska*, 248.
79 Kováč, *Dejiny Slovenska*, 252.

confirmed that the SNR was the representative organ of the Slovak nation in Prague and the state's representative organ in Slovakia, but it weakened the SNR's authority in Slovakia with the following statement:

> "Until the provisionary Czechoslovak constitutional assembly is established, the president of the republic, as suggested by the government and in accordance with the SNR, holds legislative power, executed through his decrees, over the entire territory of the Czechoslovak republic."[80]

The agreement confirmed the authority of the SNR and the board of the government trustees (*zbor povereníkov*) in Slovakia, but weakened their position by subordinating them to Prague. The board of the government trustees had to report to Prague about the execution of the president's decrees and other orders relating to common affairs. The First Prague Agreement was thus no solution to the constitutional status of Slovakia.[81]

The negotiations continued in a second round from 9 to 11 April 1946; they ended with a protocol that determined more precisely the stipulations of the First Prague Agreement. A new co-ordinating organ, reporting to the office of the prime minister, would be in charge of solving disagreements and disparities; it was composed of three Czechs and three Slovaks. The second Prague Agreement returned some of the powers the SNR had won for itself in the past to the president: he appointed university professors, judges and civil servants and granted clemency.[82] However, the Second Prague Agreement was not a solution to Slovakia's constitutional status.

A fundamental change in the relations of Czechs and Slovaks occurred only after the parliamentary elections of May

---

[80] Kováč, *Dejiny Slovenska*, 252.
[81] Kováč, *Dejiny Slovenska*, 253.
[82] Kováč, *Dejiny Slovenska*, 253.

1946. The SNR was the only organ that represented Czechoslovak state authority in Slovakia. Prior to the 1946 elections, the Czech Communists had supported the Slovak demands; in the Moscow negotiations, they had sided with the SNR against Beneš's party of the National Socialists and the Czech People's Party.[83] They had considered the issue of Slovak equality an argument that would be supportive of their fight for governmental power, but did not opt for a federation; the KSČ's principal goal was to assume total power over the entire country – which a federation would render impossible. In general, one could say that the Communists considered Slovakia's constitutional status a minor issue – supporting it for the time being was a tactical move, while their long-term strategy was total control of the country. Trying to muster as much resistance in Central Europe against the Nazis, the Bulgarian Communist and General Secretary of the Comintern Georgi Dimitrov (1882–1949), whose second wife was of Czech origin, had said in December 1944:

> "I think that the best solution to the relations of Czechs and Slovaks in liberated Czechoslovakia would be an equal status of both, with a Czech government in the Czech lands, a Slovak government in Slovakia and a common Czecho-Slovak federative government."[84]

But after the victory of 1945, the situation in Czechoslovakia changed drastically. The loss of the 1946 parliamentary elections in Slovakia made the KSS change gear. Šrobár's Democratic Party (DS) won 62% of the vote, which prompted the Slovak Communists to join their Czech comrades. They now sided with the centralist camp, counting on the support of the powerful Czech Communists. The loss of KSS support considerably weakened the SNR, a situation the adherents of centralism had

---

[83] Kováč, *Dejiny Slovenska*, 253.
[84] Kováč, *Dejiny Slovenska*, 253.

been waiting for.⁸⁵ The parties of the NF adopted the Third Prague Agreement on 27 July 1946. The SNR and the board of government trustees were reduced to a mere adjunct of the central government. The SNR was able to execute its legislative power only through the state institutions; it was bound to submit its proposals to the government.⁸⁶ Without the government's approval, the SNR could not adopt any proposals or issue orders. The board of the government trustees had the right to elect the chair of the SNR, but every Slovak *povereník* had to report to the respective minister in the Prague government.⁸⁷ The fight for a constitutional amendement granting Slovakia's self-government was lost because of the Communists' principal goal of total control of the country.

The three Prague Agreements demonstrated the power of centralism and the KSČ's dominance in the NF: the belief that the state would be strong only if governed by a centralist system from Prague won the upper hand over considerations of constitutional equality between Czechs and Slovaks. The SNR lost the once-powerful position it had achieved in the SNP.

From 1947 on, the Party stepped up its efforts; it was pressed for time since the next parliamentary elections were scheduled for 1948. The Communists had won the 1946 elections in the Czech lands with 41% of the vote; they began to orchestrate demonstrations of workers' unions and farmers' councils and increased their propaganda. The resignation of 12 of the 26 centre-right ministers in February 1948 was evidence of the pressure the KSČ was putting on the government with its maximalist demands for reforms. The most important issue was the involvement of the StB in the conspiracies against centre-

---

85   Kováč, *Dejiny Slovenska*, 253.
86   Kováč, *Dejiny Slovenska*, 253.
87   Kováč, *Dejiny Slovenska*, 253.

right politicians. The secret service, already firmly in the Party's hands, had planned attempts on the lives of Prokop Drtina, Peter Zenkl (1884–1975) and Jan Masaryk. Klement Gottwald (1896–1953), the chairman of the KSČ, simply refused to appoint an investigating commission. On 21 February, the Party called for a demonstration on Prague's Old Town Square. Gottwald accused the centre-right ministers who had stepped down of reactionary subversion and betrayal of the NF.

The Party proceeded with great aplomb: Gottwald promised that the KSČ would lead the country towards its own homemade Socialism, with no involvement of the Soviet Union. A homegrown Czechoslovak path to Socialism suggested that the country's sovereignty, a very sensitive issue, would not be touched, but it had *de facto* ceased to exist with the Christmas Treaty in 1943 and the Košice Agreement in 1945.

On 23 February, Beneš, already gravely ill, promised the centre-right parties to refuse the resignation of their ministers, but on 25 February, he appointed a new government according to Gottwald's suggestions, caving in to the carpenter from Moravia.[88] The government crisis the KSČ had artificially created seemed to be solved with the support of President Beneš – which suggested that the NF was working and Czechoslovakia was still a democracy. Yet, as soon as the KSČ was in control of the country, it embarked on a brutal course of Sovietization:

---

[88] Anatolii Sudoplatov suggested in his memoirs that Beneš had received 10,000 $ back in 1938 that had paid for his travel to London, where he had established the Czechoslovak exile government. To prevent this information from being published in the Czechoslovak press, Beneš allegedly caved in to Gottwald's pressure, *Special Tasks. The Memoirs of an Unwanted Witness – A Soviet Spymaster* (London: Little, Brown and Company, 1994), 233–235. I have no means to make a sound judgement about Sudoplatov's statements, which could be true or defamation.

> "The terror that was unleashed hit everybody. Even in the tiniest village citizens suspected of political opposition were found. The purges were carried out ruthlessly in all social strata. Privacy, a private life was completely eliminated, which hit the farmers and tradesmen particularly hard. Those who stood up against the terror had to expect that their families' fates were at stake."[89]

In the purges from 1948 to 1954, between 250,000 and 280,000 citizens were imprisoned, and 23,000 sent to labour camps.[90] The rationale of the persecution and oppression unfolded in three phases: first, mass purges to terrorize the population; second, elimination of politicians of the oppositional parties, and third, a thorough purge of the Party's top ranks, demonstrating that not even high-ranking Communists could be trusted. The third phase would become known as the 1952 show trial of the Titoist and Zionist conspiracy of Slánský et al.

Today, 25 years after the Velvet Divorce, the relations between the two sovereign states and the citizens are better than ever before. It seems to me that the principle of *rovný s rovným* (equal among equals), which had caused grievances and disappointment and enforced biases on both sides, has finally been realized, but bereft of its sense – since the state split. One can thus conclude that *rovný s rovným* never worked; it remained a mere political wish of the Slovaks that could not be realized in the common state because of both nations' biases and, first and foremost, the Communists' principal goal of assuming total power and complete control.

---

[89] Jan Kalous, "KSČ jako iniciátor a vykonavatel politických čistek a procesů", in *Český a slovenský komunismus*, 87–93, 89.
[90] Kalous, 91.

X. 3. 2. 3 The Relationship between the KSČ and the KSS (1948–1967)

On 29 July 1948, the KSS and the KSČ merged; from then on, the KSS was but an executive organ with no legislative or judiciary power. As the long arm of the KSČ, the KSS executed Prague's policy directives in Slovakia, often to the disadvantage of the Slovak citizens.[91] The KSS could not even independently issue the calls for the meetings of the CC and the CC's chairmanship – Prague had the last say in everything.[92] The Czechs' mistrust of their Slovak comrades, ever suspected of 'bourgeois nationalism,' and their former co-operation with the Slovak centre-right politicians in the SNR were the main reason for the KSČ's control of the KSS. Centralism and total control was the governing principle of the Party.

Let me briefly explain the meaning of 'Slovak bourgeois nationalism' in the context of Marxist-Leninist thought. The only feature of identity a Marxist-Leninist approves of and acknowledges is his identity as a worker: he is a proletarian, nothing else. He conceives of Nationalism and national identity as core elements of Capitalism; the bourgeois class uses Nationalism as an ideology to divide the workers, prevent their global solidarity and uprisings against their exploiters. Therefore, any attempt of Party members to pursue rights for their nation, for

---

[91] An excellent analysis of the relationship of the two CPs is Jan Pešek, "Komunistická Strana Slovenska: Od Prevratu 1948 do Pokusu o Reformu 1968 (KSČ a KSS, Členstvo, Organizácia, Stranícky Aparát, Vedenie Strany), in *Štátna Moc a Spoločnosť na Slovensku 1945 – 1948 – 1989* zhnev Bratislava: HÚ SAV, Prodama, 2013), 57–82.

[92] Stanislav Sikora, "KSS a čiastočná liberalizácia režimu na Slovensku počas predjaria (1963–1967)", in *Český a slovenský komunismus*, 132–144, 132. The latest publication about Slovakia from 1945 to 1948 is *Slováci a ľudovodemokratický režim* (Bratislava: Literárne informačné centrum, 2016).

example constitutional equality in a bi- or multi-national state, has to be condemned as reactionary.

Slovak Communists, such as Husák and Clementis, certainly were no nationalists, but they wanted a significant change towards more democracy and autonomy, within the limits of the Communist regime, of course. They thought that the Slovaks who had just survived the Tiso regime would become loyal Communists only if the Prague government would arrange for a constitutionally granted equality with the Czechs. The DS had won the parliamentary elections in 1946 in Slovakia, because the centre-right politicians had promised to negotiate for Slovak self-government within the common state, a theme the KSČ did not allow the KSS to promote. The KSS had also lost the elections, because the Slovaks traditionally voted for centre-right and Catholic parties; they liked neither social democratic nor Communist ideas. The KSS had to keep to the strict Party discipline dictated by Moscow and the KSČ. One could speak of an intra-Party centralism, which forbade the KSS to co-operate with the centre-right parties in negotiating Slovak equal status and self-government.

In the Slovak Communists' way of thinking, the KSČ should not make the same mistakes as the bourgeois governments in the First Republic; they had ruled Slovakia in centralist fashion from Prague. The Slovak Communists truly believed that the common state's future was Socialism; to achieve this goal, the Slovak citizens had to be convinced that the Communist credo was the way towards a new and better life. They thought and acted rationally: promoting Socialism in Slovakia would only improve relations between Czechs and Slovaks that had still been suffering from mistrust, grievances and contempt ever since the 1938 Munich Agreement. If the KSS established Slovak equal status with the Czechs and gave the Slovaks what they wanted, it would foster loyalty to Marxism-Leninism and the Gottwald government. Equality with the Czechs and regional self-government was thus a first step towards overcoming nationalism; Socialism could be realized only if all citizens, Slovaks and Czechs, enjoyed equal status and a fair amount of local and regional self-government, naturally within the political confines of the Party's unchallenged monopoly of governmental rule.

The view of the Gottwald government, which had taken over the centralist policy from the first post-war government from 1945 to 1948 under President Beneš, was diametrically opposed. Czech and Slovak Party members of the Gottwald government thought that Slovakia had to be ruled with a tight centralist fist, not only because the centrally planned economy demanded Prague's control. To give the Slovaks what they wanted, would only create ideological unrest and sow the seeds of anti-Communist rebellion. Particularly the Catholics and bourgeois elements in Slovakia would be trying again to drive a rift between the two nations and split the state. They had done it before, or so the CC KSČ must have thought. After the lost parliamentary elections of 1946, the CC KSS had no more say in Slovakia in terms of independent policy-making.

Had Czechoslovakia's capital been Bratislava and the Slovaks the more powerful and numerically larger nation, Stalin would have instructed them to accuse leading Czech comrades of 'Czech bourgeois nationalism' – the result, that is, the show trial, would have been the same. Had the KSS been the more powerful Party, Stalin would have dictated that they rid themselves of those Czech Party members who had had fought in Spain, spent WWII in London exile, and were intellectuals and Jews. Every comrade who had come into contact with the Imperialist West was, in Stalin's brutal logic, infected with the virus of Capitalism, Titoism and Imperialism. Thus, the Soviet camp had to rid itself of these potentially dangerous individuals.

An important aspect of the planned show trial that added to Titoism the accusation of Zionism was not only Stalin's anti-semitism, but also the hatred working class members felt towards their privileged comrades. The majority of the accused in the *monstr proces* of Slánský and co-accused in 1952 had a bourgeois background, were Jewish and had received a university education. They were not real proletarians like Gottwald, a carpenter, Novotný, a blacksmith and Široký, a railway worker.

The role model for the control of the KSS by the KSČ was the Soviet Communist Party; Gottwald's 'suggestion' to unite the two parties, or rather, to subdue the KSS under the leadership of the KSČ, met no resistance.[93] Štefan Bašťovanský, the General Secretary of the KSS in his speech at the meeting of the CC KSČ on 9 June 1948:

> "After the events of February, we all understood and believed that after we had eliminated the forces of reaction from the government [*odstráneni reakcie z vlády*, the centre-right parties, add. JB] [...] the Party shall unite. We considered this as a natural and obvious matter. Comrade Gottwald's authority is high and unchallenged in Slovakia too. We ourselves [the Slovak Communists, add. JB] wanted to come up with the initiative of uniting the Party."[94]

At the beginning of 1950, the federalization of the Party, whose purpose was to establish the KSS on an equal footing with the KSČ, was no longer a realistic option. Although the unification of the Party *de jure* foresaw a certain amount of independent decision-making for the KSS, the KSČ in Prague had the last say in even the most banal matters. The Czech comrades appointed the members of the CC KSS, the SNR, the position of the editor-

---

[93] Pešek, "Komunistická strana slovenska", 57.
[94] Pešek, "Komunistická strana slovenska", 57.

in-chief of the Party's newspaper *Pravda*, the chairmen of the regional Party sections and other societal and political positions in Slovakia.[95] Prague could interpret every demand of the KSS for more independent decision-making as Slovak nationalism; KSS members were thus afraid to protest; their support of the KSČ's unrestricted power was their duty to the Party.

This situation did not change after Dubček's election as First Secretary of the CC KSS in the spring of 1963.[96] Only in 1967, when the reform-minded Czech and Slovak Party members began to challenge Novotný's Stalinist regime, the status of the KSS, its independence and equality with the KSČ became an issue on the country's political agenda:

> "After January 1968, the relationship between the KSČ and the KSS, that is, how they should be run, became a part of the general attempt of reforming society, which meant federalizing the country. The federalization of the KSČ was only a logical precondition."[97]

X. 3. 3   Research Questions

The research questions of this study focus on two main areas:
1. Democratization and Liberalization of the Stalinist regime: Dubček grew up in a Communist environment. What were the intellectual origins of his reform course?

2. Constitutional status of Slovakia within Czechoslovakia: what constitutional arrangement did Dubček pursue for Slovakia? Was the projected constitutional arrangement the principal driving force of his reform course or a minor, collateral issue on his political agenda? What came first: Democratization then Federalization of Czechoslovakia? Or Federalization and then Democratization?

---

[95] Pešek, "Komunistická strana slovenska", 59.
[96] Pešek, "Komunistická strana slovenska", 60.
[97] Pešek, "Komunistická strana slovenska", 61.

"It smells of an Asian dwelling, of herbs and pelts. Last year's dry steppe grass is rustling lightly in the wind. The dunes are singing, where the sand, warmed by the sun, is flowing, like pearls or gentle ascending waves. [...] The air is filled with the full-throated song of fan-coloured larks. Thousands of blue and golden wings are fluttering [...] The sky is full of them, like angels. [...] There are covered bazaars that extend for several verst. It is cool there, the pigeons are cooing under the eaves. Midday's golden rain is flooding through the cracks. Left and right, on the doorsteps of the tiny shops, old men are sitting in colourful kaftans and turbans whiter than snow, wearing little beards like the Prophet. They are calculating their gains and ungainful profits, and resting, looking like gods, savouring the scent of delicate roses."[1]

"In the terrible years of the Yezhov terror, I spent seventeen months waiting in line outside the prison in Leningrad. One day somebody in the crowd identified me. Standing behind me was a woman, with lips blue from the cold, who had, of course, never heard me called by name before. Now she started out of the torpor common to us all and asked me in a whisper (everyone whispered there): 'Can you describe this?' And I said: 'I can.' Then something like a smile passed fleetingly over what had once been her face."[2]

---

[1] Larissa Reissner, *Oktober. Ausgewählte Schriften* (Berlin: Universum-Bücherei für alle, 1932), 312, 313. Reissner (1895–1926) was a Polish-Russian intellectual and Communist, who participated in the October Revolution of 1917 and wrote about the Russian Civil War. In the 1920s, she travelled to Afghanistan with her husband, a delegate of the Soviet Union. They lived two years in Kabul. In her book, Reissner described her journey to Kabul through Kyrgyzia, Tashkent and Buchara. She was appalled by the backwardness of Central Asia and eager to bring Soviet modernizing influence to the region.

[2] *Requiem* by Anna Akhmatova, on http://www.ronnowpoetry.com/contents/akhmatova/Requiem.html; accessed 2 July 2017. *Requiem* is a most touching poetic description of the *Yezhovchina*, the years of the terror and purges under Nikolai I. Yezhov (1895–1940) from 1937 to 1938. See https://www.youtube.com/watch?v=P--7yKgBfro; accessed 20 January 2018. The poet's son was arrested, her husband murdered. The only biography of Yezhov known to me is J. Arch Getty and Oleg V. Naumov, with the assistance of Nadezhda V. Muraveva, *Yezhov. The Rise of Stalin's 'Iron Fist'* (New Haven, London: Yale University Press, 2008). See also https://www.britannica.com/biography/Nikolay-Ivanovich-Yezhov; accessed 24 January 2018. An interesting interpretation of Akhmatova's encounters with the British diplomat and philosopher Isaiah Berlin (1909–1997) during WWII in St. Petersburg is György Dalos, *Der Gast aus der Zukunft. Anna Achmatova und Sir Isaiah Berlin. Eine Liebesgeschichte* (Hamburg: Europäische Verlagsanstalt, 1997 (2)).

I. Childhood, Early Years and Education (1921–1939)

I. 1 Childhood in Soviet Kyrgyzia and Gorky (1925–1938)

Alexander Dubček was born on 27 September 1921 in Uhrovec, Central Slovakia, into a workers' family. Little Sasha, whom everybody called Šaňo or Šanko, was the second child of Štefan and Paulína. Brother Július had been born in the USA in December 1919.

At the turn of the 20th century, Dubček's parents had left Slovakia for the USA, like so many Slovaks before WWI. They were driven to emigrate by poverty, the political oppression of the Magyar assimilation and the painful lack of a future in Upper Hungary, [1] where, unlike in the Czech lands, industrialization had not yet begun. But the Slovaks in the USA had not forgotten their homeland, and many were Communists, because Marxism-Leninism seemed to promise a better future.

Paulína, born in Banovce not far from Uhrovec, left Slovakia for the USA with her parents in 1909 at the age of 12; in 1912, Štefan and his brother Michal arrived in Chicago, where a large Slovak community lived and worked.[2] Both shared the same political beliefs as they were workers, members of the proletariat; Paulína was cook and housemaid to a wealthy Jewish family, while Štefan worked as carpenter in a factory that made musical instruments. During WWI, Communists did not

---

[1] For a summary of the Magyarization and how it affected the principal thinkers of the Slovak National movement see my *Revolution, Modus Vivendy or Sovereignty? The Political Thought of the Slovak National Movement from 1861 to 1914* (Stuttgart: ibidem, 2010).

[2] Dubček, *Hope Dies Last*, 5, 4.

have an easy life in the USA. Therefore, Štefan and Paulína decided to return home after the foundation of Czechoslovakia on 28 October 1918. They hoped that the new government would promote industrial development in their native Slovakia.

With hindsight, it seems almost like an omen that little Sasha was born in the same house in the Uhrovec parish[3] where Ľudovít Štúr (1815–1856), the famous father of the Slovak written language had been born 106 years before.[4] Today, Štúr and Dubček are the most famous and respected Slovaks at home and abroad.

The parents wanted to call their second son Milan, but in reverence and gratitude to the church organist Alexander Trančík who gave the young family his apartment in the parish house, they baptized their second son Alexander. Sasha spent his childhood and teenage years with his loving family in the Soviet Union; these years would form his political thought as much as his character.

In 1925, Štefan and Paulína decided to move to Soviet Kyrgyzia with the Czechoslovak Socialist cooperative INTERHELPO.[5] In the early 1920s, the economic prospects in the

---

[3] Banáš, *Zasťavťe Dubčeka!*, 21.
[4] For a first analysis of Štúr's political thought in English see my *Slavic Thinkers or The Creation of Polities. Intellectual History and Political Thought in Central Europe and the Balkans in the 19th Century* (Stuttgart: ibidem, 2007), 44–77.
[5] I thank Juraj Benko for providing me with a bibliography about INTERHELPO. A selection of studies: Mečislav Borák, *České stopy v gulagu* (Opava: Slezské zemské muzeum, 2003); Miloš Březina, *Interhelpo. Pomoc Československých dělníků při modernizaci Sovětského Kyrgyzstánu* (Pardubice: Univerzita Pardubice, 2008), Matura Thesis; Š. Fano, "Internacionálna pomoc československého proletariátu mladému sovietskemu štátu pri obnove národného hospodárstva", *Slovanské štúdie 1*, (1983): 56–70; Michail Grigar, *Žizň dlja radosti* (Moskva: Gosudarstvenoie izdatelstvo političeskoi literatury, 1962); Ladislav Hubenák, *U pramenů přátelství: k 60. výročí Interhelpa* (Praha: Lidové nakladatelství, 1984); Petr Kokaisl a Petr Usmanov, *Amirbek. Dějiny Kyrgyzstánu očima*

Slovak part of Czechoslovakia were still poor; industrialization had begun but could not absorb all workers. Also, the Russian Revolution of 1917 and the Soviet propaganda of the early 1920s that was praising the economic and political progress and fantastic conditions in the workers' paradise enticed many foreigners to seek a new life in the Soviet Union. When a cooperative of Czech and Slovak leftist workers, bound by their enterprising and adventurous spirit, clubbed together and organized a first batch of members to move to Soviet Central Asia, the Dubček family was among them.

In 1968, when her son was First Secretary of the KSČ, not only the most powerful but also the most loved and respected Czechoslovak politician since Presidents Masaryk and Beneš, Paulína Dubčeková gave an interview to *Slovenka*, a Slovak women's weekly.[6] She told the interviewer that some of the people who had enrolled with INTERHELPO had thought mistakenly that they could get rich in the Soviet Union. She and her husband, so Paulína said, had been realistic; devoid of any illusions, they had signed up, aware that they would move to a non-developed country, leading the difficult life of pioneers. In spite of the harsh conditions and unfamiliar climate, the physically fit

---

pamětníků. 1917–1938 (Praha: Nostalgie, 2012). Pavel Pollák, "Die Auswanderung in die Sowjetunion in den zwanziger Jahren", *Bohemia 10*, (1969): 287–311; Miroslav Schneider, *Die tschechoslowakische Auswanderung in die Sowjetunion in der Zwischenkriegszeit (1921–1939)*. Inaugural-Dissertation zur Erlangung der Doktorwürde der Philosophischen Fakultät III (Geschichte, Gesellschaft und Geographie) der Universität Regensburg. Regensburg 2007 http://epub.uni-regensburg.de/10791/1/Elektronische_Publikation_2008_pt11.pdf. See also the documentary about INTERHELPO by ČT 1: http://www.ceskatelevize.cz/porady/10123387 223-interhelpo-historie-jedne-iluze/; accessed 21 September 2017.

6 Naďa Roháčková, "Chvíľka s Pavlínou Dubčekovou", *Slovenka 21*, no. 21 (1968): 8. The interview took place at the community house of the local National Council in Trenčín, north-central Slovakia, where the pensioner Paulína lived in 1968.

and outspoken pensioner had fond memories of her years in Soviet Kyrgyzia. They had been the happiest years of her life:

> "We had to put up with all possible difficulties, cold, diseases, the lack of basic goods, but, you know, we were young, we felt that we were doing something useful. And also, all we Interhelpists were like a large family; we liked each other, I had never experienced such a sense of community before. I remember the happy days when a child was born. And the wedding parties we managed to organize in spite of poverty and difficulties getting hold of things. There were also some bachelors; we took care of them as if they were our family. One of them, Janko Osoha, you know, the one the Fascists murdered later, was my sons' first teacher because we did not have a school close enough. Later, after we had moved from Frunze to Gorkii, we sent the boys to the Russian school. We lived there for ten happy years."[7]

When the interviewer of *Slovenka* lit up a cigarette, comrade Dubčeková shook her head; why did young women smoke? Like his mother, Alexander Dubček would lead a healthy life; he did not smoke or drink and was known for his love of water sports and volleyball.

To put the Dubček family's years in Kyrgyzia into a wider perspective, let us have a look at an interesting historical coincidence. The Dubčeks could not possibly know that when they arrived with INTERHELPO in Kyrgyzia in 1925, a small man lived and worked close to them; he would be responsible for the suffering and death of millions of Soviet citizens.

Nikolai I. Yezhov (1895–1940), the future chief of the NKVD in the 1930s, was appointed party secretary of the Semipalatinsk provincial committee in Kyrgyzia in 1923.[8] He made a stellar career in Central Asia, mainly because of his ruthless but effective style of government, drawing the region's agricultural populace into the 20th century with an iron fist. By October 1925, Yezhov, whom comrades and enemies described as

---

[7] Roháčková, 8.
[8] J. Arch Getty and Oleg V. Naumov, 61.

courageous, energetic, modest, truthful, eager to learn, disciplined, absolutely reliable in ideological terms but no great intellectual, was deputy secretary of the Kazakhstan Territorial Party Committee and head of the personnel department.[9] Yezhov's loyalty to Stalin, his outstanding skills in personnel policy, his organization of the 1930's show trials of Lenin's old comrades and the subsequent purges did not spare him from the monstruous terror machine he had helped to create. On 10 April 1939, the chief of the almighty NKVD was arrested and executed on 2 February 1940 after his trial.[10]

Why could the Czechoslovak cooperative work and live peacefully for ten years in a region Moscow was eager to control and integrate ideologically, economically and politically? Did the Dubčeks meet Yezhov? I think the answers to these questions lie in the conditions of establishing Soviet rule in the provinces and the context of Soviet collectivization. Yezhov and his comrades had, first and foremost, to bring Soviet rule and order to the region, which was a very difficult task, given the social structure and different cultural customs of the clans in Central Asia. And as yet they had no instructions from Moscow to persecute foreigners who had come to the country to help build Socialism:

> "The huge Russian Empire had spanned a dozen time zones and encompassed more than a hundred languages and nationalities. [...] In the south, in Central Asia, and in Siberia 'bandit' gangs (political, criminal, or both) disrupted transportation and made communication difficult and administration perilous. [...] Even for someone without powerful patrons [such as Yezhov, add. JB], a desperate shortage of administrative talent in the early Soviet regime propelled skilled and

---

[9] J. Arch Getty and Oleg V. Naumov, 61.
[10] J. Arch Getty and Oleg V. Naumov, 12, 13.

loyal young administrators – cultivated or not – up the ladder as the scope of the regime's activities dramatically expanded."[11]

I cannot prove it, but I think that the paths of Yezhov and INTERHELPO did not cross. Yezhov had more pressing problems to solve with the local population, while the cooperative lived in peace with their Kyrgyz neighbours, witnessing their hardships that began with the collectivization of 1929. In 1933, the Dubčeks moved to Gorki in the Moscow *oblast'*, the former Nižnii Novgorod.[12]

I. 2 The Soviet Purges of the 1930s and Return to Czechoslovakia (1938)

In Gorkii, father Štefan worked at the GAZ (*Gorkiovskii avtozavod*), a Soviet automobile factory, which was overseen by experts from the US company Ford, who helped with establishing a Ford assembly line, an invention of modernity and US industry alike.[13] Štefan often had to translate for them, and many Americans were guests at the Dubček family's home.

An incident, however, ended the happy years in the Soviet Union: in the first months of 1935, brother Július got involved in a fight with some boys in the neighbourhood and hurt one of them. The parents decided that Paulína and Július should leave immediately for Czechoslovakia, since such an incident could prompt serious consequences. Alexander and his father would stay in Gorki until 1938.

Young Sasha's account of the atmosphere in the years of the *Yezhovchina* are interesting from a viewpoint of his political and national identity. The parents had educated their sons as

---

[11] J. Arch Getty and Oleg V. Naumov, 37, 213.
[12] Dubček, *Hope Dies Last*, 23.
[13] Dubček, *Hope Dies Last*, 24.

Czechoslovaks and Socialists; they spoke Slovak at home and never considered adopting Soviet citizenship. During the Munich crisis in 1938, the Soviet government issued a decree: any foreigner should either adopt Soviet citizenship or leave the country.[14] Štefan and Alexander would return to Czechoslovakia in the autumn of 1938, leaving a country that subjected its citizens to a hitherto unknown terror, organized by Yezhov and Andrei Y. Vyshinsky. The purges had begun after the show trial of Lenin's old comrades:

> "This is the production [the show trials of Sinoviev, Kamenev, Radek and Bukharin in 1936, 1937 and 1938, and the subsequent purges under Yezhov, add. JB] Stalin entrusted to Vyshinsky. He had been watching him closely for a very long time, and now made a perfect choice. [...] There were stacks of ready-made statements like these lying in safes, which, if the Leader and Teacher so wished, could be instantly put in front of him. [...] In the meantime, the population was subjected to a powerful and subtle campaign of brainwashing. What mattered most was to create the general atmosphere of a happy life, bubbling over with optismism, a festival of triumphant youth, regardless of age, 'because everyone here is young now in our youthful and beautiful country', as a popular song of the time went."[15]

In the brutal years of the purges and show trials, many male members of INTERHELPO were arrested, convicted and executed. They left behind wives, sons and daughters who were forced to adopt Soviet citizenship. The Dubček family was lucky: they survived the terror, most probably because of Štefan's language skills and his job at the GAZ, which was of strategic importance to the Soviet government that was eager to industrialize the country. The poet Daniil I. Kharms (1905–1942) wrote about the individual's utter defencelessness in Stalin's lawless Soviet Union in his absurdist poem *The Dream*.

---

[14] Dubček, *Hope Dies Last*, 28.
[15] Arkadi Vaksberg, *Stalin's Prosecutor. The Life of Andrei Vyshinsky* (New York: Grove Weidenfeld, 1990), 73, 201, 77.

Kalugin was subject to the regime's absolute arbitrariness and lack of predictability. A Soviet citizen could be punished for everything – even for his dreams:

> "Kalugin fell asleep and had a dream that he was sitting in some bushes and a policeman was walking past the bushes.
>
> Kalugin woke up, scratched his mouth and went to sleep again and had another dream that he was walking past some bushes and that a policeman had hidden in the bushes and was sitting there.
>
> Kalugin woke up, put a newspaper under his head, so as not to wet the pillow with his dribblings, and went to sleep again; and again, he had a dream that he was sitting in some bushes and a policeman was walking past the bushes.
>
> Kalugin woke up, changed the newspaper, lay down and went to sleep again. He fell asleep and had another dream that he was walking past some bushes and a policeman was sitting in the bushes.
>
> At this point Kalugin woke up and decided not to sleep any more, but he immediately fell asleep and had a dream that he was sitting behind a policeman and some bushes were walking past.
>
> Kalugin let out a yell and tossed about in bed but couldn't wake up.
>
> Kalugin slept straight through for four days and four nights and on the fifth day he awoke so emaciated that he had to tie his boots to his feet with string, so that they didn't fall off. In the bakery where Kalugin always bought wheaten bread, they didn't recognize him and handed him a half-rye loaf.
>
> And a sanitary commission which was going round the apartments, on catching sight of Kalugin, decided that he was unsanitary and no use for anything and instructed the janitors to throw Kalugin out with the rubbish.
>
> Kalugin was folded in two and thrown out as rubbish."[16]

Dubček remembered the terror in his memoirs: from mid-1936 on, strange things were happening that were hanging over the

---

[16] Kharm's *The Dream* on http://absurdist.obook.org/kharms/display.php?p=26; accessed 6 August 2018. I thank Lukas Joos for recommending this poem to me.

country like a dark cloud.[17] Lenin's old comrades, the revolutionaries of the first hour, were accused of high treason, espionage for imperialist Capitalism, subjected to show trials and executed. To express doubt was highly dangerous, and the government made sure that the people believed in the accusations:

> "In school, we were instructed to cut whole pages from our textbooks as truth changed, often overnight. I vividly remember some of the textbooks we were using at that time, particularly one with a photograph of Marshal Tukhachevsky in full regalia – that page had to be cut out with scissors after his execution in the spring of 1937. The removed pages were meticulously collected and counted by our teachers. [...] Parents of some of my schoolmates suddenly disappeared, and when I asked their sons or daughters what had happened, they were never able to explain. [...] The whole picture could not be put together for many years. For many of us it was Khrushchev's historical revelations in 1956 that finally made it all clear. "[18]

A couple of weeks after the signing of the Munich agreement on 30 September 1938, the Dubček family were reunited; they lived in Trenčín in Central Slovakia. From 15 March 1939, clerical Fascism ruled in Slovakia, and Tiso (1887–1947) was the head of the totalitarian-antisemitic government.[19] The Communist Party was declared illegal, and the Party's leadership

---

[17] Dubček, *Hope Dies Last*, 26.
[18] Dubček, *Hope Dies Last*, 26, 27.
[19] Although the Slovak state referred to itself as "Republic", the regime had nothing at all in common with a republic; clerical Fascism ruled in the puppet state that was at Hitler's beck and call. For a chronology of the most important events of the Slovak state see František Cséfalvay a Ľubica Kázmerová, *Slovenská republika 1939–1945. Chronológia najdôležitejších udalosti* (Bratislava: HÚ SAV, 2007). A recommendable collection of historical analysis is *Slovenská Republika 1939–1945* (Bratislava: Veda, 2015). For an excellent analysis of how Germany carved up Czechoslovakia and pressed Slovakia into pseudo-sovereignty see Valerián Bystrický, Miroslav Michela, Michal Schwarc a kol., *Rozbitie alebo rozpad? Historické reflexive zániku Česko-Slovenska* (Bratislava: VEDA, 2010).

went underground. Father Štefan was among them. In 1939, Sasha made a decision that would change his life forever:

> "From its inception in spring 1939 until March 1940, the Slovak Communist program consisted largely of three clear points: nonrecognition of the Slovak state, overthrow of fascism, and restoration of the Czechoslovak Republic. These aims were clear enough for me, at the age of seventeen, to follow my father's example and advice and join the Party in mid-1939. [...] joining the Communist Party at that time was not like joining a pigeon breeders' club. It was a very dangerous step that promised only negative rewards."[20]

As a worker in the Dubnica arms factory's toolmaking workshop, Sasha ran dangerous errands for the Party; he and his mother distributed illegal publications, hiding them in the doghouse.[21] In those hard times, he found happiness: the old friends from Pishpek, the Ondris family, lived in Velcice, a village between Nitra and Trenčín. Sasha and Anna Ondrisová, who had grown up together in Kyrgyzia, fell into each other's eyes, as a Slovak saying goes; they would marry in September 1945 and have three boys.

---

[20] Dubček, *Hope Dies Last*, 34.
[21] Dubček, *Hope Dies Last*, 34.

"Against the functionaries under scrutiny and other Party members, the security service began to make up accusations, which should prove that they not only committed political mistakes or deviated from the Party line but had engaged in hostile and anti-state activities. [...] The author of the speech did not even care about the logical chaos he created; claiming, in one breath, that they had considered Clementis an agent of Beneš [...], and, at the same time, portraying Clementis as the leader of Slovak nationalism and separatism. [...] Also, one has to mention that at the top echelons of the KSS, Lenin's norms and the norms of Party work had been destroyed. That is why the former Party leadership in Slovakia is fully responsible for the violations of Socialist law in the times of the personality cult, especially from 1949 to 1952, when Štefan Bašťovanský was First Secretary KSS, and Comrade Široký Prime Minister. [...] Now, we have to deal with these issues in a correct manner, scrutinizing them for subjectivist interpretation. A very challenging task is thus awaiting our scientific workers, especially the historians. We are expecting that they are going to face this task in a responsible fashion, in the sense of the Party and Marxism-Leninism."[1]

"That I gave Novotny an opportunity to remove from his office some secret files is nonsense. There would have been no way other than a strict police search to separate his personal things from official papers, and I wanted to avoid that by all means. [...] When it was all over, I left for Bratislava, quite exhausted. [...] I went straight home and spent some time with my wife and children. In the evening, I went to an ice hockey game at Bratislava Winter Stadium. [...] I enjoyed the game, and I felt good there among the cheerful crowd."[2]

---

[1] "1963, 8. Apríl, Bratislava, Prejav Alexandra Dubčeka na zasadaní ÚV KSS o výsledkoch činnosti tzv. Kolderovej rehabilitačnej komisie", in *Alexander Dubček: Od totality* ..., 35–43, 39, 40, 42. Dubček referred to the 1952 Prague show trial of Slánský, Clementis and co-accused, mentioning also the 1954 Bratislava trial of the Slovak 'bourgeois nationalists' Husák, Novomeský and co-accused, which had been conducted behind closed doors. Bašťovanský had accused the top Slovak Party members in his speech at the CC KSS in February 1951, when the planning of the 1952 show trial in Prague was in full swing, logistically led by Soviet NKVD agents. In his speech, Dubček expressed the widely felt dissatisfaction in the KSS with the more than meagre results of the Kolder Commission, which prompted the establishment of the Barnabite Commission.

[2] Dubček, *Hope Dies Last*, 126–127.

II. Dear Sasha – A Career in the Communist Party (1939–1968)

In this chapter, I shall describe Dubček's rise to power that began in 1963, when the CC KSS elected him First Secretary. The focus of this chapter is on what Slovak historians call the Slovak Pre-Spring (*predjarie*); Khrushchev's thaw of 1956 was the principal impulse for the Soviet bloc states to re-arrange domestic and foreign affairs. But first, let us have a brief look at Dubček's activities for the illegal KSS during WWII.

II. 1 The Slovak National Uprising (1944)

In the above-mentioned interview with *Slovenka*, mother Paulína remembered the hard years during WWII and the SNP. Her sons had asked her whether they should join the partisans in the mountains. She said:

> "Go, join them. There is no other way!"[1]

The 23-year-old Alexander and his brother Július fought in partisan units in the autumn of 1944.[2] Július died in the fighting against the Germans; Alexander was wounded twice. The

---

[1] Roháčková, "Chvíľka s Pavlínou Dubčekovou", 8.
[2] A selection of studies in chronological order: Alice Dubova, "War experiences with Slovakian partisans (1958)", Yad Vashem Archives, Israel, Wiener Library Collection, record group 0.2, file no. 668, 14 pages; Terézia Kováčiková, "Ženy v národnooslobodzovacom zápase (1939–1945)", in *Zborník múzea Slovenského Národného povstania 7* (Martin, Múzeum SNP v Banskej Bystrici: Osveta, 1982), 5–24; Jozef Jablonický, *Z ilegality do povstania. Kapitoly z občianskeho odboja* (Banská Bystrica: Muzeum SNP, 2009 (2)); Miroslav Pekník, ed., *Slovenské národné povstanie 1944. Súčasť európskej antifašistickej rezistencie v rokoch druhej svetovej vojny* (Bratislava: Veda, 2009) and Rudolf M. Viest, *General Viest's notebooks. Call to arms came in 1938* (Breinigsville, PA: JMV, 2009).

Germans sent father Štefan, a member of the illegal CC KSS, to Mauthausen concentration camp; unlike many others, he survived.[3]

After the war, father Štefan wrote a brief report about the activities of the illegal KSS, explaining in a somewhat simplistic manner that the Communists had been the only ones active in the resistance; their first task had been to establish the printing of leaflets, brochures and, most importantly, the newspaper *Hlas Ľudu* (*The People's Voice*).[4] Jan Osoha, their old INTERHELPO comrade from Kyrgyzia, had been one of the members of the first CC KSS. The co-operation with the Czech comrades in the protectorate and the Austrians beyond the border had worked very well; the illegal KSS had also been in steady contact with Moscow.[5] From 1941 to 1942, the CC KSS had organized the building of revolutionary national councils (*revolučné národné výbory*) in cities, towns and villages. Dubček senior was convinced that after the liberation from the clerical-fascist Tiso regime and the defeat of Nazi Germany, these councils would be ready to seize power.

"That's what our great teacher, the genius Lenin, had taught us."[6]

The members of the first two illegal CC KSS had been betrayed to the Tiso regime, and Osoha, who had evaded arrest, had put together the third CC, appointing Dubček senior as member. It

---

[3] Ivan Laluha, "Alexander Dubček. 1921–1992", in *Alexander Dubček: Od totality...*, 14–29, 15.
[4] AMSNP, "Spomienky Š. Dubčeka", Fond XII, 16 pages, typewritten, p. 1, undated. The report is well structured; Dubček senior expressed himself in a matter-of-fact, down-to-earth manner, in simple language, with short sentences, presenting facts as he had learned about them and what he had experienced. The reasons why the KSS was not allowed to participate in the SNP have never been convincingly explained.
[5] AMSNP, "Spomienky Š. Dubčeka", Fond XII, 16 pages, typewritten, p. 3.
[6] AMSNP, "Spomienky Š. Dubčeka", Fond XII, 16 pages, typewritten, p. 5.

was a pity, as Štefan wrote, that they had not been allowed to participate in the uprising, because some members of the CC did not agree. After the members of the third CC KSS had been arrested and imprisoned in the district prison in Bratislava, the regime had handed them over to the Germans, who had deported them to Mauthausen concentration camp.[7] American fighter planes had bombed the transport in the Austrian town of Melk; many comrades had died, among them Osoha. Štefan finished his report with typical Communist newspeak, praising the glorious Soviet Union and the perennial gratitude and loyalty of the Slovak Communists, which in those days had some bearing. From the Communists' perspective, this way of expressing themselves was not newspeak; it was their regular and normal use of language in communication with fellow Party members. Štefan's view of the future was very clear:

> "The main task of the Party as organized leader of the working class was to grant that the KSČ shall build Socialism after liberation."[8]

The SNP was as much an uprising of leftist and democratically minded citizens against the Tiso government as against the Germans who had invaded Slovakia on 29 August 1944 – yet, the KSČ would claim after its seizure of power on 25 February 1948 that the Communists had been the only ones fighting in the SNP.

On 29 August 1944, the Tiso regime had called in the Germans to fight the partisan movement and block the rapidly advancing Red Army. The uprising as a concerted effort was not successful; it lasted roughly two months, but it was one of the largest anti-Nazi rebellions in Europe. The Czechoslovak army commanders Ján Golian (1906–1945)[9] and Rudolf M. Viest

---

[7] AMSNP, "Spomienky Š. Dubčeka", Fond XII, 16 pages, typewritten, p. 8–9.
[8] AMSNP, "Spomienky Š. Dubčeka", Fond XII, 16 pages, typewritten, p. 14.
[9] http://www.muzeumsnp.sk/historia/osobnosti/general-jan-golian/; accessed 9 February 2018.

(1895–1945),[10] who would be captured, sent to Flossenbürg concentration camp and shot there, faced immense difficulties, as they were unfamiliar with the territory. Materiel support and troops could be sent in only by air.[11] The population supported the uprising, whose centre was Banská Bystrica. 60,000 men of different national origins[12] were fighting in the resistance army and 18,000 in partisan groups. Yet, the German Army that had called in additional troops from Hungary was too strong; Banská Bystrica fell on 27 October. At the end of 1944, the Red Army and the 1st Czechoslovak battalion led by General Ludvík Svoboda (1895–1979)[13], a veteran of Masaryk's *legia*, liberated eastern and south-eastern Slovakia, which Hungarian troops had occupied since the Vienna Arbitrage of 1938. Thanks to the Czechoslovak army, Beneš's war effort in Great Britain, Operation Anthropoid[14] and the SNP, re-united Czechoslovakia would be on the victorious side.

---

[10] http://www.muzeumsnp.sk/historia/osobnosti/general-rudolf-viest/; accessed 9 February 2018.

[11] Kováč, *Dejiny Slovenska*, 237.

[12] For the details of the call to arms in Banská Bystrica see my *A Life Dedicated to the Republic*, 235–239; see also the portrait "Chaviva Reiková (1914–1944) – a Jewish resistance fighter" in my *Seven Slovak Women*, 61–83. Chaviva Reiková (Adele Rosenbergová) left for Palestine in September 1939, trained with the British Army in Egypt and joined the SNP as a radio operator. After capture, the Germans tortured her for two months and then shot her.

[13] For a brief biography of Svoboda, Czechoslovak President from 1968 to 1975, see https://www.hrad.cz/en/president-of-the-cr/former-presidents/ludvik-svoboda; accessed 24 January 2018.

[14] The Czechoslovak exile army in Great Britain planned Operation Anthropoid; officers Jan Kubiš (1913–1942) and Jozef Gabčik (1912–1942) shot *Reichsprotektor* Reinhard Heydrich on 4 June 1942 in Prague. For details see http://www.ww2inprague.com/operation-anthropoid; accessed 24 January 2018. The Germans took cruel revenge with the destruction of the villages of Lidice and Ležaky: http://www.lidice-memorial.cz/en/; accessed 24 January 2018; http://www.holocaustresearchproject.org/nazi occupation/lidice.html; accessed 24 January 2018.

Sasha fought bravely and was shot in the foot. He hid at the house of friends in Velcice, where Anna joined him. Physical pain was nothing compared to his emotional suffering:

> "I was limping around the house at the time of the first thaw, in February 1945, when I learned that Julius had been killed. After our parting in the thick of the battle, he, like me, had made the transition to guerrilla warfare. He had stayed with his partisan group, which in the late fall of 1944 retreated to the wooded area between the Nitra and Hron rivers; we had not been far from each other. There he was killed by a German patrol on January 28, 1945. Julius had not been a political person – just a decent, regular fellow. He fully shared my parents' and my beliefs but never joined the Communist Party. [...] He did not try water twice before jumping in. And I'm sure that was how he died. Since the news arrived that February, I have never stopped remembering my brother's last smile as we parted on that hill above Nitra River, less than six months before liberation."[15]

The end of the war and the immediate post-war years brought happiness and hope to Sasha. The Germans who had immersed the world in unspeakable suffering, were defeated, and Europe, or so he must have thought, could finally be reconstructed according to a body of thought that would bring about a new dawn for mankind. Marxism-Leninism would protect the citizens from exploitation and poverty, establish a just world and efface from the world, once and for all, racism and antisemitism, cynical tools of the exploiting capitalist class.

The Sovietization of Czechoslovakia began on 25 February 1948, when the Communist Party led by Klement Gottwald seized power. Dubček got a job as a mechanic at a yeast factory in Trenčín.[16] He was a grass-roots member of the KSS and did not think about a political career until the Party approached him. The KSS was in need of young, loyal members, and Sasha was the perfect candidate: he was the son of a member of the

---

[15] Dubček, *Hope Dies Last*, 56, 57.
[16] Dubček, *Hope Dies Last*, 60.

illegal CC KSS during the war; he was from a proper proletarian family, had joined the Party when the Communists were being persecuted by the Tiso regime and he had fought in the SNP. Owing to his activities in various Party positions, dealing with administration and economic planning, he was promoted within the Party's rank and file. Simultaneously, Sasha was studying law at Bratislava's Comenius University by correspondence course. He would not graduate, because, in 1955, he got an offer from the Party, which he could not reject.

II. 2 Political Training in Moscow (1955–1958)

With Czech and Slovak comrades, among them Miloš Jakeš (*1922) and Jozef Lenárt (1923–2004), who would both betray him in 1968, the Party sent Dubček to the prestigious Higher Political School in Moscow. He felt at home in the Soviet Union, remembering his childhood in Kyrgyzia. Owing to his fluent Russian, he was able to understand the political situation in the Soviet Union – and the consequences it seemed to promise for the bloc states. Approximately one thousand foreign students lived in Moscow, ten percent being from the East European satellite states.[17] The foreign students lived quite isolated; the majority of them did not yet speak Russian. Because of his fluent command of the language, Alexander was treated like a Russian student. The foreign students received a somewhat less strenuous education than their Soviet peers. Sasha's main interests were history and political economy.[18] He felt that some of Khrushchev's revisions of Stalin's foreign policy were the right way to go, the path to the future of Socialism:

---

[17] Dubček, *Hope Dies Last*, 67.
[18] Dubček, *Hope Dies Last*, 71.

> "Deep in my heart, I had never quite reconciled myself to the idea that Tito was the traitor described in Soviet propaganda in the years after his break with Stalin. With Khrushchev's public apology, I felt a great inner satisfaction, even if Tito, his party, and his country did not formally return to the group of Soviet-led states and continued to pursue their own goals, internally and externally. *Khrushchev's act legitimized a socialist country's independence from the Soviet Union for the first time.*"[19]

Khrushchev's secret speech at the 20th Congress of the Soviet CP, about which he learnt from Soviet friends, convinced the young Slovak that better times were coming. He was shocked to learn about Stalin's crimes and decided to think things through before he spoke about them to his Czechoslovak comrades.[20]

I think that this characteristic trait of Dubček's, that is, keeping things to himself until he was certain to have a proper understanding of the matter that allowed him to make the right move or decision, would later be interpreted by his political adversaries and critics as having doubts, of being naïve and irresolute, as lack of energy or efficiency, of stalling instead of making a courageous move. The difference between theory and practice, between Marxism-Leninism by the book and how it was being realized, was a considerable problem to him.[21] According to his biographer Ivan Laluha, Dubček's contacts with Soviet students, who confided in him and explained what a hero Khrushchev was to them, can be understood as the beginning of his reformist political thought: he was eager to learn how people were thinking, what they were concerned with in their real lives – and thought about reforming the entire socio-economic system.[22]

---

[19] Dubček, *Hope Dies Last*, 71, italics by me.
[20] Dubček, *Hope Dies Last*, 72.
[21] Laluha, "Alexander Dubček …", 16.
[22] Laluha, "Alexander Dubček …", 17.

Dubček was no intellectual like Václav Havel (1936–2011), Vladimír Clementis (1902–1952) or Gustáv Husák, but he had a truthful and genuine interest in realizing Marxism-Leninism, of making the lives of Slovaks and Czechs better. He was an intelligent worker and pragmatic, knowing how the Party worked – and how it could improve the political, economic, cultural and societal atmosphere in the country. I think that in Moscow, he was beginning to form his own ideas, having perhaps already the basic principles of *Socialism with a human face* in his mind. Certainly, the three years in Moscow had a first and crucial influence on his political thought and activities.

Dubček truly believed that Socialism was a system that could be reformed; Khrushchev's tolerance of Yugoslavia's own path to Socialism and his trip to the USA in 1959, where he met US president Dwight D. Eisenhower (1890–1969) proved to the young Slovak that a thorough reform of Czechoslovakia's Stalinist system was not only possible, but that the Soviet Union would approve of it. After all, did Khrushchev not apologize to Tito for Stalin ousting Yugoslavia from the Socialist bloc back in 1948? Inspired by the new freedom of speech, Dubček *ex post* described the Stalinist stranglehold that was still suffocating Czechoslovak society:

> "I was overwhelmed by these events, and, as my stay in Moscow approached its end, I thought more and more about the situation back home. I remember complaining about the restrictions on home visits to an official of the personnel department of the Czechoslovak Communist Party Central Committee in Prague at the end of a leave. Her response was: 'Nor could we come home to visit from the German concentration camps!' I could not help but tell her, 'But we are not in a concentration camp, Comrade. We are at school!' This episode may show how slowly the thaw was making its way into Czechoslovakia."[23]

---

[23] Dubček, *Hope Dies Last*, 73. The response of the comrade of the CC KSČ who rejected Dubček's reasonable complaint demonstrates the tunnel

Zdeněk Mlynář (1930–1997), a young Czech Party member who lived in the Soviet capital before Dubček arrived in Moscow and who would be a principal supporter of Dubček's reforms in 1968, remembered the impact of Soviet de-Stalinization. During his years in Moscow, Mlynář had befriended a young Soviet Party member, who was also studying at the prestigious Moscow State University MGU (*Moskovskii Gosudarstvenii Univerzitet*, also referred to as Lomonossov Moscow State University). The young Mikhail S. Gorbachev (*1931) was a student from a farmer's family from Stavropol in today's Ukraine, and the two young men began a friendship that would last longer than Communism in Europe:

> "Newspapers ignored the first anniversary of Stalin's death in 1954. It wasn't until February 1956, after Gorbachev had graduated from MGU, that Krushchev directly attacked Stalin in his famous secret speech to the Twentieth Party Congress. Meanwhile, the mood at MGU, as in society at large, began to change. Mlynář realized that his MGU friends 'sensed and knew far more about the reality of Stalinist terror in their country than I had gathered from them while Stalin was still alive. In 1954 and 1955, such things were spoken of more and more openly.' Upon his return to Prague in 1955, he found that his compatriots were more afraid than his fellow students in Moscow."[24]

Back home from Moscow, the KSS elected Dubček as a candidate for the political bureau of the CC KSS (*kandidát byra ÚV KSS*); in spite of his doubts, which he would admit in his autobiography later, the young Party functionary published an ideologically impeccable article in *Hlas ľudu* (*The People's Voice*), following

---

vision of Party cadres in the late 1950s; she overreacted with a moral argument, thereby stifling any criticism of procedure and organization with her remark about her past in a Nazi concentration camp. Psychologically understandable, the comrade clung to Stalinism after the trauma of surviving a German concentration camp.

[24] Taubman, *Gorbachev*, 58.

Novotný's line to the letter.[25] As a veteran of the SNP, he praised the Slovak and Czech citizens who had fought in partisan units. Much like his father Štefan in his report, Dubček junior followed the Party line. The intention of the article was to introduce the Party's promising young member to a wider public, since *Hlas ľudu* was the newspaper of the KSS and thus had the largest distribution network in Slovakia. Slovaks should get to know the young Dubček, a potential future leader of their Communist Party. And he obliged, writing about the Communist Party's leadership in the SNP:

> "The Slovak nation rose up. [...] At the forefront of the fight were always and only the Communists. [...] One CC KSS after another was destroyed. [...] Also, nationalists like Husák and Novomeský had made their way into the leadership of the KSS where they did a lot of damage." [26]

When Dubček published this article in August 1959, Husák, Ladislav Holdoš (1911–1988), Ivan Horvath (1904–1960), Daniel Okali (1903–1987) and Laco Novomeský were still in prison. They had been given long sentences; Husák had received *doživotný* (life imprisonment). Husák and Novomeský had been Clementis' best friends. With the trial of the 'Slovak bourgeois nationalists' in 1954, the KSČ thus had rid itself of the leading Slovak Party members of the inter-war generation, slavishly following Stalin's command to get rid of any Party member who was capable of independent thinking or had been in contact with the Capitalist West. Clementis had been in exile in London, working for the Czechoslovak war effort at the BBC; Holdoš had fought in the Spanish Civil War, and Husák was unlucky to have been born too early and befriended Clementis.

---

[25] Alexander Dubček, "Zostaneme verní", *Hlas ľudu VI*, no. 34, 26 August 1959, 1–2, 1.
[26] Dubček, "Zostaneme…", 1.

In his article *Faithfully we stand*, Dubček *expressis verbis* confirmed the fabricated accusations of the trial of 1954 and thus also the Stalinist politics after 1948, referring to Husák and Novomeský as 'nationalists'. Husák and co-accused would be released in Novotný's presidential amnesty of 1960.

I think that, in psychological terms, Husák never forgave Dubček for calling him a traitor in public in the article published in 1959. From Husák's point of view, young Dubček lacked courage, while he had been tortured for "a thousand and two hundred days and nights", courageously withstanding false accusations, signing nothing and facing a lifetime in prison.[27]

II. 3 The Slovak *predjarie* (Pre-Spring) (1963–1967)

How did the *predjarie* begin, and what was Dubček's involvement?

Let us first have a brief look at a fantasy, a utopian future that Czechoslovak and Soviet Party members seemed to seriously believe in. The following extract is from a position paper presented at the conference of the Association of Czechoslovak and Soviet Friendship (*Sväz československo-sovietský priateľstvo*) that took place in Bratislava in November 1961:

> "Over the next twenty years, the Soviet Union will build the material and technological basis of Communism. In view of the diverse development of the powers of production and the high level of engineering, cultural and living standards, the Soviet Union will overtake the USA

---

[27] Gustáv Husák, "Barnabitky a čo im predchádzalo", *Nové slovo*, 20 June 1968, no. 5, p. 16. Husák's article in *Nové slovo* consisted of seven parts, in which he described in detail his ordeal that had begun in 1950 with the Party cancelling his membership. It is an interesting account, revealing the Party's publication policy: only in 1968, *Nové slovo* was allowed to publish excerpts of Husák's report he had submitted to the CC KSČ in 1962. This text was a revelation to the citizens who wanted to know the whole truth; finally, the trials and show trials made sense – all accusations had been false.

in per capita industrial production, becoming number one in the world. [...] By 1980, the Soviet Union will possess the financial means to grant free education for children in kindergartens and primary schools, material support for those who cannot work, free education in schools at all levels of instruction, free medical care and stays at health spas, rent-free apartments and free community services, free public transport and a step-by-step transition to free public food for all. These are the achievements of Communism – rewards according to needs."[28]

The Communist paradise on earth, indeed, and who would not like to live in a state that was paying for everything? But by definition utopia cannot be realized; it is a paradise, a place beyond earthly reality, a place that does not exist.[29] Not only the ideologically blind Party members of that era believed in such utopia; in recent memory, some citizens of the oldest democracy in Europe, a market economy, seemed to have lost their power of reasoning when, in 2017, Swiss citizens rejected a leftist initiative that demanded an "unconditional basic income" for all.[30] What they failed to convincingly demonstrate was who was going to pay for this basic income.

In this subchapter, I present three political events in Czechoslovak domestic affairs that were not only significant aspects of the developing Slovak *predjarie*, but also demonstrated

---

[28] Slovenský národný archív (SNA), fond (f.) Ústredný výbor Komunistickey strany Slovenska (V KSS), zasadanie (zas.) byra ÚV KSS 6.10.1961, krabica (kr.) číslo (č.) 1068, quoted from Stanislav Sikora, "Rehabilitácie v roku 1963 a ich politické dôsledky", in *Predjarie*, 15–20, 16.

[29] The definition of utopia on https://www.etymonline.com/word/utopia; accessed 24 May 2018.

[30] See https://www.admin.ch/opc/de/federal-gazette/2015/9553.pdf; accessed 24 May 2018. I thank Lukas Joos for sending me this link. My former teacher Hermann Lübbe, professor emeritus of political philosophy, referred to political moralism as "the triumph of attitude over reason"; *Politischer Moralismus. Der Triumph der Gesinnung über die Urteilskraft* (Berlin: WJS Corso, 1987 (2)).

that the Party was changing its Stalinist ways, merely aping the new Soviet course.

Studying the *predjarie* reminded me of the period of European integration in the early 1990s. The EC (European Community) was preparing to become the EU, with the *acquis communautaire* for prospective members from the former Soviet bloc, the Visegrad Four: the Czech Republic, the Slovak Republic, Poland and Hungary. Much like the basic idea behind 'European integration', the concept of *predjarie* seems to me to be of a similar twofold nature. First, the *predjarie* was a goal that was achieved by 1967, and second, it was a movement that began with Dubček's election as First Secretary in 1963.

One could say that an ordinary and intellectually independent Slovak citizen was politically oppressed in a threefold fashion: first, by the KSS, which had, second, to obey totally the KSČ, which was, third, forced to follow Khrushchev's new course. Prior to the beginning of the Slovak Pre-Spring, the Slovak Communists had to report to Prague. This all-encompassing system of hierarchical command connected Bratislava first and foremost to Prague; the top echelons of the KSS did not communicate independently with the Soviets.

First, I shall present a brief subchapter about the currency reform of 1953; second, the attempt to catch up with the more advanced Western economies by way of the so-called 'scientific-technical revolution'; and third, a brief summary of the rehabilitation commissions investigating the Stalinist trials of the 1950s.

II. 3. 1 Currency Reform and the Consumer Goods Industry (1953–1958)

Khrushchev's thaw set off a wave of reforms in domestic affairs and relations to the Capitalist West that would affect each country of the Soviet bloc. Why was Czechoslovak de-Stalinization so protracted, beginning in 1957 and ending in 1967? While Moscow was experiencing an unprecedented spring, Czechoslovaks still felt Novotný's iron fist.

Yet, owing to the new Soviet course, Novotný did have to arrange for some reforms. Czechoslovakia's economy was stagnating, and the regime desperately needed foreign currency. The helpless citizens referred to the currency reform of 1953 as *The Big Theft* (*velká krádež* in Slovak, *velká loupež* in Czech),[31] since the regime had taken away their savings. Parliament adopted the law on currency reform on 30 May 1953 and implemented the change on 1 June 1953; because the authorities had not properly informed the International Monetary Fund (IMF), Czechoslovakia was excluded from this important institution.[32] The overall loss to the citizens amounted to 22 billion Czechoslovak crowns (KČS):

> "Human creativity knows no limits and that is why the reform left its imprint on society: people used to say that in February 1948, Gottwald had promised that we are going to be the best-dressed nation wearing the best shoes [*najlepšie oblečeným a obutým národom*] – but after the spring of 1953 they said: 'now, we are not only de-scarfed but also de-coated [*už sme ošálení a i okabátení*].'"[33]

---

[31] Oral History interview with Vlasta Jaksicsová and Jaroslava Roguľová, 3 December 2017, Bratislava, Slovak Republic.

[32] The best analysis of the 1953 currency reform known to me is Miroslav Londák, "Príčiny peňažnej (menovej) reformy z jari 1953 v Československu so zreteľom na vojenské súvislosti", *Vojenská história* 19, no. 2 (2015): 73–82. I am indebted to the author who sent me his article as a Word document in A4 format, 11 pages. I quote from Londák's Word document. For more details see the IMF Annual Report of 1954, page 86, on http://www.imf.org/external/pubs/ft/ar/archive/pdf/ar1954.pdf; accessed 1 March 2018.

[33] Londák, "Príčiny ...", 4. Londák in an e-mail conversation from 16 February 2018 about today's value of those KČS 22 billion: "I am guessing, as you cannot compare the value of money from, for example, 1985 with today's value. But we can say that in 1954 – according to official statistics – the

Besides the currency reform that was the basis of a new economic system with Soviet-style five-year plans, which the economists in 1968 would try to reform, an international incident affected the top echelons of the KSČ. Czech and Slovak Party members were shocked by the Hungarian uprising of October 1956; they were genuinely afraid that a similar uprising could happen in Czechoslovakia too. After all, they had strung up Communists on lampposts in Budapest. These conditions resulted in a new economic policy that concentrated on the consumer goods industry.[34]

Textiles, cosmetics, furniture and telephones appeared. A comparison: in 1957, one self-service food shop served 53,303 Slovak citizens; in 1959, such a food shop served 2,333 citizens – thus, a massive improvement.[35] The textile industry began to show fashion from the West, which was no longer considered the ideological enemy, at least not when it came to catching up

---

state revenue was KČS 84.2 billion. As far as the revenue of the citizens was concerned: in 1954, the average salary was KČS 1,171. The loss was thus immense. People not only lost the savings they had at home (50:1), but also money they had saved in various insurances and other institutions. For example: the small farmers and craftsmen were so hard hit by the currency reform that they vanished as a social class – these small entrepreneurs had at home so-called operational capital (they did not have the money in a bank like today) and so they lost their entire capital, everything. This was a tragedy, compared with what happened to the small farmers – these were under such pressure from the Communist regime in economic and micro-economic terms that collectivization was accomplished in Slovakia at the end of the 1950s. 80% of all agrarian land was in the so-called Socialist sector, that means, owned by the state. Essentially, the nationalization of autumn 1945 and later, after February 1948, and after the 1953 currency reform made the Communist state the owner of the large majority of the means of production, while a major part of the citizenry had nothing left to own – only its labour force. That's how the citizens became fully dependent on the regime."

[34] Oral History Interview with Vlasta Jaksicsová ...
[35] Jaroslava Roguľová, ed., *Pramene k dejinám Slovenska a Slovákov, XIIIC: Slováci a nástup socializmu* (Bratislava: Literární informačné centrum, 2017), 176.

with Western living standards and economic development. Czech and Slovak women saw in their journals *Vlasta*, *Slovenka*, *Žena a Život* and *Žena a Móda* what women in Paris and Rome were wearing. After the monotone and monochrome years of brutal Sovietization, citizens were craving new products, colour and diversity.

Fashion became de-politicized; unlike in the late 1940s and early 1950s, fashion no longer followed the ideological line that had prescribed simple and functional clothes for working women. In the Party's mind back then, the proletariat did not need bourgeois luxury.[36] A particularly important year was 1958: Czechoslovakia had a pavilion at the EXPO in Brussels. In 1965, the country participated at an international salon for fashion in Paris, and in 1966, Christian Dior was able to show his collection in Prague.[37]

II. 3. 2 The Scientific-Technical Revolution (early 1960s)

The second factor of the economic change was the so-called scientific-technical revolution.[38] Against the background of the new course, the KSČ saw itself forced to accept that without a 'revolution' in science and technology it could not keep up with the more advanced industries of the West. The regime thus had to invest in automation, cybernetics and electronification.

---

[36] Konstantína Hlaváčková, *Móda za železnou oponou. Společnost, oděvy a lidé v Československu 1948–1989* (Praha: Grada Publishing, Uměleckoprůmyslové museum v Praze, 2016). The exhibition *Let us sow! (Nech šije!)* at the Slovak National Gallery in Bratislava in summer 2017 on https://www.sng.sk/sk/vystavy/1046_nech-sije-moda-na-slovensku-1945-1989; accessed 27 December 2017. A similar way of ideological thinking can be observed in Mao's China: the Mao suit on http://www.sacu.org/dresspolitics.html; accessed 13 March 2018.

[37] Hlavačková, 38, 39.

[38] Stanislav Sikora, "Slovensko v predjarí – na ceste k roku 1968", in *Od predjaria …*, 14–24, 14, 17.

Compared with Western states, the conditions in the service industries, public transport and production of electronic devices and machines were alarmingly bad.[39]

The concept of 'revolution' should not be taken too seriously in this context; it was Marxist-Leninist newspeak, a smoke screen intent on convincing Party cadres about the plan for a cosmetic change of the economic system. The idea was to increase economic output under the conditions of the centrally planned economy. It was no revolution in the true sense of the word – just the idea that something in the economy had to change. The Czech sociologist and academic Radovan Richta (1924–1983) in 1966 about the necessity of catching up with the West in science and technology in the post-industrialist world:

> "In the current conditions of two competing systems, the scientific-technological revolution [*vedecko-technická revolúcia*] is a process that shall necessarily turn against anybody who is not capable of following it or catching up with it in time. [...] Now, it is about everything."[40]

The problem was, of course, that in a totalitarian state that was micromanaging citizens' lives and selecting students for universities and technical colleges according to their class background and not their individual talents, scientific innovation and enterprise were suffocated. Children of the proletariat were selected to study engineering, physics and philosophy – regardless of whether they had any talent for these subjects, while children from the wrong class background, that is, from families of

---

[39] Sikora, "Slovensko v predjarí ...", 14.
[40] RICHTA, Radovan a kol. *Civilizácia na rázcestí*. Bratislava: VPL 1966, s. 50, quoted from Sikora, "Slovensko v predjarí ...", 14. Sikora quoted from the Slovak translation of Richta's study. The study in original Czech was called *Civilizace na rozcestí* and can be found on http://www.sds.cz/docs/precte te/eknihy/rri_cnr.htm; accessed 10 February 2018.

former entrepreneurs or the intelligentsia, were sent to vocational training; the regime banned children of bourgeois families from higher education.[41] This social change was indeed a revolution – but for the worse; it undermined the basis of Czechoslovak society, causing a general and painful lack of expertise, motivation and education worthy of the name.

Scientific creativity and innovation need liberty, or, at least, a certain amount of independent thinking and scope for decision-making. The regime thus had to allow for a basic minimal tolerance of individual talent. Furthermore, the 'civilizational aspect' of the scientific-technical 'revolution' required that pressing problems be discussed and solved in order to improve the economy. The Soviet bloc wanted to prove to the world the superiority of its socio-economic regime and ideology: it had to face up to the challenge of the West. As soon as the KSČ began to loosen its ideological grip to some extent, citizens demanded answers about the past.

II. 3. 3 The Rehabilitation Commissions (1955–1968)

The third aspect, or condition that led to the *predjarie* and was also a part of it was rooted in the past: one could say that Czechoslovak civil society was slowly emerging because of that past – and the Party's more than reluctant way of dealing with it. The rehabilitation commissions and the historians' analysis of the commissions' modest achievements overall should be

---

[41] A telling example of this policy was former Czechoslovak and Czech president Václav Havel (1936–2011), who was from a bourgeois-capitalist family and hence not allowed to study at university. He embarked on vocational training as a chemical laboratory assistant; because he suffered from vertigo, the planned vocational training as carpenter was cancelled. Havel wrote in his spare time. In the early 1960s, he worked as handyman and sceneshifter at the *Divadlo na zábradlí* theatre in Prague; Josette Baer, *Politik als praktizierte Sittlichkeit. Zum Demokratiebegriff von Thomas G. Masaryk und Václav Havel* (Sinzheim: Pro Universitate Verlag, 1998), 99.

scrutinized with a critical eye since the persecution of the non-Communist citizens was ignored.[42] All historians employed in the rehabilitation commissions were Party members; they had, first and foremost, the task to investigate the persecution of the Communists. The persecution of the Lutheran and Catholic priests, centre-right politicians, officers and soldiers loyal to the Beneš government during WWII, that is, all non-Communists, were legitimate in ideological terms, since the non-Communists were widely considered 'enemies of the people'. In this regard, the KSČ's ideological brainwashing from 1948 on proved a success. Vlasta Jaksicsová about the persecution of the 1950s in the context of the rehabilitation commissions:

> "The Communists thought: that had happened only to us!"[43]

The Czech historian Václav Veber listed five commissions the KSČ established to find out the truth about the past, or rather, lukewarmly pretended to do so. First, the Barák commission (*Barákova komise*) of 1955, named after Interior Minister Rudolf Barák (1915–1995); second, the Kolder Commission (*Kolderová komise*), named after Drahomír Kolder (1925–1972), secretary of the CC KSČ and head of the commission that was active in 1962 and 1963 with Dubček and Lenárt as board members. The third was the Barnabite Commission (*Barnabitská komise*) of 1963, which emerged as a protest commission against the ignorance of the fate of the Slovak Party members the Kolder Commission had failed to investigate.[44]

---

[42] Václav Veber, "O rehabilitacích a o tom, co s nimi souvisí", *Securitas Imperii* 16, no. 1 (2010): 10–29, 28–29. I am indebted to Miroslav Londák who recommended Veber's study to me.
[43] Oral History Interview with Vlasta Jaksicsová ...
[44] Veber, 17–18. The Barnabite Commission was named after the Barnabite monastery in the Prague Castle district, where the commission met.

A further commission, active from 1966 to 1967, was an independent initiative of the Czechoslovak union of writers (*Svaz československých spisovatelů*). The future Nobel laureate Jaroslav Seifert (1901–1986)[45] was the chairman of the commission, which rehabilitated persecuted members, non-Communists and Communists alike, by asking the Ministry of Culture and Information to return the books of forbidden authors to the libraries.[46] The commission also demanded the re-edition of books that had been put on the index and asked for higher pensions for persecuted members.

The Seifert Commission divided the persecuted writers into four groups: first, those who were released from prison, but rehabilitated only in secret, since the public should not learn about their persecution; second, those, who were still waiting for a re-trial; third, those who had suffered from the savage criticism of Ladislav Štoll (1902–1981), literary critic and member of the union, who allegedly had wormed his way into his high position with political intrigues, displaying a painful lack of academic expertise. The fourth group consisted of everybody else, among them the internationally respected Czech literary critic Václav Černý (1905–1987).[47]

The fourth commission established by the KSČ came into being after Novotný's amnesty of 1960; soldiers who had been interned in labour camps demanded the establishment of a commission that should investigate their persecution. In 1963,

---

[45] See https://www.nobelprize.org/nobel_prizes/literature/laureates/1984/seifert-bio.html; accessed 8 March 2018; see also his autobiography and some of his most famous poems on https://www.nobelprize.org/nobel_prizes/literature/laureates/1984/seifert-poetry.html; accessed 8 March 2018.
[46] Veber, 19.
[47] For a brief biography see http://www.slovnikceskeliteratury.cz/showContent.jsp?docId=357; accessed 14 February 2018.

and 1964, the Mírov Commission (*Mírova komise*), named after the labour camp at Mírov in the Olomouc region of Moravia, postponed the publication of its 'investigation'.[48] The persecuted soldiers were neither rehabilitated nor did they receive financial compensation.

The new law about public rehabilitation in court (*zákon o soudní rehabilitaci*), law no. 82/1968 Sb., adopted on 27 April 1968, when Dubček was First Secretary of the KSČ, prompted consequences in society: former prisoners of the Communist regime founded the independent club K 231 (*Klub 231*), named after law no. 231 from 1948 that had been the 'legal' basis for their imprisonment.[49]

The last and fifth rehabilitation commission the CC KSČ initiated in April 1968 was the Piller Commission (*Pillerová komise*), named after Jan Piller (1922–1995), naturally a member of the KSČ.[50]

The rehabilitation commissions that investigated the show trials and persecution of the 1950s inspired more hope than they presented facts – in many cases, justice was not served to the full. But the rehabilitation law of April 1968 served one important function; to the citizens, it was a symbol of the Dubček government and all it stood for – *liberalizácia*:

> "The law on rehabilitation gave back to the people the belief in the grand idea of Communism. It re-established the belief in a government that acknowledged its mistakes and took responsibility to correct them – as far as this is in human power at all. It was adopted to purify

---

[48] Veber, 21.
[49] Veber, 21, 22.
[50] Veber, 22. In his above-quoted article "The Barnabite findings and what preceded them", Husák delivered a thorough account of his fate, but did not criticize the various commissions; the parts that *Nové slovo* published contained no criticism of the Kolder and Barnabite Commissions nor of the Party's policy of organizing the commissions and publishing the results.

> the party from its top, so one could live and work with a clear conscience. It revived the faith of the public, regardless whether citizens were Party members or not; it gained the support of the young generation and became one of the symbols of the pure and heartfelt post-January effort."[51]

Basically, we can state that the commissions' results were lukewarm and half-baked, because of their composition: all commission members were Party members. The regime followed the rationale: 'Admit that some unlawful decisions in the 1950s had been made, but do not admit that the Party was completely wrong. The KSČ is never wrong; only some individual Party members committed injustices, got carried away in their eagerness to establish Socialism in the difficult times of the personality cult.' Yet, the rehabilitation commissions were a start, a modest beginning of a new course that would be admired in the West and raise hopes for an authentic Socialism with a human face in Czechoslovakia.

Finally, in the context of protracted de-Stalinization, we should mention two further aspects or phases of domestic affairs that had considerable influence on the emergence of the Slovak *predjarie*. The Pre-Spring, as I have come to understand it, was much more complicated than a slow thawing of the ice on command from above, that is, the Party. The *predjarie* was half – and half-heartedly – initiated by the Party, at its helm Novotný, and pushed forward by the citizens who wanted to know the truth about the brutal Sovietization of the 1950s, while the Party was still clinging to its old Stalinist ways.

I think we would be gravely mistaken to conceive of the late 1950s and early 1960s as the beginning of Czechoslovak Reform Communism. Reform Communism as a concerted

---

[51] Anna Tučková v článku Kdo seje neklid (*Reportér*, 1969, č. 5, s.11n, citát je na s. 13), quoted from Veber, 29, footnote 29; "post-January effort" refers to the election of Dubček as First Secretary KSČ in January 1968.

political programme could not get underway until the reformers had the upper hand in the Party, when the KSČ rid itself of Novotný in January 1968, electing Dubček First Secretary, who had the judicial, executive and legislative power to initiate political change. But without the Slovak *predjarie*, the liberalization that had encouraged people to speak their minds and had taken away their fear, the Czechoslovak Spring of 1968 could not have happened.

II. 4 First Secretary of the KSS (1963–1968)

When the CC KSS elected Dubček First Secretary on 8 April 1963, a change began in Slovakia that would spill over to the Czech lands and peak in the Czechoslovak Spring of 1968. I will proceed with a description of how the *predjarie* slowly changed the political atmosphere in Slovakia, focussing on archive material available to the Western reader for the first time. I do not claim to present a complete description, let alone a thorough analysis of how the *predjarie* affected citizens' lives from 1963 on; such an endeavour would involve several aspects of society, politics and economy that would probably fill two volumes in their own right.

The examples I chose demonstrate how total the Party's control had been since 1948. Even if one is fairly familiar with the totalitarian regimes in Eastern Europe in the second half of the 20th century, one is baffled by the arbitrariness and lawlessness of the Party's style of ruling. But first, a brief word about Dubček's election.

Why did the CC KSS elect young Comrade Dubček and not an older Slovak protégé of Novotný's? And how much room for manoeuvre did the KSS have in its relationship with the more powerful KSČ? According to my friend Miloslav Liška, the Soviet government had had its eyes on Dubček ever since he had attended the Moscow Party school from 1955 to 1958, and, following Khrushchev's course of criticizing Stalin's personality cult, they might have hinted to the CC KSČ to have the young Slovak elected First Secretary of the KSS.[52] This is an absolutely plausible explanation, which, however, does not withstand closer scrutiny.

My esteemed colleague Jan Pešek,[53] a historian and specialist on the history of the KSS, thinks that there was no Soviet influence on Dubček's election at all, since Slovakia was a minor, hence negligible, issue for the Soviets. The Soviet government was only ever interested in who was at the helm of the KSČ in Prague; to them, Slovakia was a province. Naturally, they knew Dubček, since he had studied in Moscow, and held him in high regard, but in 1963, Novotný's influence was of decisive importance. He did not manage to get his protégé Michal Chudík (1914–2005) elected First Secretary; furthermore, his men at the CC KSS Karol Bacílek (1896–1974) and Pavol David (1899–1970) had to step down owing to their involvement in the trials of the 1950s.[54] The KSS leadership simply did not want a Novotný man, so they elected Dubček, a young Party member, unstained by the 1950s and fluent in Russian. I consider it likely that the CC KSS hoped that they might establish an independent line of communication through Dubček to Moscow, to persuade Moscow to make Prague change its ways in regard to Slovakia – but this is speculation. Dubček's election was an internal affair

---

[52] Oral History Interview with Miloslav Liška in Podolí, Czech Republic, 7 January 2018.
[53] E-mail conversation with Jan Pešek on 28 and 29 January 2018.
[54] The CC KSS removed Bacílek and David from their functions in the CC KSS at its meeting on 6 June 1963, three months after Dubček's election; *Chronológia Dejín Slovenska a Slovákóv II*, 859.

of the KSS. Pešek on the KSS's room for independent decision-making:

> "The KSS had absolutely no room for independent manoeuvring, not even after 1956. They obsequiously executed the commands from Prague and asked Prague to give them instructions. This was the situation in the autumn of 1956 with regard to what was happening in Hungary, and in 1960 too, when the new constitution became effective, defining the rights and duties of the Slovak national organs. The triumvirate of Bacílek, David and Rudolf Strechaj (1914–1962) were Novotný's men; he supported them and kept them at the helm of the KSS. A certain limited room for independent decision-making was opening up after Dubček's election as First Secretary, but the fight between Novotný and his protégés Chudík and Michal Sabolčik (1924–1995) against Dubček prevailed."[55]

The atmosphere of liberalization in Slovakia and the half-hearted work of the rehabilitation commissions prompted Gustáv Husák to make a courageous move; the reckless doctor of law, who had been imprisoned for ten years and withstood psychological and physical torture, wanted justice at all costs. He appeared at the meeting of the Bratislava section of the KSS on 14 and 15 March 1964 and strongly criticized the KSS' failure to properly investigate the trials of the 1950s and their overall neglect of efforts to build Socialism.[56] Because of his fierce speech, the CC KSS, at its helm Dubček, rejected his applications to Party and state functions. From Dubček's point of view, Husák's criticism only made matters with Prague unnecessarily complicated, since the principal interest of Slovak domestic affairs was to realize the stipulations of the 1960 Czechoslovak constitution: equal rights for the Slovaks with the Czechs. And this should be realized, first and foremost, in the relationship between the KSS and KSČ.

---

[55] E-mail conversation with Jan Pešek on 28 and 29 January 2018.
[56] *Chronológia Dejín Slovenska a Slovakóv II*, 861–862.

The fact that Dubček was First Secretary of the KSS did not mean that he immediately stood up against Novotný. Like a marathon runner, Dubček was well aware of the power relations in both parties. It would take him five long years to gain the upper hand over the Stalinists in both Parties and, finally, Novotný.

Meanwhile, US president John F. Kennedy's visit to West Berlin on 26 June 1963 seemed to promise a further rapprochement of the two ideological blocs. Yet, while Kennedy's famous *Ich bin ein Berliner* speech conquered West Germany and proved to the free world that the USA was willing to listen to its ideological adversary, politics in the East were changing – but not too much and not too fast. The visit of the most famous Soviet woman to Czechoslovakia in August 1963 demonstrates totalitarianism in practice, but also, the Czechoslovak citizens' interest in the first woman in space.

II. 4. 1 A Soviet Cosmonaut (1963)

From a file classified top secret (*přísně tajné*):

> "Resolution for the 33rd meeting of the presidium of the CC KSČ on 13 August 1963. Ad 15). Programme of the visit of Comrade V. Tereshková to the ČSSR (compiled by Comrade J. Hendrych). The programme of the visit of Comrade V. Tereshková to the ČSSR consists of the following points."[57]

It was an honour for the Czechoslovak government to host the first woman[58] in space; the visit of Soviet cosmonaut Valentina

---

[57] "Usnesení 33. schůze předsednictva ÚV KSČ ze dne 13. srpna 1963", SNA, Fond ÚV KSS, tajomniki, A. Dubček, 1963–1968, carton 2380, nine pages, typewritten, 1. The document is not dated, but I deem it safe to assume that it was written two or three days prior to the meeting of the presidium of the CC KSČ, that is, around the 10 or 11 August 1963.

[58] How Russia honours Valentina Tereshkova: https://www.rt.com/news/379550-tereshkova-facts-80-anniversary/; accessed 9 March 2018. The first woman in space about visiting Mars: https://www.theguardian.

V. Tereshkova (*1937) in August 1963 was meticulously planned. Looking at the demanding and tight schedule, one almost feels sorry for Mrs Tereshkova, but she probably liked the admiration and well-deserved attention, the good Czech food and Czechoslovakia's famous tourist spots such as Prague Castle, the Pilsen breweries and Karlovy Vary, a beautiful spa resort in the west of Czechoslovakia that had a long-standing tradition of celebrity guests, ever since Goethe had visited in the 18th century.[59] The CC KSČ begrudged neither cost nor effort to make Comrade Tereshkova's stay in Czechoslovakia an unforgettable memory – to her, the Party and the people.

Because of security, state visits are always meticulously planned, regardless where they take place; yet, Comrade Tereshkova's visit in Novotný's Czechoslovakia significantly differed from a visit, let's say, of a Swiss federal councillor to France or Italy in 1963.

In the West, citizens usually show up voluntarily to greet an international guest or demonstrate their criticism of the visit with protest banners, gathering at a crucial place the foreign guest has to pass through. In Switzerland, for example, you would gather in front of the Bundeshaus in Bern to protest against the visit of a prime minister or president of a state that is violating human rights on a daily basis, imprisoning journalists and oppressing people's free speech. Such protest is directed not only against the guest, but also against one's government that issued the invitation.

---

com/global-development-professionals-network/2017/mar/29/valentina-tereshkova-first-woman-in-space-people-waste-money-on-wars; accessed 9 March 2018.

[59] Goethe in Karlsbad on https://www.karlovyvary.cz/en/bust-johann-wolfgang-von-goethe; accessed 10 March 2018.

No rule-of-law state can whip in citizens, pupils and students from offices, factories, schools and universities and herd them into the streets. To voice one's critical protest or enthusiastic welcome of an international political guest is a democratic right. It is also a democratic right NOT to be interested in politics at all, that is, to boycott voting and abstain from having a political opinion, to stay at home, grow carrots in one's garden or engage in online gambling, or whatever takes one's fancy. However, I am certain that many Czechoslovak citizens were curious, hence gladly gathered in the streets to see Comrade Tereshkova in the flesh; but that is not the issue here. The issue is that they had no choice but to turn out to greet her.

Let us now have a closer look at the programme of the visit. Comrade Tereshkova would arrive at Prague Ruzyně airport at 9 am on Thursday 15 August 1963, welcomed by Secretary of the KSČ Hendrych and two female comrades. No speeches were planned. Delegates of the most important economic and political institutions such as the Union of Youth, the National Front, the Women's Association and other institutions would be present; besides representatives of the Prague government, delegates of the Soviet Embassy would greet her at the airport.

> "Furthermore, 10,000 to 12,000 workers from Prague factories are going to participate; they will be gathered in front of the main airport building. [...] The convoy will follow this route: Kladenská, Starodejvická [...] through the Letná tunnel. 70,000 to 80,000 Prague citizens will participate, welcoming her along the route Švermův most, Revoluční [...] to Klárov. Then, the car with Comrade Tereshkova will head for the government villa, where she is staying."[60]

The welcome festivities would be broadcast live on national TV. At 12 noon, welcome festivities at Prague Castle with President

---

[60] "Usnesení 33. schůze ...", 2.

Novotný and a handful of selected members of the CC KSČ would begin. The president would award Comrade Tereshkova with the order of Socialist Work for her long flight in orbit. From 1.15 pm lunch in private at the government villa; at 3 pm, Comrade Tereshkova would participate in a discussion with members of the presidium of the Czechoslovak Academy of Sciences ČSAV and members of the academy's commission for space technology. From 5 to 7 pm, festive reception at Prague Castle, hosted by First Secretary and President Novotný with approximately five hundred guests, Party members, artists, actors and sportsmen and sportswomen.[61]

The next day, Friday 16 August, was also planned to the minute: at 8 am Comrade Tereshkova would meet delegates from the Czechoslovak Women's Association and other societal organizations. The guided tour through Prague would lead her to the Tesla Moskva factory in Karlín, the Vyšehrad castle complex, the Strahov monastery and the Old Town guildhall. After lunch in the government villa at 12 noon, the guest would be driven to the TIBA Beroun textile factory in the south of Prague. Around 4 pm the convoy would drive to Lidice, where the mayor would show her around, explain the tragedy of the people of Lidice, after which she would sign the guest book. She would be back in Prague at approximately 7.30 pm to attend a festive reception with delegates from the youth organizations and workers in the sports hall of the Park of Culture.[62]

The programme contains important information that helps us understand the immense lengths the government went to: continuous and controlled broadcasting on national TV and radio; the appearance of thousands of citizens welcoming the

---

[61] "Usnesení 33. schůze ...", 2.
[62] "Usnesení 33. schůze ...", 3.

honoured guest, standing at the sides of the streets the cosmonaut was driven through, forming a jubilant throng; festive dinners; discussions; visits to factories; speeches; toasts. According to Slavic tradition, the hospitality of the Czechoslovak Socialist society had no limits – only the best was good enough for Comrade Tereshkova.

On day 3, 17 August, the government delegates showed Comrade Tereshkova the Pilsen breweries, a pioneer camp close by and then drove her to Karlovy Vary, where she was put up at the Grand Hotel Moskva, today's Grand Hotel Pupp.[63] On day 4 she was walked through the beautiful colonnades and surroundings of the spa town and visited the famous Moser factory that specialized in glass and crystal; around 5 pm she was driven back to Prague. Day 5, 19 August, eventually brought the comrade to the other part of the country; at 8 am, she was flown to Bratislava, where First Secretary KSS Dubček gave her a festive welcome at 9 am.[64]

In the list of the top functionaries welcoming the Soviet cosmonaut, Chudík is named in second position;[65] Novotný's man in the CC KSS was thus still around. So was David, who would be asked at the bottom of the document to pay the bills incurred with the visit of Comrade Tereshkova in Slovakia, pocket money included; the state funds for international top guests would foot the bill.[66] In the Slovak capital, Mrs Tereshkova was put up in the luxurious Hotel Carlton in the centre of the old town on Hviezdoslavovo namestie. She was invited to discussions and another *kulturní večer* (evening cultural

---

[63] On the history of the grand hotel Pupp see http://www.pupp.cz/en/section/15-history.html; accessed 22 April 2018.
[64] "Usnesení 33. schůze ...", 6.
[65] "Usnesení 33. schůze ...", 7.
[66] "Usnesení 33. schůze ...", 9.

programme) the KSS had organized. She spent day 6, 20 August, in Ostrava in Moravia and was then flown back to Prague at 5 pm. The Soviet embassy in Prague held a festive reception, starting at 8 pm.

> "7). 21. August 1963 (Wednesday). At 10 am, Comrade Tereshkova will be on her way back to Moscow. At the airport, Comrade Hendrych and other comrades, the same individuals who welcomed her when she arrived, will bid her farewell. Only 3,000 persons will be at the airport; the participation of the masses in Prague [when she would be driven to the airport through Prague, add. JB] is not granted [*Po Praze účast zajistována nebude*]."[67]

What does this programme tell us? First, the meticulous planning of Comrade Tereshkova's visit to Czechoslovakia speaks for itself, or rather, the totalitarian government. Almost every minute was planned; the Novotný government showered her with attention, gifts and honours; tens of thousands of factory workers were herded into the streets of Prague. The cosmonaut had to visit, greet, listen, discuss, receive honours, visit some more, sign guestbooks – all in the spirit of Socialist Internationalism.

Second, I find it most telling that Comrade Tereshkova spent only one day in the Slovak capital Bratislava. According to the Czechoslovak constitution of 1960 that had put Slovakia theoretically on an even footing with the Czech part, her visit should have been planned accordingly: three days in the Czech part and three days in the Slovak part would have been fair. Had the KSS top functionaries had any say in the planning of the visit, that is, had the KSS enjoyed equal rights with the KSČ, I am quite certain that they would have suggested showing Comrade Tereshkova as many beautiful spots, factories and institutions

---

[67] "Usnesení 33. schůze ...", 9.

in Slovakia as the KSČ had suggested for her visit to the Czech part.

I deem it realistic, albeit I am speculating here, that had Dubček had any say in the planning, he would have drawn up a Slovak programme: he would have been proud of showing the Soviet cosmonaut the beautiful city centre of Košice, Nitra and Trnava's medieval old towns and their historical significance for Slovak national identity. A discussion with Slovak astronomers and mathematicians of the Academy of Sciences SAV would have been planned as well as a visit to Devín, an architectural site close to Bratislava that has a symbolic meaning for the Slovak nation ever since Ľudovít Štúr and his adherents' romantic excursion and celebration of Slovak patriotism in the ruins of the medieval castle on 24 April 1836.

The programme of Comrade Tereshkova's visit clearly demonstrates that Novotný and the KSČ were still very much in command. This did not change eight months later in 1964, when a courageous doctor of medicine insisted on his right to openly speak his mind.

II. 4. 2 A Rebellious Party Member (1964)

When Vladimír Maňák, doctor of medicine, candidate of the prestigious Slovak academy of sciences (MuDr, CSc.) and member of the KSS, published two articles in the Slovak journal *Kultúrny život* (*Cultural Life*) in 1963, the CC KSČ obliged (!) First Secretary Dubček on 19 February 1964 to organize a hearing of the physician's incorrect opinions at the upcoming meeting of the Western Slovak section of the KSS; members of the journal *Life of the Party* (*Život strany*), the organ of the CC KSČ, would be present – the text of the CC KSČ sounds rather threatening, revealing the power relations between the two Communist Parties.⁶⁸

In theory, the CC KSS in Bratislava had more power and say in Slovakia than journalists of the organ of the Prague CC KSČ. What did Comrade Maňák write to draw the attention of the almighty CC KSČ to him? And what can this document tell us about the political atmosphere in Slovakia and the relationship of KSČ and KSS??

I do not have Maňák's original texts at my disposal, but we do not need them, since his views are not important; for our purpose, much more interesting is how the CC KSČ reacted and instructed its people at *Life of the Party*. From the report to the CC KSČ of the journalists of *Life of the Party* about the hearing:

> "The journal 'Cultural Life' published in its issue no. 28 of 1963 the article 'The task of the creative intellectuals in building socialism and communism' and in issue no. 41 of 1963 the article 'Trust for trust'. The author of both articles is Comrade Vladimír Maňák, member of the KSS at the department of physiology and medicine at the Slovak Academy of Sciences in Bratislava. Besides some correct thoughts, the author's articles promoted incorrect views [*proklamoval nesprávné názory*] that are in conflict with the basic Leninist principles concerning the Party's development and activities."⁶⁹

Furthermore, the report reads, in a letter to the editors of *Life of the Party*, Maňak had glossed over the mistakes in his articles, expressing a distinct lack of trust in the Party's organs and apparatus. He had recommended the Party members' search for mistakes in the resolutions and decisions before carrying them out. I understand this as Maňák's call for individual responsibility, which was no issue to the journalists. *Life of the Party* had reacted to these incorrect views in issue no. 21 of 1963 with a

---

⁶⁸ "Usnesení 39. schůze sekretariátu ÚV KSČ ze dne 19. února 1964, k bodu: 11) Články s. dr. Vladimíra Maňáka, CSc. (s. J. Valenta)", Fond ÚV KSS tájomniki, A. Dubček, 1963–1968, karton 2384, four pages, typewritten, 1.
⁶⁹ "Usnesení 39. schůze ...", 2.

polemic by Comrades Marton and Hrabovski. The authors had written in their text "Party discipline and the struggle against the residues of the personality cult" about the positive aspects of Party discipline when accomplishing political tasks. Comrade Maňák, however, had rejected that positive criticism and asked the editors of *Life of the Party* to publish his reply to Comrades Marton and Hrabovski.[70] The editorial board had given an assurance that the journal would publish his article if he stuck to the political line.

In the meantime, *Cultural Life* had reacted in issue no. 47 of 1963 to the article of Marton and Hrabovski in the column "The Classics are polemicizing", making fun of the authors' views. The author of the polemic who had signed with the pseudonym Cervantes[71] had accused Marton and Hrabovski of preaching water while drinking wine; they did not uphold the ideological principles they were preaching to others. They were criticizing a different view of the Party's work while insisting on the rightfulness of their view, that is, they rejected the objective reality of two differing views. Cervantes argued here with the Leninist theoretical principle of thesis, anti-thesis and synthesis – which the Prague comrades should have applied in their criticism if they took seriously the Leninist principle of ideological scrutiny, that is, dialectical materialism. In Cervantes' view, they just insisted on their own view (antithesis) without objectively analysing his criticism (thesis) and then finding a solution (synthesis) after proper analysis. According to Cervantes, "they were the right ones to speak up, convinced that they had done their deed!"[72]

---

[70] "Usnesení 39. schůze ...", 2. The concept 'polemic' is positively connoted in Czech and Slovak; in English, it would mean 'discussion'.
[71] "Usnesení 39. schůze ...", 2.
[72] "Usnesení 39. schůze ...", 2.

The sharply intelligent and mocking polemic compared the author to Cervantes' hero Don Quixote, who had entered world literature as a symbol of courage in a hopeless situation: Don Quixote fights windmills, that is, a battle he cannot possibly win.[73] It was no surprise that Cervantes was Maňák, which the report confirmed on the next page.[74]

I am quite certain that the readers of *Cultural Life* were highly amused by Cervantes' polemic, understanding his irony that revealed the dominance and dictate of the KSČ, whose acknowledgement of the KSS's equal standing was nothing more than paying lip service. Furthermore, these top journalists, who were, after all, employed at the CC's main organ, were not even capable of properly applying Lenin's method of theoretical scrutiny! The learned readers of the well-read Cervantes in Slovakia understood the author's criticism and its theoretical and national aspects: the comrades in Prague still thought it was their right to tell the Bratislava comrades what to do in their own country – which went against the 1960s constitution. From the perspective of the Czech journalists who were under much more pressure from the KSČ, the Slovak doctor's article was short of rebellion, but he was a Party member and candidate of the prestigious academy, so one had to walk a fine line. One could simply not put him into prison or send him to a labour camp – those times were definitely over.

Maňák's reply to Marton and Hrabovski submitted to *Life of the Party* was discussed in an editorial meeting; the editors decided to reject it because the issue was not a discussion, but a basic difference of opinion. The author opposed the Party line

---

[73] A short biography of the author of the famous Don Quixote de la Mancha can be found on http://cervantes.tamu.edu/cervantes/biography/new_english_cerv_bio.html; accessed 18 March 2018.
[74] "Usnesení 39. schůze ...", 3.

and Lenin's teachings about the Party. The editors invited Maňák to the journal to explain to him their reasons for refusing to publish his text.[75] In more than two hours of discussion, the editors tried to explain to Comrade Maňák, why he was mistaken, why not every individual could decide for himself what the Party's tasks were and how to exercise them. Comrade Maňák insisted on his views and said that he would never fulfil a task he deemed damaging to the Party; were the Party a true Communist Party, he would not be criminally liable,[76] that is, not politically persecuted on the basis of a phoney accusation, as it had been practised in the years of the personality cult.

The report of the journalists of *Life of The Party* ended in a quite unspectacular, rather banal fashion: the Czech comrades had to let Maňák return to Bratislava. Most probably, they lacked clear instructions from the CC KSČ. The rebellious doctor announced that he would continue with his criticism; if *Life of the Party* would not publish him, he would write directly to the CC KSČ.[77]

II. 4. 3 Ideological Unity and Party Discipline à la Novotný (1964)

Changing a political system in the Soviet bloc requires a loosening of the ties of control and surveillance – at least, if one thinks in terms of actually improving the political system. How uninterested the Novotný regime was in changing its ways is visible in the resolution of the 44th meeting of the CC KSČ on 20 May 1964.[78]

---

[75] "Usnesení 39. schůze ...", 3.
[76] "Usnesení 39. schůze ...", 3.
[77] "Usnesení 39. schůze ...", 4.
[78] "Usnesení 44. schůze sekretariátu ÚV KSČ ze dne 20. května 1964, k bodu: 3) Usnesení sekretariátu ÚV KSČ k posílení a prohloubení ideologické

We cannot possibly find out if Comrade Maňák's criticism and refusal to toe the Party line had any direct consequences at the Party's higher echelons. I do not think that the rebellious physician was important enough, but his brazen behaviour – or so the Stalinists must have thought – was proof of a new style of governing in Slovakia, which prompted their anger. They decided to evaluate the current ideological guidelines, which was a perfect pretext for forcing the KSS to re-tighten the screws.

On 18 December 1963, the Barnabite Commission had submitted its report to the CC KSČ, demanding full rehabilitation of the Slovak members persecuted in the 1950s trials. Dubček had been a member of the Kolder Commission; as First Secretary KSS, he was informed about the progress and findings of the Barnabite commission; he considered the endorsement of the Barnabite report by the CC KSČ a success for the Slovaks and himself.[79]

Let us have a look at the minutes of the meeting of 20 May 1964: reading the promising title, one expects to find clear and precise instructions how the Party should tackle the issue of ideology, for example, what amount of criticism would be allowed and where to draw the line; instructions about Leninist principles and how to apply them in practice; the impact of the Soviet Union's new course on Czechoslovak domestic and foreign affairs. Nothing of this can be found in the document. The resolutions' key concept and principal idea was 'strengthening and deepening the unity of the Party'. What did this mean?

On 11 March 1964, the Department of Ideology of the KSČ had submitted to the secretariat of the CC KSČ a report about

---

jednoty strany (s. J. Hes)", SNA, Fond ÚV KSS tájomniki, A. Dubček, 1963–1968, karton 2384, typewritten, 13 pages.

[79] Dubček, *Hope Dies Last*, 92–93. Dubček did not mention this resolution in his memoirs.

the current conditions at the "ideological front [*na ideologické frontě*]".⁸⁰ The secretariat had discussed the report on 6 and 13 May, focussing on youth organizations, national committees and Party organizations. On page 1, the minutes admitted to conditions that required correction and improvement, but naturally, these bad conditions were not the Party's mistake:

> "In the phase of transition from the dictatorship of the proletariat towards the People's Republic [*v období přechodu od diktatury proletariátu k všelidovému státu*], the KSČ is neither breaking with class politics nor its Communist basic principles. At the same time, the KSČ is removing the mistakes of the past, strengthening Lenin's norms of party work in its daily practice."⁸¹

Theoretically correct in Marxist-Leninist terms of building Socialism, the KSČ defined the transitional phase. Furthermore, the Party was also correct in its way of thinking that ideology was the responsibility of every Party member and citizen. The ideological unity and strength of the entire country required workers, farmers, teachers, professors, kindergarten teachers, journalists, artists and students to follow and realize Party discipline on a daily basis. The protocol of the meeting listed four main points the Party should concentrate its efforts on: continuous and immediate information of the entire Party; concentration of goal-oriented and active attention to those sections of Party and society that were still falling short of ideological unity and strength; the work of the Party cadres, and, finally, the CC KSS and its regional and district committees.⁸²

So much for the theory; the practice was an entirely different issue. What at first looked like democratization, of transferring responsibility from the top of the Party down to the citizens, proved at second glance to be the establishment of even

---

80 "Usnesení 44. schůze …, 1.
81 "Usnesení 44. schůze …, 1.
82 "Usnesení 44. schůze …, 10–13.

more control, an attempt to control citizens' minds. One cannot help but think that while Khrushchev, certainly no democrat, let alone a champion of pluralism, was trying to overcome the old Stalinist ways of governing in the bloc's centre in Moscow, the comrades at the periphery were clinging to power, ignoring the Soviet thaw. But then, the thaw was a new instrument of Soviet foreign policy in the relationship with the class enemy of the USA and the Capitalist world. One did not have to implement the thaw in one's domestic affairs, as the Soviet suppression of the Hungarian anti-Communist rebellion in 1956 had demonstrated – or so Novotný must have thought. He had the power to rule Czechoslovakia without embarking on a course of change, let alone to acknowledge Slovakia's equal standing, regardless of the 1960 constitution.

What reads at the beginning of the document like a plan for improvement or perhaps principal instructions for more inner-Party tolerance turns into a vague text with a clear statement of hostility: no instructions of how to strengthen Party discipline, only instructions of how to implement the dictates of the CC KSČ in an improved fashion, read, extending the KSČ's control to the tiniest parts of state and society. The resolution was geared to more control, not less. The belligerent concept of 'ideological front' reminds one of the Stalin years; it is not only because of the war-like language that we can consider this resolution a Stalinist one, or perhaps, an attempt to keep de-Stalinization at bay.

The control of the CC KSČ and its idea of Party discipline and ideological unity had to be followed by every collective, working place, cultural institution, political committee, school, university and the press, national radio and television. It actually cemented the power of the CC KSČ by establishing the smoke screen of a 'new' ideological course by calling Party cadres and citizens to the 'ideological front'. The basic principle of domestic politics was not more tolerance or intra-Party discussion, nor Lenin's democratic centralism, but absolute obedience and complete lack of independent thinking.

Summarized under point 2 was the concentration of goal-oriented and active attention to those sections of Party and society that were still falling short of ideological unity and strength; the instructions prescribed focussing in particular on national television and radio that should implement discipline and ideological unity in their documentaries and broadcasts.[83] Nihilistic black comedies, satirical comedies or theatre plays considered belonging to the genre of absurdist theatre should not be allowed to express anti-Party views; theatre, especially the plays of the Prague comedy theatres should be strictly monitored.[84] Newspapers and journals should draw special attention to cartoons and satirical articles; the schools should make sure that the young generation properly understood the Party's mission so that they could later contribute to the development of society as scientific and technical specialists.

Most prominent and telling in the document was point 4 that revealed Novotný's aversion to the Slovaks, Slovakia and the KSS; members of the CC KSS must have been offended by the seventeen instructions (!) listed in alphabetical order, which extend to four pages, roughly a third of the entire document. A lesson one can learn from point 4 is how NOT to rule a country whose history is a difficult one, to say the least. One can easily provoke and promote national hatred by pushing a nation politically to the wall, clubbing it down verbally and letting it feel inferior in official documents and communication.

---

[83] "Usnesení 44. schůze …, 4.
[84] "Usnesení 44. schůze …, 6–7.

The instructions summarized under point 4 gave the impression that the KSS was incompetent and untrustworthy, that Slovakia as a whole was a potential nest of traitors and fascists, class enemies and enemies of the Czechoslovak people. Clearly, these instructions were aimed at Dubček who had 'allowed' Husák to speak openly about his ordeal in the 1950s, let *Cultural Life* publish Comrade Maňák's criticism and permitted the writer's congress of 1963 to demand liberalization and the truth about the trials of the 1950s.

Point a) on the extensive list of 'suggestions', or rather, commands as to how the KSS should improve ideological unity and Party discipline was addressed to the CC KSS and the Party's regional and district committees. They should stand up against all mistakes in terms of ideological work by using to the full their press organs such as *Pravda*, the regional newspapers and the broadcast media. Second, the KSS should mobilize wide sections of the population for the ideological struggle by integrating them into the preparations for the celebration of the 20th anniversary of the SNP. Third, the regional and local Party cadres should organize reading circles and committees, which would implement ideological unity; in those circles and gatherings, they should use the political material the KSČ had approved. Point f) was particularly humiliating:

> "Every two weeks, the youth organizations, the national council and workers' committees shall, together with the Department of Ideology of the KSČ, evaluate the decisions of political and ideological work aimed at the masses, and discuss the operational basics. They are obliged to translate to the masses the suggestions of the secretariat of the CC KSČ."[85]

As if these 'suggestions' were not enough, KSČ members would supervise KSS members on a regular basis. One is reminded of

---

[85] "Usnesení 44. schůze ...", 10.

Slovakia's past: the brutal Magyarization policy in the late Hungarian kingdom prior to the foundation of Czechoslovakia in 1918 was child's play compared with the CC KSČ's control and supervision of the CC KSS in 1964. *Nota bene*, this resolution was published just five months before Khrushchev's stopover in Bratislava and Prague on his way to the Paris conference with US President Kennedy. Thus, while the super powers were adamant in improving their relationship, trying to make the nuclear world a safer place, Novotný and his adherents were trying to suffocate the tiniest signs of a modest thaw in Slovakia.

Point j) of the minutes can be referred to as an attempt to reverse the findings of the Barnabite Commission, another proof of Novotný's deep hostility to the Slovaks. The KSS should intensify the work with older Party members:

> "Choose groups of elder comrades, gather them around the sections of the Party organizations, youth organizations and national committees and the KSČ's Department of Ideology and engage them in the active part of the ideological struggle (for example, in lessons about the Party's historical tasks, Party commandments and discipline; in the Party's view of the sectarian politics of the Chinese Communist Party; and in support of the Party against the revisionist and liberalist distortion of Party politics)."[86]

---

[86] "Usnesení 44. schůze …, 11. Mao Tse-tung condemned Khrushchev's new course as revisionist, on https://www.marxists.org/reference/archive/mao/works/1964/phnycom.htm; accessed 21 March 2018. The fact that the CC KSČ condemned Mao's 'sectarian politics' but did not follow the Soviet thaw should be understood as paying lip service; as long as Czechoslovakia slavishly obeyed Moscow in terms of bloc loyalty, the power of the old guard was safe. My friend and colleague Marc Winter, a specialist on the Chinese Communist Party and senior lecturer in Chinese Studies at the UZH, in an e-mail conversation of 20 and 21 March 2018: "Principally, we can say that from the mid-1950s on, the Communist world experienced a split, because the two alpha males Stalin and Mao could not agree on the principles of the global Communist movement. Mao decided to leave the COMINTERN and created an alternative Socialist International Movement. Yet, only Albania and Tito's Yugoslavia joined his movement. The word 'sectarian' refers to the fact that Mao decided to go his own way, while the

What elder Party members, that is, the generation born before WWI, could contribute to the programme of promoting ideological unity and Party discipline commanded by the CC KSČ was unquestioning loyalty, blind obedience, memoirs of the alleged 'persecution' of the Communists in Masaryk's Republic and the real brutality they had suffered in the Nazi concentration camps. But they could also provide witness statements about the persecution of their comrades during the 1950s, be it from the viewpoint of the persecutors such as Široký or the experience of the persecuted. Since the CC KSČ did not specify which comrades should be invited to the lectures and instruction courses, one could actually obey – and invite, for example, the critical Husák, who would not shy away from telling what had really happened in the 1950s. Holdoš too could tell his story. But I do not think that Novotný had these two Party members in mind, when the CC KSČ thought about activating the older generation of Slovak and Czech Communists. He continued to fight Dubček with the help of his supporters in the KSS. After having received Khrushchev in Prague and Bratislava, where the young Dubček had won the sympathy of the Soviet leader[87] who in a few months would be ousted by Brezhnev, Novotný enjoyed his power – and the comfortable feeling of knowing that he soon would be 're-elected'.

II. 4. 4 'Electing' the President and the Tasks of Loyal Journalists (1964)

So far, we have mentioned the concept of personality cult in the context of the bloc's de-Stalinization, that is, Khrushchev's revealing of Stalin's crimes. All CPs in the bloc had more or less

---

members of the Warsaw Pact stayed with the Soviet Union. The term 'sectarian' thus means that Mao did not want to play along with the others."

[87] Dubček, *Hope Dies Last*, 99–101.

enthusiastically followed the new Soviet course, which was, naturally, geared to strengthening the bloc, not disrupting it. Yet, thinking about the meaning of 'personality cult' in the context of Czechoslovak domestic affairs, I find that the cult of personality of the leaders of the KSČ prevailed to some extent ever since Gottwald had come to power through a putsch in February 1948. Compared with Stalin's purges and his reign, we could thus speak of a *non-violent personality cult* of the Czechoslovak president on the one hand and the First Secretary KSČ on the other. This cult would end only with Husák stepping down as General Secretary of the Party, and the Velvet Revolution of November 1989.

Furthermore, one could say that the personality cult[88] was a vital element of the power of the Communist parties of central, eastern and south-eastern Europe that served as blueprint for the Chinese, North Korean and Vietnamese Communist regimes. From the more liberal Yugoslavia governed by the hero of the partisans Tito to Romania's 'titan of the Carpathians' Nicolae Ceaușescu to the somewhat dry East German Walter Ulbricht and the narcissistic, Stalin-mimicking North Korean Kim Il-sung, all leaders held absolute power and decided about the fate of their nations, enjoying admiration and fear.

Because of the hierarchical and undemocratic structure of the Party, Communist regimes were particularly prone to develop *systematic and continuous mass activities of admiration, obedience and loyalty*, if we want to avoid the term 'cult' that originates in religion. The leader's reliable executioners and functionaries in the Party apparatus made sure that the citizens paid him continuous respect and gratitude in parades,

---

[88] An interesting analysis is Anita Pisch's study about the Stalin cult on http://press-files.anu.edu.au/downloads/press/n2129/pdf/ch01.pdf; accessed 21 March 2018.

speeches, quotations, posters, conferences, forewords to scientific studies and pledges of fulfilling economic norms and plans. The leader was infallible: he was not only above the law, but also above criticism. He was almost a deity, but often also presented as the father of the nation. This *system of enforced admiration* was one aspect of totalitarianism in practise. The people had no right not to participate in the rituals of admiration and obedience. Naturally, the systematic admiration was a crucially important element also of non-Communist totalitarian regimes, such as Hitler's Nazi regime and Mussolini's Fascist Italy.

Now, what did the personality cult in Czechoslovakia in 1964 look like? First, no Czechoslovak leader had been criticized and accused of crimes the way Khrushchev had chipped away at Stalin's image in 1956, although they had been equally responsible for immense suffering of the people, particularly in the early years of Sovietization. However, unlike his more modest predecessor Zapotocký, Novotný used his power to the full, creating a dangerous anti-Slovak bias that was threatening the state's unity. In November 1964, he was still firmly in power. From a document classified top secret (*přisně tajné*):

> "Before the election of the president of the republic publish in Rudé právo, Pravda and Uj szó and other press organs a comment about the significance of the election for current domestic affairs and the international situation. Broadcast the same comment in national radio and television."[89]

The document originating in the secretariat of the CC KSČ gave clear instructions to the Slovak and Czech comrades how to

---

[89] "Usnesení sekretariátu UV KSČ, schválené per rollam dne 29. října 1964, k bodu: Zajištění publicity volby presidenta Československé socialistické republiky (s. J. Hes)", SNA, Fond ÚV KSS tájomniki, A. Dubček, 1963–1968, karton 2384, typewritten, 3 pages, dated 3 November 1964, 2. *Uj Szó* was the newspaper of the Hungarian minority in Slovakia. It still exists today: https://ujszo.com; accessed 22 March 2018.

report about the election. The KSS leadership should make sure to point out the positive consequences of the election for the fulfilment of the general line of the 12th Party plenum, particularly in the broadcasts directed to foreign countries.[90] On the evening before the election, radio and television should again stress the importance of this act. The following press organs, newspapers and journals would be provided with pictures and live coverage of the election, representative rooms in Prague castle and the friendly meeting of the president with workers in the third courtyard of the castle: Czechoslovak radio, Czechoslovak television, *Rudé právo, Pravda, Uj szó*, ČTK, *Práce, Práca, Mladá fronta, Večerní Praha, Smena, Zemědelské noviny, Rolnické noviny, Svobodné slovo, Lidová demokracie, Ľud*.[91]

The Foreign Ministry would provide the foreign accredited journalists with conditions for reporting about the election and necessary information. On the day of the election, all daily newspapers should present perfect layouts, and after the election of the president of the ČSSR, publish his portrait and congratulatory telegrams.[92] These instructions are proof that the 'election' was not only completely rigged, but also how the domestic press should report, including congratulatory telegrams. Praise of the acting and future president also came from foreign journalists. The 'election' was a farce, an absurd theatre play that had nothing in common with a real election, but it served one particularly important function: to pretend that the

---

[90] "Usnesení sekretariátu UV KSČ …", 2. I think the foreign countries referred to in the document were the bloc member states, since the election of Novotný meant that Czechoslovak domestic affairs were stable and reliable – no surprises from Prague.
[91] "Usnesení sekretariátu UV KSČ …", 2. The list contains the newspapers and journals in Czech and Slovak that had the largest readership, of course, all under the control of the Party.
[92] "Usnesení sekretariátu UV KSČ …", 3.

'parliament' that 'elected' the president had a real say, that the People's Republic was a true democracy.

Besides reporting about political rituals such as 'elections', spartakiades, the annual harvest or industrial production, Czechoslovak journalists, at least those who wanted to get ahead or truly believed in Socialism, had a particularly important task. A top-secret document of the CC KSČ, dated 16 November 1964, informs us about the planning of an international meeting of journalists in March 1965.[93]

The meeting would take place in the High Tatra in Slovakia, organized by the Czechoslovak professional association of journalists (*Svaz čs. novinářů*).[94] Apart from some budget issues, that is, that the *Svaz* would receive only KČS 150,000 to 200,000,[95] the document defined the task of the carefully selected journalists:

> "Use the 11th international meeting of journalists to achieve the following goals: establish relations with progressively and realistically minded bourgeois journalists [*navázat styk s pokrokově a realisticky uvažujícími buržoazními novináři*] and strengthen ties with the organizations of journalists of the Socialist countries. Support exchanges of opinion and establish as many contacts as possible. With these relationships, develop the promotion of the ČSSR to achieve the most positive reports about the 20th anniversary of the liberation and stimulate tourists' interest in our country. [...] Inform the Department of Ideology on a regular basis about the preparations for the meeting; by 15 February 1965, submit a report about the preparations to the

---

[93] "Usnesení sekretariátu ÚV KSČ, schválené per rollam dne 16. 11. 1964, k bodu: Uspořádání XI. mezinárodního zimního setkani novinářů v Československé socialistické republice (s. J. Hes, s. O. Kaderka)", SNA, Fond ÚV KSS tájomniki, A. Dubček, 1963–1968, karton 2384, typewritten, 3 pages, dated 16 November 1964, 2.

[94] "Usnesení sekretariátu ÚV KSČ ...", 2.

[95] This amount was a fortune, compared with the average monthly salary of less than KČS 1,000; e-mail conversation with XY, 27 March 2018.

Department of Ideology and the Department of Foreign Affairs of the CC KSČ."[96]

By 1965, Czechoslovakia was a progressive Socialist state – or so the West must have thought. The film *Obchod na korze* (*The Shop on Mainstreet*),[97] with the famous Slovak actor Jozef Kroner (1924–1998) in the leading role portraying a decent citizen standing up against the deportation of Jews in an Eastern Slovak town, won the Oscar for best foreign film. For Dubček, 1965 would prove a significant year: the fight against Comrade Cvik would begin in 1965. Who was this Comrade Cvik and what did he stand for?

II. 4. 5 Comrade Cvik (1965)

A good example of how the KSS under Dubček's stewardship was slowly de-Stalinizing the Party, introducing new moral values and behaviour and forming a front against Novotný, is the case of Comrade Rudolf Cvik (1923–1996).[98] Cvik was a conservative hence loyal to Novotný, and many Party functionaries in the countryside supported him against the fresh wind from Bratislava, embodied in Dubček. On 6 April 1965, Dubček informed Comrade Novotný in Prague about the discussions of the CC KSS that had taken place at the Party meeting on 27 March 1965. What did Comrade Cvik do to arouse the anger of his colleagues?

Rudolf Cvik, a car mechanic from the Nové Zámky district in south-western Slovakia, had had a stellar career in the Party, which he had joined in 1945; at the age of 27, the Party had made him secretary of the OV KSS (*okresný výbor*, the Party

---

[96] "Usnesení sekretariátu ÚV KSČ …", 2–3.
[97] *Obchod na Korze* on http://www.imdb.com/title/tt0059527/; accessed 27 March 2018.
[98] "Informácia", SNA Bratislava, ÚV KSS, tájomniki 1963–1968, A. Dubček, carton 2380, typewritten, three pages.

committee of a rural unit) in Bratislava.[99] Such a quick career was not unusual after the KSČ had assumed power on 25 February 1948, since the Party had needed reliable functionaries in those years. From 1960 to 1968, Cvik was secretary of the KV KSS (*krajský výbor*) in Banská Bystrica in Central Slovakia.[100] His power base was the Slovak countryside, where every party functionary knows everyone, and networks of friends and family relations go a long way back. One can regard Comrade Cvik as an instrument Novotný used to get at Dubček and his followers.

The comrades of the CC KSS stated unanimously that since the 12th Party congress, Comrade Cvik had developed activities that were damaging the Party and its work. He was creating mistrust among the members of the CC KSS, abusing his power and sugar-coating facts. According to Dubček, Novotný used Cvik, Sabolčik and Chudík to sabotage him, waging "a guerrilla war" through his Slovak confidants.[101] The report of the CC KSS about Cvik addressed to Novotný was thus a clear signal – the First Secretary KSS took up the challenge from his Prague adversary with the support of the majority of the members of the presidium of the CC KSS, confronting Novotný but sticking to correct Party procedure.

Indeed, Dubček's was a clever move: by being openly honest and direct, he provoked a reaction on the part of Novotný, which would tell him where he stood in the balance of power. How would Novotný react to the letter from the CC KSS? I think the psychological dictum 'the best prognosis of future behaviour is past behaviour' is pretty much applicable to every

---

[99] Jan Pešek, "Cvikiáda. Rudolf Cvik v konflikte Antonína Novotného a Alexandra Dubčeka", in *Storočie škandálov*, 233–244, 233.
[100] Pešek, "Cvikiáda", 233.
[101] Dubček, *Hope Dies Last*, 96.

situation, and one could hence expect Novotný to reject the accusations and side with his man. According to the modernizers in the CC KSS, Comrade Cvik seems to have been quite a nasty person:

> "Lately, many complaints and grievances arrived about the behaviour of Comrade Cvik, who apparently is giving himself to excessive drinking. There is a lot of talk about his relationships with women, and many citizens have expressed reservations about his moral and political integrity. As the members of the presidium of the KSS recall, his behaviour had been subject to much discussion when he was district chairman of the Party in Bratislava. [...] The comrades criticized his lack of honesty, careerism and sectarian-bureaucratic methods."[102]

Furthermore, the report said, Comrade Cvik was eager to create the impression that he and his followers were the only ones that defended the correct Party line. The wording of the report was forthright: Cvik was an intrigant, careerist – and, as the comrades thought, also a shameless liar. The Party had taken away the honorary medal he had received for his alleged participation in the SNP.[103]

Not surprisingly, Novotný not only reject the letter of the CC KSS, but ostentatiously defended Cvik in a letter to the CC KSS of 15 March 1966[104] – the best prognosis of future behaviour is past behaviour. Comrade Cvik and his colleagues from the KV KSS Banská Bystrica would step down in protest when Dubček was elected chairman of the CC KSČ in January 1968. Cvik would return to Slovak politics after the invasion of 1968,[105] wholeheartedly defending and implementing the politics of Normalization.

---

[102] "Informácia", 2.
[103] "Informácia", 3.
[104] Pešek, "Cvikiáda", 243.
[105] Pešek, "Cvikiáda", 243.

II. 4. 6 A Failed Intrigue: The Dubčeks in the SNP (1965–1967)

A quite elaborate intrigue the StB concocted at Novotný's behest would drag on for almost two years, from the summer of 1965 to January 1967.[106] The archive material[107] is copious, and the 'case' confusing, since it involves letters from witnesses, summaries of the Control and Revision Commissions[108] of both KSČ and KSS and protest letters from Dubček.

What the intrigue that failed can teach us is to what lengths the hopeless and hapless Stalinist Novotný went to discredit Dubček: had the intrigue proved successful, rumours spread and the accusation gone to court, Dubček's spotless reputation would have been destroyed, or at least gravely damaged – and his power in the KSS would have been on shaky ground. What saved the First Secretary KSS was the loyalty of his comrades who felt that something was being fabricated against him by the president and First Secretary KSČ; they warned him, keeping to the Party's communication channels. A further factor, I think, was that most of the higher KSS members were no

---

[106] Dubček did not mention the details of this intrigue in his memoirs; ever the gentleman, I think he wanted to protect the reputation of his wife who died in 1991 while he was writing his memoirs. Anna had suffered enough from the psychological terror mounted against the family by the StB, so he wrote only that the StB was preparing a case against him in the spring of 1966; *Hope Dies Last*, 107.

[107] SNA Bratislava, ÚV KSS, tájomniki 1963–1968, A. Dubček, carton 2395, file 113, typewritten, 51 pages. The following documents I quote are all in file 113; therefore, I shall use only the titles of the documents as reference in my footnotes.

[108] The Control and Revision Commissions of the Central Committees had the task of scrutinizing research results of the StB for their ideological impact. Thus, the StB investigated, handed its results to the ÚKRK, which then interpreted the material according to the Marxist-Leninist state ideology. In a third step, the ÚKRK then submitted its interpretation to the CC KSČ, which had the last say, the power of decision-making; Skype conversation with XY on 23 April 2018.

longer afraid of the Stalinists in both KSČ and KSS, because the Barnabite and Kolder Commissions had proved beyond any reasonable doubt the guilt of the Stalinists in both parties. Now, in 1965, they were standing up for their First Secretary, who had been standing up for them against Novotný and the conservatives since his election in 1963.

The intrigue involved the doctoring of facts in the protocols, fabrication of contexts that seemingly had nothing to do with each other and, most probably, the use of a former Nazi collaborator and HSĽS member. Note that I cannot prove anything by quoting from the documents; this subchapter is based on careful assessment of the archive material. Here is what I think happened.

The intrigue consisted of two schemes that did not seem to be related, appearing, at first glance, to be independent affairs. Yet, both plots had the same goal: to smear the name of the First Secretary KSS and his then-girlfriend-now-wife by casting doubt on their activities in the Slovak clerical-fascist state during the SNP. The first plot concerns the part played by Comrade František Boháč from Bratislava; the second one the questioning of Citizen Rudolf Mikuláš, a car mechanic from Topoľčany, who believed that the two men who had visited him in August 1965 were StB agents. Let us first have a look at the first plot involving Boháč.

In a letter dated 14 October 1965, Comrade Vincent Lukáč from Bratislava informed the presidium of the CC KSS about a strange occurrence: around 21 August 1965, Comrade Boháč had paid him a visit at his place of work at the state inspectorate of the food industry in Bratislava.[109] After some chit-chat about the current state of affairs, Comrade Boháč had asked Comrade

---

[109] "Lukáč Vincent, Bratislava, Ružová dolina č. 22", typewritten, 2 pages, 1.

Lukáč whether he knew Comrade Dubček from the times of the SNP and was he aware that Comrade Dubček had been active in the Šrobár group that had been working with the Edelweiss group.[110] Lukáč wrote that Boháč had convinced him of the importance of these facts; also, Comrade Boháč had told him that he would present Dubček's collaboration with centre-right politicians, the Tiso regime and the Germans during the SNP in his report to the CC KSČ in Prague; Comrade Zeman would take care of it. Then, as Lukáč wrote, Comrade Boháč had said that Comrade Dubček's wife was also involved; apparently, she had worked for the Germans in Dubnica nad Vahom in a control office.[111] Boháč had said that if Lukáč now told him everything he knew about Dubček's involvement in the SNP, Prague could

---

[110] "Lukáč Vincent, ...", 1. Not only the Communists, but also centre-right Slovaks had formed resistance groups, among them former Slovak governor Vavro Šrobár. They had been in contact with the Beneš exile government in London, supporting the Allies. Some resistance groups had code names, while others referred to their leaders; the best-known groups were *Obrana národa, Justícia, skupina Jána Lichnera, Demec, Victoire, Flóra, skupina Dr. V. Šrobára, Hela, skupina Fedora Zorkócyho*, Daniela Baranová, "Evanjelickí antifašisti v odbojových skupinách", in *Slovenské národné povstanie 1944*, 105–114, 107–108. *Edelweiss* and *Schneewittchen* were special SS groups the Germans had sent to Slovakia to fight the partisans of the SNP. https://plus7dni.pluska.sk/Domov/SNP-Mali-Edelweiss-zastavit-partizani-Takto-vycinali-Niznanskeho-zlocinci; https://www.vtedy.sk/prislusnikov-oddielov-edelweiss-postavili-pred-ceskoslovensky-sud; accessed 14 April 2018. See also the report about the Munich trial of Ladislav Nižňanský, a former Edelweiss commander and war criminal: http://www.spiegel.de/spiegel/print/d-32060815.html; accessed 14 April 2018. The implication of *Edelweiss* was crystal clear: Šrobár's group had been collaborating with the Germans against the partisans – and Dubček had been part of it! I am indebted to my colleague Ivan Kamenec who recommended the following studies about Edelweiss: "Jozef Šufliarsky, *Akcia Edelweiss* (Bratislava, 1963); Dušan Halaj, ed., *Fašistické represálie na Slovensku* (Bratislava, 1990), 48–52. In the weekly *Protifašistický bojovník* (no 1 from January 1963), the historian Jaroslav Šolc had published the article 'Smrť sa tentoraz volá Edelweiss'." E-mail conversation with Ivan Kamenec, 14–17 April 2018.

[111] "Lukáč Vincent, ...", 1.

close this important affair and would show its gratitude. But Lukáč was not as gullible as Boháč had thought:

> "I immediately informed Comrade Šalgovič. Back then, I was not sure if this was a provocation or an intrigue, because it is unthinkable and impossible that our Party employs persons who are acting without the knowledge and approval of the institutions in charge, which have the authorization to conduct inquiries of such importance."[112]

What Comrade Lukáč failed to mention in his letter is why he waited almost two months before informing the CC KSS. Did he expect that Šalgovič would inform Dubček and the other members of the CC KSS, as the Party communication channels prescribed? Did he, after some deliberation, not trust Šalgovič and decided to make sure that Comrade Dubček was informed? We can only speculate.

From the report of an unknown author and member of the CC KSS, it transpires that Comrade Boháč had not only paid a visit to Comrade Lukáč. In August 1965, he had shown up quite brazenly at the Archives of the Department of Military History in Prague and demanded to see archive material about the SNP, making negative remarks about some KSS

---

[112] "Lukáč Vincent, ...", 1. Viliam Šalgovič (1919–1990) was a supporter of Novotný's and would join the anti-reform movement after the 1968 invasion, thus the organizers of the Normalization. From 1962 to 1968, he was the head of the Control and Revision Commission of the CC KSS (ÚKRK KSS). I think that Lukáč first contacted Šalgovič to be on the safe side, since in October 1966, it was not yet clear how the struggle of the Dubček innovators-modernizers against the Novotný conservatives in the KSS would turn out – the author made sure he had all his angles covered, which is understandable in such circumstances. 'Provocation' [*provokace; provokácia*] was based on the stretch paragraph 101 of the Czechoslovak Constitution; it was a criminal offense, involving the spreading of anti-Socialist thinking, speaking, writing, in general, casting doubt about the rightfulness of the Party's ways and decisions. Any harmless phrase could be interpreted as provocation and criticism of the Party; Skype interview with XY on 23 April 2018.

functionaries.¹¹³ Boháč had also said that for his report to the CC KSČ, he was collecting information about the Comrades Dubček, Dvorský, Šalgovič and Biľak. Furthermore, Boháč had told the unknown author "that there are people in the leadership of the CC KSS who do not have a clean past and who are therefore supporting Husák and through him activating clerical Fascism in Slovakia [*podporujú Husáka a cez neho aktivizujú na Slovensku ľudáctvo*]".¹¹⁴ The unknown author finished his report with the suggestion of interrogating Boháč, whose activities were proof of his nasty character – he was a plotter who had schemed against Party functionaries before. Who was this Comrade Boháč? And how could he, apparently without the knowledge of the almighty StB, roam about the republic, even demand material at the closely watched archives (!) and interrogate a member of the CC KSS about the First Secretary KSS?

From a report of the Control and Revision Commission of the CC KSČ,¹¹⁵ we learn about Comrade Boháč's past – if the StB had not made up his identity: allegedly, Boháč was a former Catholic priest who had founded in Sokolniky, district of Nitra, the local branch of the HSĽS in 1943. He had left the Catholic Church, married and become a tax inspector, enjoying the trust of the Fascist authorities of the Slovak state. Thanks to the statement of Reverend Dr Lasíka, Boháč had not been put on trial at

---

[113] "Vyjadrenie k šetreniu okolo s. Dubčeka a s. Dubčekovej", typewritten, six pages, signature not legible, dated 12 March 1966, 3. According to the report, Major Benčik and Captain Kural from Prague had informed the unknown author about Boháč's appearance at the archives. The unknown author knew Boháč from the Department of Education and Culture of the CC KSS.
[114] "Vyjadrenie k ...", 4.
[115] "Opis", typewritten, five pages, dated 14 March 1966, investigation conducted by Comrades Uhlíř, Tondl and Šalgovič, 4.

the People's Court after WWII, but because of his past, the KSČ had cancelled his membership in 1950.¹¹⁶

Let us now have a look at the second part of the intrigue: Citizen Rudolf Mikuláš. I assume that in his letter addressed to the CC KSS, Citizen Mikuláš had made a mistake in the first sentence: he had indicated 6 to 8 October 1965 as the date of the visit, but I think he meant 6 to 8 August 1965.¹¹⁷ He was not a Party member, hence under continuous suspicion from the authorities; he was most probably very nervous while writing the letter, since he could not know what consequences it might prompt. With this letter, he might call the StB on him. Nevertheless, he courageously reported a visit of two comrades who had introduced themselves as members of the CC KSČ.¹¹⁸ They had asked him questions and wanted to know could he confirm that Comrade Borseková had worked in a German control office in Dubnica nad Vahom from 1942 to 1944?¹¹⁹

Citizen Mikuláš remembered Comrade Borseková very well; like her, he had also been on special working assignment for the Germans but had committed sabotage whenever an opportunity arose. He had trusted Comrade Borseková because she had once warned him: the German authorities had been

---

[116] "Opis", 4.
[117] "Mikuláš Rudolf, Topoľčany", typewritten, two pages, dated 8 October 1965, signed by Rudolf Mikuláš, 1. October makes no sense since his letter was dated 8 October. Also, the visit of Boháč to Lukáč had happened in the second half of August 1965.
[118] "Mikuláš Rudolf, Topoľčany", 1.
[119] According to Dubček's memoirs, Anna's maiden name was Borseková, the name of her mother's first husband who had died in WWI. Anna had never known her biological father; her mother had married Mr Ondris with whom they had moved to Kyrgyzia with INTERHELPO. Anna had worked at the Škoda factory in Dubnica nad Vahom during WWII; 35. In Tiso's Slovak state, all unmarried women and all men had to work for the Slovak industry that had catered to the German war effort. Married women had been forced out from their employment, since their tasks were the three Cs: cooking, Church and the production of children.

onto him – he should hide the sweepings from the sabotaged work. This meant that she too had been a member of an illegal resistance group. The two comrades kept asking him:

> "Would I not know that Comrade Dubček had worked with a group that was planted amongst us [the resistance groups; add JB] by the HG? Then, they wanted to know could I not remember that in the Šrobár group there was a cell acting on behalf of Edelweiss, and was Comrade Dubček not a member of that Šrobár group at the beginning of the SNP [*Ďalej mi dali otázku, či sa nepamätám, že v skupine 'Šrobár' pracovala skupina pre 'Edelweis', a či nebol v obdobi začiatku SNP s. Dubček členom tejto skupiny 'Šrobár'*]?"[120]

Mikuláš wrote that he had answered truthfully: during the SNP and the Slovak state, Comrade Berseková had been very reliable and honest with all resistance members, and he knew that Comrade Dubček had been a member of a partisan brigade called Suvorova in the SNP.[121] The two comrades had then told him that he could not possibly know that – he would be surprised.[122] All of a sudden, as Citizen Mikuláš wrote, he had become aware of the fact that he did not know with whom he was speaking. He had demanded to see some ID or a document from their office or institution that legitimized them to question him. The comrades had refused; if they needed to contact him again, they would call him officially, they had said. Then, they had walked away; although they had paper prepared, they had not taken any notes.[123]

---

[120] Mikuláš Rudolf, Topoľčany", 1.
[121] Alexander Vasilievič Suvorov (1730–1800) was a Russian war hero the CP of the Soviet Union had co-opted during WWII to boost morale through national identity. The fact that the partisan group Dubček had joined was called *Suvorova skupina*, the Suvorov resistance group, tells us that its members were Communists.
[122] Mikuláš Rudolf, Topoľčany", 1.
[123] Mikuláš Rudolf, Topoľčany", 2.

Citizen Mikuláš, a simple car mechanic from Topoľčany,[124] nevertheless had had the education, IQ and courage to write well, showing the readers of his letter how suggestively the two comrades had formulated their questions and how menacingly they had reacted to his demand to see some identification. The suggestive inquiring by the two comrades was a method of psychological pressure; any individual less courageous would have just answered yes, yes, yes, confirming the allegations and making the two men go away.

Why do I believe that Mikuláš and Lukáč, the latter a bit more cautiously than the former, told the truth in their letters? Let me elaborate, based on my interpretation of the archival material.

First, the timeline: top StB confidants of Novotný's most probably started to plan the operation in late 1964 or early 1965. Dubček's popularity in Slovakia was a serious threat to the conservatives, and I think that domestic affairs were the principal motivation for the intrigue, less so the ČSSR's relationship with the Soviet Union. I am speculating here, but if Novotný, as Dubček wrote in his memoirs, was unhappy about Khrushchev's removal, [125] it was because he feared loss of power at home. Brezhnev now at the helm of the Soviet CP made everything a bit more complicated, but, in general, the Soviet

---

[124] File 113 also contains an individual assessment by Vincent Lukáč from 10 July 1953, most probably to protect Mikuláš from persecution by the StB, which, back then, was 'searching' for enemies of the state. Lukáč wrote in this letter of assessment that he knew Rudolf Mikuláš since 1940. Mikuláš was a good person, "hard-working, honest and direct [ako človeka pracovitého, čestného, priameho]". He was neither politically engaged nor interested in politics, concentrating on his professions as steelworker and car mechanic. His view of the People's Republic and its society and the working class was positive and honest. He would also recommend Citizen Mikuláš for a higher function with responsibility. "Individuálny posudok", typewritten, one page, dated 10 July 1953.

[125] Dubček, *Hope Dies Last*, 100.

CP's course seemed to be geared to a reversal of Khrushchev's reforms, not continuing the liberalization.

I am certainly no specialist on secret service operations and how much time it requires to plan an operation, but I think that Novotný just wanted to have some 'material' about Dubček, which he could present at a CC KSČ plenary session at any point in time, that is, when he would see fit. The intrigue that failed was a tool of Novotný's to fight Dubček, since he had to expect attacks from Dubček and the CC KSS.

Second, the two parts of the intrigue: both parts were not only identical in their content, that is, the allegations against Dubček and his wife, but also exercised in an identical fashion. Like the two StB agents who had questioned Citizen Mikuláš in Topoľčany, Boháč had asked Lukáč the same questions in the same suggestive manner. On top of that, Boháč had shown up at the archives in Prague, not making it a secret that he was writing a report for the CC KSČ, which must have intimidated the officials working there.

Third, the target: *cui bono*? Who would benefit from smearing the Dubčeks? Someone who believed that Slovak 'bourgeois nationalism' was behind the liberalization, hence a factor in Slovak politics – even within the CC KSS. Novotný's aversion against the Slovaks was well-known, and the fact that among the Slovak politicians mentioned in the documents his men Šalgovič and Biľak were listed, did not counteract the allegations against the Dubčeks, but was a step that was easy to see through: it distracted attention from the Dubčeks, shuffling it onto other Slovak politicians. Had Novotný used the 'material' at a Party meeting, I doubt that he would have accused his own men in the CC KSS of collaboration with the SS in the SNP.

Dubček's anger about the intrigue was tangible in his letter to Novotný, dated 28 February 1966. In previous communications with the CC KSČ, he had always been polite and correct, addressing the president with *Vážený sudruh* [Dear Comrade], but not this time:

> "Comrade Novotný, I have verified information at my disposal that the organs of the State Security Service investigated and possibly are still investigating a case against me and my wife. [...] I have trustworthy information about the details of the investigation from courageous persons – most of them Communists. [...] I am a member of the CC KSČ and its board and cannot agree with such practices by the security organs. I am writing this letter demanding a conversation in person [*so žiadosťou o prijatie na osobný rozhovor*]."[126]

The whole affair petered out – what else could the responsible persons do since Dubček had evidence, and the witnesses Lukáč and Mikuláš could not be intimidated? Naturally, the Control and Revision Commission of the KSČ found out neither the identity of the two men[127] who had interviewed Citizen Mikuláš in Topoľčany, nor could they find Comrade Boháč – although they had divulged quite precise information about his past in their previous report. Not surprisingly, there was also no evidence that state or Party organs had been involved.[128] The spin-doctors of the ÚKRK got out of the affair in a rather lame fashion:

---

[126] "Sudruh Novotný", typewritten, one page, dated 28 February 1966, signed by Dubček, 1.

[127] XY thinks that the only logical explanation was that the two men had been KGB agents, owing to their well-practised interrogation technique; Skype interview with XY on 23 April 2018. We can only speculate here, but I deem it also possible that the two men were StB agents, because they spoke Czech and Slovak. True, the KGB had trained the StB from 1945 on, but by 1965, the StB was absolutely capable of planning and carrying out such an operation without instructions from the KGB. For the development of the StB as the Party's instrument of power, see Karel Kaplan, *Protistátní Bezpečnost 1945–1948. Historie vzniku a působení StB jako mocenského nástroje KSČ* (Praha: Plus, 2015).

[128] "Zpráva o výsledcích šetřenístižnosti soudruha Alexandra DUBČEKA, prvního tajemníka ÚV KSS a člena předsednictva ústředního výboru KSČ", typewritten, five pages, dated 4 January 1967, prepared by Comrade P. Hron, 5.

> "The ÚKRK's investigation confirmed that unknown individuals [*neznámí lidé*], whose identity could not be asserted, did ask about Comrade Dubček, and also his wife, in Dubnica and Topoľčany [...] This case, and others, demonstrate that unsanctioned investigations of Party cadres and members of the Party organs are indeed happening."[129]

The lessons learnt from this incident, the report stated drily, was that the Party and state organs should be informed that, without positive confirmation by the responsible organs, nobody was allowed to conduct such investigations, and that every Party member who was asked to answer questions about Party cadre's details, had to demand identification and authorization of those who were conducting the investigation. Obviously, the instigators of the intrigue that failed had to save face.

Finally, what about Comrade František Boháč, the former Catholic priest who had boasted about his report to the CC KSČ? If he existed, he was obviously a survivor and well connected in Slovakia; in 1950, the KSS had abrogated his membership, but in 1965, he was already a member of the CC KSS, according to the unknown author's letter. If we trust the information about his past, he was a savvy turncoat, at best. What did he do to get back into the Party's top echelons? Might he have been the mastermind of the plot, approaching Novotný, who was unfamiliar with Slovakia and the Slovaks' way of life? Did he offer Novotný the plot of the intrigue in exchange for membership in the CC KSS that meant money and status? According to the final report of the Control and Revision Commission KSČ, Boháč had demanded revision of his Party membership abrogation, which the ÚKRK had rejected on 11 June 1964.[130] How come he was a member of the CC KSS only a year later, in 1965?

---

[129] "Zpráva o výsledcích ...", 5.
[130] "Zpráva o výsledcích ...", 3.

Or did the StB rehabilitate him by using him for the plot against Dubček? I can imagine the following: we have moved you up to the CC KSS, now, you go to the archives, demand to see material, make it crystal clear to everybody that you are writing a report for the CC KSČ. Then you are going to intimidate Comrade Lukáč in Bratislava and get him to confirm the Dubčeks' collaboration with the enemy in the SNP. Mind you, this is for Comrade Novotný. He will be grateful.

Was Comrade Boháč victim or perpetrator or both? We shall never find out. The intrigue that Dubček would fend off would not be the last. The next one would begin at Easter 1966 and involve a bear.

II. 4. 7 The Affair of the Bear (1966)

The bear is not only the symbol of Russian political power,[131] but also a popular animal in Slovakia – especially when they rummage in rubbish containers close to playgrounds in their hunt for food, frightening mothers and children.[132]

To Dubček, the brown bear he shot at Easter 1966 was a symbol of "Novotný's desperation and declining power".[133] The story of Dubček's bear is amusing because it demonstrates the way the Party worked – and what the functionaries sometimes had to waste time with. But let us have a look at Dubček's political situation before he headed up to the High Tatra for a well-deserved Easter rest:

> "I frequently clashed with the conservatives over investment policy [...] I kept pushing for more investment in Slovakia because it was in

---

[131] http://russia-ic.com/culture_art/traditions/1074#.Wr9N9mW_1PM; accessed 31 March 2018.
[132] A recent invention tested by 370 kg male brown bear Šabo, an inhabitant of the Tatra National Park TANAP, is a bear-resistant container, see http://slovakwildlife.org/en/news; accessed 31 March 2018.
[133] Dubček, *Hope Dies Last*, 111.

the interest of the country as a whole to have more balanced economic development. Given its lagging behind the Czech lands, there were even sound reasons to favour development in Slovakia and to urge the creation of more Slovak enterprises producing finished goods, instead of semi-finished ones to be completed in Bohemia or Moravia."[134]

Novotný and his supporters considered the First Secretary KSS's activities 'bourgeois nationalism', although Dubček's suggestions about promoting Slovakia's economic development withstood the scrutiny of economic facts. The president blocked Dubček efforts and did not hide his contempt for Slovakia – a part of the common state he was neither familiar with nor interested in getting to know.

According to Dubček, the president also seemed to suffer increasingly from paranoia: at a lunch at the Carlton hotel in Bratislava in honour of the 20th anniversary of the liberation of Czechoslovakia by the Red Army, where he had to show up, Novotný had the waiter open a bottle of vermouth in front of his eyes, obviously suspecting that some Slovak Fascists were intent on poisoning him.[135] Dubček's position in the KSS and the Czechoslovak Party presidium was not yet firm enough to directly confront Novotný, and after another intrigue mounted against him from Prague, the one about his and Anna's past in the SNP, he and some friends, among them František Barbírek (1927–2001), head of the Department of Industry at the CC KSS, left for the mountains.

They arrived at a small chalet close to the village of Javorina near the Slovak-Polish border. The mountains were still covered in snow, and the group learnt that a bear hunt was going on because the animal was attacking sheep, crossing the border back and forth.

---

[134] Dubček, *Hope Dies Last*, 105.
[135] Dubček, *Hope Dies Last*, 106.

> "We waited for two nights in vain, and on the third day, the foresters decided to call the hunt off. [...] My friends decided to return to Bratislava, and I almost left with them, but something told me the bear was still around."[136]

Dubček stayed on, sighted the bear in the night of Good Friday and shot him. At the following KSS Party meeting, Novotný and his Slovak confidants did not manage to get enough votes to have Dubček removed. The Slovak-Polish bear prompted political consequences, which demonstrated that Dubček was popular in Slovakia – and Novotný seeing himself forced to use desperate methods to get at him. In his memoirs, Dubček did not explain in detail why he suspected his principal adversary had initiated the investigation,[137] and we cannot possibly find out the identity of the person who initiated the investigation. The affair of the bear began when the First Secretary KSS shot the sick animal.

On 17 May 1966, Dubček received a letter from Comrade Ladislav Novák, the head of the Chancellery of the President; attached was an anonymous letter addressed to Novotný, dated 24 April and sent from the village of Ždiar, which was close to Javorina.[138] The author(s) of the letter wrote that they had learnt that on Easter Sunday a bear had been shot in the TANAP, the Tatra National Park.[139] They would normally have written to the CC KSS in Bratislava, but as the shooter was Comrade Dubček, they had decided to address the president in person.[140] Since the citizens in the Tatra villages were not even allowed to shoot a hare or a fox that had scabies, and since even shouting

---

[136] Dubček, *Hope Dies Last*, 110.
[137] Dubček, *Hope Dies Last*, 111.
[138] "Opis!", SNA Bratislava, ÚV KSS, tájomniki 1963–1968, A. Dubček, carton 2393, typewritten, two pages.
[139] The website: http://www.tanap.org/english/; accessed 31 March 2018.
[140] "Opis!", 1.

was forbidden in the forests of the National Park, it was strange that Comrade Dubček had shot a bear that was protected by law just like that. The author(s) further stated that "even Prince Hohenloche (!) [*aj firšt Hohenloche*] had thought twice about shooting a bear – and Javorina had been his, and there had been no national park, and bears had not been protected by law."[141] Did the laws of the National Park apply only to normal citizens and not to the masters? And had Comrade First Secretary KSS no other concerns than hunting? The citizens had also heard that there was drinking going on at the Javorina castle and the shooting of stags.[142]

A couple of rather roughly formulated statements complained about the director of the National Park, who had studied at the cost of the workers, and was neglecting his duties to such an extent that the foresters had not seen him once in the last three years; he used to drive around in his car and cared only about his new house – and most of the people did not understand him when he was speaking, so not even ten titles would help him.[143]

The anonymous letter had quite an impressive display of orthographic mistakes and logical inconsistencies, and we cannot possibly make any sound judgement about its authenticity. Either, Dubček was right, and the letter was a forgery concocted by Novotný's minions in Prague Castle; or the letter was authentic and some concerned citizens had complained to the president about the bad state of affairs in the TANAP – which

---

[141] "Opis!", 1. The Hohenlohe's family property in today's Tatranská Javorina on http://slovakia.travel/en/hunting-chateau-hohenlohe-is-now-open-to-the-public; accessed 31 March 2018.
[142] "Opis!", 1.
[143] "Opis!", 1–2.

Novotný might then have used to have another go at the young Slovak.

Dubček replied to Novotný's Chancellery on 23 May 1966, asking Comrade Novák to forward his letter to the president, thereby following official channels.[144] His statements were brief, a show of correct procedure. He began by saying that the anonymous letter was the first ever that expressed complaints about his governance; it was biased and not trustworthy.[145] His second point was formulated rather shrewdly, since it was aimed at Chudík, Novotný's man in the CC KSS, insinuating that Novotný must have known about the dangerous Javorina bear for two years – and with this letter, Novotný knew that Dubček knew:

> "How it came to the shooting of the bear. [...] Comrade Boďa, povereník of the Slovak National Council SNR for agriculture, and Comrade Chudík informed me that the bear in the area of Javorina *oblasť* had not yet been shot. He was doing a lot of damage, and if I was interested and courageous enough, I could participate in the hunt for him. I declined, saying that this could hurt somebody."[146]

Dubček further wrote that he, his family and some comrades had spent Easter in the Javorina castle, which the CC KSS owned and managed. As was the rule, every guest had paid for his stay; his payment could be verified in the TANAP's financial reports.[147] Together with two workers of the National Park, he

---

[144] "Letter from Alexander Dubček to Ladislav Novák", SNA Bratislava, ÚV KSS, tájomniki 1963–1968, A. Dubček, carton 2393, typewritten, two pages.
[145] "Letter from Alexander Dubček ...", 1.
[146] "Letter from Alexander Dubček ...", 1. A *povereník* was a member of the Slovak government with the duties and rights of a minister; Comrade Boďa had executive power in agricultural matters.
[147] "Letter from Alexander Dubček ...", 1. There are some discrepancies between Dubček's letter to Novotný and his memoirs. In *Hope Dies Last*, he did not mention that his family came to Javorina. He might have omitted this detail in his memoirs to avoid making the chapter too long or

was tracking the bear for three days, mainly in the early morning hours. From a distance of one to two kilometres from the place where the bear had threatened their horses the day before, Dubček and the two foresters finally found the bear. He shot twice, and the bear escaped, but fell down after 30 to 40 meters and died.[148] Dubček wrote that the foresters confirmed his description of the shooting of the bear – he had two witnesses. The bear had been dangerous, and not only the employees of the TANAP knew this, but also the citizens of the village

---

complicated, or he simply forgot about it. My friend Vlasta Jaksicsová: "The journalist Jiří Hochman who lived in the USA after 1968 offered to write Dubček's memoirs. Dubček knew him from 1968 and trusted him. According to my information, Hochman wrote the entire text on the basis of Dubček's answers to his questions and Dubček then corrected the text. Dubček did have a memory like an elephant, but with certain facts and events in Slovakia he was helped by Ivan Laluha and Ján Uher, for example the events in the High Tatra. Dubček was unable to read the final chapters of the text because of his tragic car accident." E-mail conversation on 2 April 2018. Furthermore, he got the date wrong: he shot the bear on 11 April, not on Good Friday, which was on 8 April. Moreover, he wrote in his memoirs that he had stayed in a small chalet; according to his letter to Novotný, the whole Easter party, the First Secretary of the KSS, his family and the comrades in the CC KSS stayed at the castle. I can only speculate: either, for some reason, Dubček did not want the English-speaking reader to know that he had stayed at Javorina castle with his family. After 1989, he was a committed Social Democrat. His international reputation as the father of the Czechoslovak Spring might have been damaged if readers learnt that he had spent Easter 1966 with his family in the Hohenlohe Hunting Lodge at Javorina Castle. Or, what I deem much more realistic, is that he simply could not remember the details. I think the version closer to the truth is the description of Easter 1966 in his letter to Novotný, since he wrote it six weeks after the incident in the High Tatra. I am certainly not saying that Dubček deliberately lied in his memoirs. One's memory does play tricks after thirty years, especially after years of psychological terror and surveillance by the StB. And I also deem it safe to assume that Dubček went to the Tatra quite often with his friends and comrades of the CC KSS.

[148] "Letter from Alexander Dubček …", 2.

Javorina.[149] Finishing his letter to Novotný, the First Secretary addressed the accusations against the director of TANAP:

> "As far as the management of the director of TANAP is concerned, I have informed Comrade Boďa, the povereník of agriculture. Comrade Boďa told me that the employees of the National Park shoot some eighty to ninety animals annually; guests shoot only five animals, because it is a protected game reserve. The shooting is allowed because it is necessary to regulate the numbers of animals. He told me that his little house with three rooms is being built according to the legal norms; the house is not yet finished. I asked him to scrutinize the management of TANAP [*Požiadal som ho, aby si hospodárenie v TANAP-e povšimol a veci preveril*]."[150]

If the statement of the First Secretary KSS was not enough, Comrade Boďa wrote to Novotný, confirming Dubček's version.[151] He had learnt about the anonymous letter sent to the president and deemed it his duty to confirm that the shooting of the dangerous bear had been within the legal norms. The comrade described briefly the legal basis, which the SNR had defined for the National Park in 1952, listing some successes of the measures to protect flora and fauna:

> "To illustrate this practice, in ten years, from 1952 to 1962, the herds of deer increased from 182 to 457 animals; stags from 447 to 1,200; chamois from 295 to 915; wild boar from 12 to 80 and bears from 15 to 21."[152]

To protect the vegetation and keep the animal population in check, hence the natural equilibrium of plants and animals, the SNR had issued a new directive on 23 January 1964; in 1965, for example, 276 stags had to be shot. The Park's personnel had executed this task. In very precise terms and wording, Boďa

---

[149] "Letter from Alexander Dubček ...", 2.
[150] "Letter from Alexander Dubček ...", 2.
[151] "Odpis", SNA Bratislava, ÚV KSS, tájomniki 1963–1968, A. Dubček, carton 2393, typewritten, three pages, dated 24 May 1966, signed by Boďa.
[152] "Odpis", 2.

further stressed that it had been him who had ordered the shooting of the dangerous bear already "on 12 December 1964, order number 1.461/2/CH/1964". [153] The bear had attacked horses in their stables, was hence also a danger to the population and was either sick or had suffered a trauma; he had not gone into hibernation, roaming through the region. The *poverenik* had repeatedly asked the First Secretary KSS to shoot the bear; Comrade Dubček had finally accepted after thorough analysis of the procedure and shot the bear on Easter Sunday, 11 April 1966.[154]

On 12 April, experts of the scientific department of the National Park conducted an autopsy; the veterinarians confirmed that the old bear, a loner, had had to be shot since one of his forepaws was fifteen centimeters shorter than the other and caused by an old fracture, and his teeth were worn down. These physical injuries had caused his disability to gather food in a normal way. The body was sent to the department of helminthological research of the SAV Košice for thorough investigation.[155] The *poverenik* finished, stressing that the anonymous

---

[153] "Odpis", 2.
[154] "Odpis", 3.
[155] My colleague Michael Hässig, professor of veterinary medicine at the University of Zurich UZH, about the helminthological investigation: "It was obvious to the experts that the bear stood no chance of survival with a fractured leg that was badly healed and hence shortened. Because of his worn-down teeth, he could eat only soft things and had to chew using his gums. The cause of death was clear-cut; a dissection superfluous. However, we know very little about parasitosis (infestation with parasites) in bears. Trichinae are the most frequent parasites living in bears. Earlier, they were highly feared because they cause deadly food poisoning. That is one reason why people are still afraid of eating raw meat. Until the 1970s, the large abattoirs in West Germany had a special inspector for trichinae. In this context, it is reasonable that they sent the bear to the Department of Helminthological Research. Today, such departments are mostly referred to as institutes of parasitology. In Zurich, we have only one institute of parasitology that analyses human and animal samples. If somebody

letter contained incorrect statements and the unscrupulous denunciation of a Party functionary.[156]

II. 4. 8 Anonymous Letters (1963, 1966)

Anonymous letters to the government were not uncommon in the mid-1960s. My friend and colleague Karen Henderson[157] thinks that the Communist regime overrated the anonymous letters. I completely agree: the Party was in firm control of the country, with no opposition to its rule. But, one should keep in mind the principal goal of Communism: to change people's way of thinking, to rid them of Capitalist greed – that is why the government and the StB thought that anonymous letters had to be taken seriously.

Once Pandora's box had been opened with the investigation commissions of the late 1950s and early 1960s, citizens were becoming increasingly angered, but also increasingly courageous because of the changing political atmosphere; to let off steam, some of them decided to put their anger in written form. Under the political conditions prevailing at that time, one would have had to be either an idiot,[158] in the perfect sense of the medical-psychological concept, or then a saint, intent on making oneself a martyr by signing a critical letter to the government. One would have most certainly have prompted the StB knocking on one's door. To voice one's criticism of the government was still dangerous, and from the memoirs of a former StB officer we learn that one of the tasks of the secret service was to

---

brings back a 'souvenir' from the tropics, the diagnosis is done at the veterinary clinic." E-mail conversation from 4 April 2018.
[156] "Odpis", 3.
[157] Discussion with Karen Henderson in Bratislava, 30 July 2017.
[158] For a definition see https://en.oxforddictionaries.com/definition/idiot; accessed 28 May 2018.

identify authors of anonymous letters, since they were considered internal enemies of the regime.[159]

Naturally, I do not claim that the two anonymous letters I have found in the SNA are the only ones; I am quite certain that one would find many more in the Prague Party archives. I have selected these two letters, because they specifically inform us what citizens in Slovakia and the Czech lands were concerned with – and how Dubček as First Secretary was changing the oppressive atmosphere of late Czechoslovak Stalinism.

The first anonymous letter is from 1963;[160] the authors were really clever, astute. First, they sent a covering letter to the General Consulate of the Soviet Union in Bratislava,[161] asking the consul to accept the enclosed copy of their letter to Comrade President Novotný. I think that they were well aware that the Soviet consul in Bratislava would forward it to the Soviet ambassador in Prague. The Soviets would thus be informed how domestic affairs looked from a Slovak perspective, with independent information that differed from the usual reports from the Prague comrades. Second, the authors could expect that the Soviet embassy in Prague would forward the letter to President Novotný – who in turn would have to count on the fact that the

---

[159] Karol Urban, *Sledoval som Dubčeka. Spomienky eštebáka* (Bratislava: Trio, 2012), 30. XY commented on those years and the StB tracking down authors of anonymous letters: "As far as I can remember, the situation was getting better, people started to tell jokes in pubs, the first lucky ones were allowed to travel to the West. I was able to go to Austria in 1963; theatres were staging authors younger than Shakespeare and Shaw, and literary revues started to publish existentialists. The StB had strict rules; finding anonymous authors was probably a 'safe' case to be followed; it was time-consuming and proof of one's working effort without results." E-mail conversation from 2 April 2018.

[160] "Vážený súdruh prezidente!", SNA Bratislava, ÚV KSS, tájomniki 1963–1968, A. Dubček, carton 2393, typewritten, two pages, dated 18 June 1963.

[161] "Vážený Generálny konzulát SSSR, Bratislava", SNA Bratislava, ÚV KSS, tájomniki 1963–1968, A. Dubček, carton 2393, typewritten, one page, dated 18 June 1963, signed by V. M. and R. K.

Soviets had read the letter, which put him under some pressure. Fact is that Soviet General Consul I. Šuľgin sent the letter to Dubček on 21 June 1963, which was standard procedure in a Communist state in its relationship with the leading state of the bloc; it was an exchange of important information.[162]

In their covering letter, the authors V. M. and R. K. stressed that they trusted the consul and particularly the Russian brotherly nation, hoping that he would have the letter translated into Russian and hand it over to the Russian nation and Comrade Khrushchev, whom the Slovaks held in particularly high regard for his reasonable leadership of the entire camp of peace and Socialism.[163] They apologized for omitting their addresses, since this might prompt severe reprisals from the Czech comrades. What did they complain about in their letter to the president?

I have rarely seen such an amusing and well-composed letter: straightforward, rational, logically structured, grammatically correct, save for a few typos, open-hearted and, above all, self-confident. I am speculating here, but I think it is quite possible that the authors were academically trained and members of the KSS. Addressing the president with the Communist informal you (*Ty*), the authors went straight to the heart of the matter, presenting themselves as ordinary working people who had participated in the SNP. The president had inspired them to write this letter: in his speech of 12 June 1963 in Košice, Novotný had criticized the increasingly liberal atmosphere in

---

[162] "Pervomu sekretariu TSK KPS tov. A. Dubčeku", SNA Bratislava, ÚV KSS, tájomniki 1963–1968, A. Dubček, carton 2393, typewritten, one page, dated 21 June 1963, in Russian Cyrillic, signed by Soviet General Consul I. Šuľgin.

[163] "Vážený Generálny konzulát SSSR, ...", 1.

Slovakia.[164] The authors wrote that some articles and speeches of Slovak writers and journalists were a thorn in his side, but the majority of the Slovak public regarded them with great sympathy, hoping for a better future. The authors further had the impression that he had come to Slovakia only to suffocate the free current of liberal ideas:

> "Really, you would have been much more welcome here had you done the opposite: praising what has been happening lately in Slovakia. But you have brought only disappointment to our country and to a certain extent frustration and the undermining of the relationship between Slovaks and Czechs [*priniesol si sem len rozčarovanie a do istej miery sklamanie a sklatenie nášho vzájomného pomeru Slovákov a Čechov*]."[165]

For some time now, the authors stressed, every Slovak citizen was shaking his head about the fact that the officially declared policy of ending the personality cult had prompted only the removal of Stalin's statues – nothing else had changed. The ordinary Slovak citizen had the impression that those 'above' who had, under pressure, expressed criticism of the personality cult at the 20th and 22nd Party conventions were not at all interested in or capable of removing the well-known Stalinists from the Party and state apparatus, because they themselves would fall. And this was the very reason why their country remained

---

[164] "Vážený súdruh prezidente!", 1. Dubček wrote about Novotný's visit in Košice: "Novotný demonstrated again his complete ignorance of Slovak affairs. He said that there was no substance to calls for a revision of the new constitution because the abolished Slovak Board of Commissioners had not worked well. Then he tried to defend the repressions by repeating absurd arguments about bourgeois nationalism, naming Husák and Novomesky again as culprits. This was a political blunder of remarkable proportions, given that the main findings of the Kolder Commission were soon to be published. I wondered what drove him to such silliness." *Hope Dies Last*, 91.

[165] "Vážený súdruh prezidente!", 1.

the last Socialist state that had not yet undergone a thorough purge of Stalinists from public life.[166]

The authors, referring to the KSS (we, *my*), went on to criticize the Slovak authorities, which had also made grave mistakes in the past. The KSS was to blame for the miserable life of the farmers who had had to 'voluntarily' join the collective farms – no wonder the farmers had lost interest and joy in their work. The poor farmers in the mountain regions, whom the government had allowed to keep farming privately, had been burdened with unbearable output quotas. As the holder of power, Prague should hence unburden those farmers and cancel the quotas.[167] The authors described the lack of humanity and decency that dominated the unhealthy schools policy: to some students, access to higher education, to enrol at high school or university, was denied, only because somebody had spotted them in church.[168] Even if they, as Communists, were inclined to atheism, every reasonable citizen and comrade had to condemn such inhuman and nasty methods, which had been carried out deliberately and against the civil rights granted by the Czechoslovak constitution.[169]

So far, the anonymous letter must have confirmed Novotný's anti-Slovak bias: I can vividly imagine how the president either turned pale or was foaming at the mouth in rage. In his view, the letter confirmed four 'facts': first, the Slovaks were still nationalists and bourgeois ones at that, because, second, they mentioned the church, a relic of the exploitative system of Capitalism; third, not only were they always complaining but they were incapable of achieving anything on their own, see

---

[166] "Vážený súdruh prezidente!", 1.
[167] "Vážený súdruh prezidente!", 1–2.
[168] "Vážený súdruh prezidente!", 2.
[169] "Vážený súdruh prezidente!", 2.

their economic policy; and fourth, they were ever quick to blame the Czechs for their misery. The authors' statements, or rather, warnings, about the relationship of Slovaks and Czechs must have been too much for the president:

> "The current mood circulating among the Slovaks is gaining momentum to such an extent that they are thinking that the best way forward for the future and the common state is to establish a full confederation with a Slovak president governing Slovakia [*vybudované na základe úplnej konfederácie a to i s vlastným prezidentom na Slovensku, inač v jednom štátnom zväzku*]. Only this solution would definitively remove the lack of trust between Slovaks and Czechs. [...] If things continue as they are now, if the current conditions and methods of ruling from Prague do not change, the anger of our people is going to increase to such extent that it will soon be too late. This could lead to a complete rupture between Slovaks and Czechs. We comrades certainly do not want that, but first and foremost, Prague has to understand the situation [*To si iste ako súdruhovia neprajeme ale to musí pochopiť v prvom rade Praha*]."[170]

It was ironic, as the authors wrote, that African states were achieving independence, while the Slovaks were not. After all, it was the 20th century. The Comrade President should openly condemn the bad conditions mentioned above, and ensure their improvement, and the Slovak nation would be immensely grateful to him; such action would improve the relationship between Slovaks and Czechs. If he did not, then they could only say that "a fish rots from the head [*ryba smrdí od hlavy*]", which they would rather not.[171] That was really quite a pun – the final statement comparing the First Secretary KSČ and president of the republic to the stinking head of a fish! What they meant was, of course, that the Prague government was the origin of the Slovaks' complaints and grievances – and it was up to Prague to improve the conditions in Slovakia.

---

[170] "Vážený súdruh prezidente!", 2.
[171] "Vážený súdruh prezidente!", 2. In English, this idiom means something like 'the rot starts at the top'.

The second anonymous letter I have chosen is not as funny or brazen as the first one, but equally interesting.[172] On ten pages, the author wrote quite a detailed description of the current state of Czechoslovak domestic affairs from the ordinary citizen's view. The letter was not clearly structured, more an essay, free floating and in the tradition of Michel de Montaigne (1572–1675). The contents reminded me of Václav Havel's descriptions of how the Party's rule affected the citizens in psychological terms: fear, careerism, lies, resignation, in brief, the destruction of civilized behaviour in social interaction.

The author began with the statement that he had been following the life in the republic; he was trying to objectively and dispassionately judge what was happening. Referring to the thesis of the 13th Party congress of the KSČ, his letter was a contribution to an open and general discussion; his was an opinion that one surely would not hear at official meetings or in news broadcasts and discussions with citizens, but it was what the citizens of the republic were talking about, regardless of Party

---

[172] "Příspěvek do diskuse na teze k XIII. sjezdu KSČ", SNA Bratislava, ÚV KSS, tájomniki 1963–1968, A. Dubček, carton 2391, typewritten, ten pages, date-stamped upon reception 1 February 1966 signed "A citizen of the republic [*Já, občan republiky*]". Dubček received the anonymous letter from *Pravda* on 5 February 1966; the editor wrote in his covering letter that they had received the letter from Prague. On page 1, the author listed the recipients of a copy: Novotný; the chairman of the parliament Bohuslav Laštovičký; prime minister Jozef Lenárt; minister of justice Alois Najman; minister of education and culture Jiří Hájek; the Czechoslovak union of writers; the Czechoslovak radio in Prague, Brno and Bratislava; the editorial offices of *Rudé Právo, Pravda, Literárné Noviny* and *Kulturní Tvorba*, all Czech journals and newspapers. The last recipient listed was the dyed-in-the-wool actor, cabaret artiste and humourist Jan Werich (1905–1980). The author obviously hoped that Werich would support his arguments. The author must have had access to a typewriter, enough paper and possibly an offset printing machine, which is why I suppose he could have been a journalist, academic or teacher.

membership.[173] Lenin had said go among the people and listen to what they were saying.

In historical terms, twenty years was a short time, but not for the individual who well remembered the theories and promises that the welfare of the next generation was being built by the increased effort and material sacrifices of this generation. The continuous search for new approaches was nothing other than smearing ointment on a sick organism that was suffering a protracted ailment. To remove that ailment, one had to remove its origins:

> "With a reorganization that replaces a previous reorganization, we won't remove the causes, the origins of the ailment. We must, above all, have the courage to call the origins of the ailment by its name [*Musíme najít především odvahu a nazvat příčinu neduhu pravým jmenem*]. If you, like Lenin, go among the people, you are going to be astonished, how deep the gulf between the people and the KSČ is and how gravely the Party has forfeited the people's trust."[174]

The reason for this gulf was fear; fear was everywhere and people with fear in their souls would certainly smile and clap their hands enthusiastically, but what they really thought, was quite different. 'Duplicity [*dvojí tvář*]' was a deformation of the character and the most terrible element of the politics of the previous twenty years.[175] Duplicity dominated the entire life of the citizens: already small children joined the pioneers to gain advantages. Parents told elder children to join the Communist Youth Organization (ČSM) to become somebody, and the saddest thing was that teachers taught the children what they themselves did not believe. The result was that the young were squinting to the West, forgetting about their Slavic origins.

---

[173] "Příspěvek do diskuse …", 2.
[174] "Příspěvek do diskuse …", 3.
[175] "Příspěvek do diskuse …", 3.

Criticism of the Party's privileges and violation of equal rights was the author's main argument: against the Party's viewpoint, its power monopoly without objective control by other parties or independent institutions meant neither democracy nor equal rights.[176] The elections were a farce, pure formalism, since 99.99% of the citizens voted for the Party only because they had to agree with everything. If those in power were really interested in improving the socio-political and economic conditions, they should give independent citizens legal security, that is, protection from being legally persecuted. Citizens who had not joined the Party were realistically thinking citizens – they could contribute to the state to the benefit of the whole country.[177]

The author finished his letter with the call that the Party had to regain the trust of the people and signed with 'A citizen of the republic'. In his postscript, he added an interesting and courageous promise:

> "I have always been just a small Czech person and that's why my name is not important. For the first time in my life, I am using anonymity, because I am aware that I have important reasons for doing so. If, however, I find that the press reacts positively to my opinion, I shall identify myself to support it [přihlasím se]."[178]

The intention of the author was clear: he demanded democracy and a rule-of-law state; he criticized the ideological power base of the KSČ and argued with the psychological consequences of the Party's rule. The psychological damage to the people's morale and the lawlessness of the single-Party state was causing the citizens' duplicity; from childhood on, Czechoslovaks were learning to hide what they really thought, say X when they

---

[176] "Příspěvek do diskuse ...", 6–7.
[177] "Příspěvek do diskuse ...", 9.
[178] "Příspěvek do diskuse ...", 10.

thought Y and join the Party's organizations to get ahead. The Party suffocated individual talent, innovation and independence of thinking. Was the author a psychologist? We shall never find out.

II. 5 The Eight Months of the Czechoslovak Spring (1968)

To the Western reader, the concept of the *Prague Spring* is well known. It is, however, imprecise: it focuses on the Czech part of the country, because the Czech capital was the city where the important events of 1968 took place. From the perspective of Czechoslovak domestic affairs, historically and chronologically correct would be *Slovako-Czech Spring* or *Bratislava-Prague Spring*, because de-Stalinization had begun in Slovakia under Dubček's stewardship. From Bratislava, the liberalization spread to Prague, the capital Western journalists, once the borders were open, were flocking to in 1968 to report about the hitherto unheard-of liberalization of a Communist bloc state.[179] For reasons of simplicity, I shall use the term *Czechoslovak Spring*. This last subchapter is brief, since the events of 1968 have been sufficiently analysed by historians and political scientists. I shall thus present only a summary of the events that led to the invasion of the Warsaw Pact troops in the night of 21 August 1968, focussing on the fight between the conservatives

---

[179] Western journalists' ignorance of the Slovak part of the country prevailed after the 1989 Velvet Revolution; we could say that the majority of Western media reported about Czechoslovak affairs from a Prague viewpoint. Highly recommendable in this context is Slavomír Michálek and Peter Weiss, "The Foreign Policy Context of the Break-Up of Czechoslovakia from 1989 to 1992 and the Relations of Prague and Bratislava with Washington", in *Slovakia. A European Story*, 117–160.

and the modernizers, embodied in the duel between Novotný and Dubček.

So far, we have portrayed Novotný as a conservative politician who was trying to disempower the First Secretary KSS by all possible means; to be fair, however, we should note that it was he, in February 1967, who rejected the Soviets' request to station two divisions on Czechoslovakia's Western border.[180] But let us get back to the army later.

Although Novotný's many intrigues against the First Secretary KSS did not get results, he did not tune down his anti-Slovak bias, on the contrary: I consider Dubček's former statement that he suspected the president was suffering from paranoia an apt psychological analysis. If the above-mentioned incident with the bottle of Vermouth at the Bratislava Carlton Hotel in 1964 could be topped, the president's behaviour during his state visit to Slovakia in the summer of 1967 definitely topped it. What happened?

> "The president's visit to Martin and the Matica Slovenská in Slovakia from 26 to 27 August 1967 to celebrate the 100th anniversary of the foundation of the first Slovak secondary school (*gymnasium*) can be seen as an overture to the inner-Party crisis, which would emerge in the autumn of 1967 and lead to the fall of A. Novotný. Until today, it remains unclear why he left for Slovakia in the middle of the government-instigated campaign against the Czech writers [who had sharply criticized the government; add JB] at the 4th Convention of the Czechoslovak Union of Writers."[181]

---

[180] KURAL, V. – MORAVEC, J. – JANÁČEK, F. – NAVRÁTIL, J. – BENČÍK, A.: ref. 426, s. 18, quoted from Stanislav Sikora, "Dubček kontra Novotný", in *Predjarie*, 137–152, 147.

[181] Sikora, "Dubček kontra Novotný", 142–143. The union's meeting had taken place in Prague from 27 to 29 June. Havel went as far as to reproach the union for taking a pseudo-critical attitude towards the government; the *Svaz* had not protested against the government shutting down the Czech independent literary revues *Květen* (*May*) and *Tvář* (*Face*), Baer, *Politik als praktizierte Sittlichkeit*, 107. I would like to take issue with the

Dubček and the renowned Czech historian Jan Rychlík think that Novotný's trip was a spontaneous decision: aware that the majority of Slovak writers did not share their Czech colleagues' political criticism expressed at the union's meeting in June 1967, he was determined to capitalize on what he must have deemed Slovak loyalty. He wanted to polish his image among the Slovak cultural intelligentsia and writers.[182] However, it very quickly became obvious that Novotný was not capable of garnering the sympathy of the Slovaks.

In political terms, the most important part of Novotný's journey was the visit to the Matica Slovenská in Martin. Dubček commented on the circumstances of Novotný's visit that reveal to us the rather significant room for independent manoeuvring of the Matica Slovenská as a cultural institution – and the CC KSS' conscious loosening of the tight reins of Stalinist totalitarian control of all institutions:

> "Thus, the hundredth anniversary of the foundation of the lycée was an important event in Slovak cultural history. Neither we in the Slovak Party leadership nor the Presidium of the Slovak National Council had taken the initiative to invite Novotny to attend the celebration. [...] It was the idea of the leading officials of Matica Slovenska to invite him in his role as head of state. They needed no permission from Bratislava, so they acted on their own. They did not even inform us until after Novotny surprisingly accepted. Not having been officially informed by either the presidential office in Prague or the Czechoslovak Party, I could avoid going to Martin myself. Still, Novotny was the president of the Republic, so I instructed Vasil Bilak, a Slovak Party

---

concept 'inner-Party crisis'; what happened from autumn 1967 to January 1968 in the CC KSČ was not a crisis in the truest sense of the word, that is, a phase that must end either in death or life, but a simple fight between two factions for power: the modernizers led by Dubček against Novotný's conservatives. The KSČ's monopoly of power was never in danger, not for a second.

[182] Sikora, "Dubček kontra Novotný", 143.

> Presidium member and the Central Committee secretary responsible for cultural affairs, to attend the event."[183]

The First Secretary KSS did not show up, since he had received no invitation. Would you crash a party you are not invited to? Would you welcome your fiercest enemy to your own turf? I think that Dubček used Novotný's visit to his own advantage in a twofold fashion: first, no invitation – no show; second, by sending members of the lower echelons of the CC KSS to attend the festivities, he signalled to Novotný that he respected him and his visit, but that it was he who was ruling in Slovakia. Had he shown up without an invitation, it would have been an act of pre-emptive obedience. And by August 1967, after years of Novotný hatching intrigues against him and his wife, Dubček, ever the clever strategist and supported by the majority of CC KSS members, must have thought: just let him come to Slovakia. I bet he is going to act in a fashion that will only estrange him further from us – which I then can use against him in the forthcoming meeting of the CC KSČ. The best prognosis of future behaviour is past behaviour. Dubček would prove right. From Biľak's report to the CC KSS:

> "First, he refused to welcome to his entourage representatives of Slovak political and public life. [...] When President Novotný arrived at the National Cemetery, where thousands of citizens were awaiting him, expecting to witness the festive laying of a wreath, he refused to do so. [...] It was planned that he should stay overnight in a holiday resort for Martin builders, in Gaderská Dolina, but, claiming that he was afraid of an attempt on his life, he left for Rajecké Teplice. His journey led him and his entourage also to Mošovce, the birthplace of J. Kollár, the great poet and ideologue of Panslavism (and also Czecho-Slovakism). Yet, the citizens of Mošovce waited in vain [meaning that the president did not get out of his car to greet the citizens, his convoy just rushed through the village, add. JB]. On the second day, local dignitaries laid wreaths on the monument to Soviet soldiers, but A. Novotný

---

[183] Dubček, *Hope Dies Last*, 114–115.

> sharply and insensitively refused to accept the expressions of sympathy of ordinary citizens from Martin and surrounding villages [*A. Novotný ostro a necitlivo odmietol prejavy sympatií prostých obyvateľov Martina a okolia*]. [...] After the faux pas in the Matica Slovenská, the festive dinner was about to begin, but half of the invited guests did not show up, and so A. Novotný left Martin and Slovakia. The anger of the Slovak people peaked when the Chancellery of the President returned the beautifully sewn fur coat and hand-made embroideries given as a gift of the Slovak people to the president's wife."[184]

Novotný's visit to Slovakia proved to be a complete disaster – he not only offended the comrades of the CC KSS and the chairman of the Matica, but above all, the people. Returning a gift in a Slavic country, the Slavs being traditionally and famously known for their hospitality and friendliness, is like a slap in the face – and in just two days, Novotný managed to slap the Slovaks in the face, not once but three times. Why did the president behave in such an abominable way? What was his motivation? The Slovak historian Michal Štefanský:

> "The conflict in Martin was staged; its purpose was to demonstrate that the official policy of rapprochement and union of the Czechs and Slovaks on Slovak territory had failed [for which the Slovaks were to blame, according to Novotný's view, add. JB]. Its further goal was to frighten the KSS leadership before the September and October plenary sessions of the CC KSČ, that is, before the voting about the discontent of the Slovaks [what Dubček wanted to discuss, on the basis of the

---

[184] BIĽAK, V: Míľniky môjho života, ref. 91, s. 188–194, quoted from Sikora, "Dubček kontra Novotný", 143, footnote 430. Novotný's discussion with Juraj Paška, the chairman of the Matica Slovenská was about the Matica's representative functions for the Slovaks abroad. Novotný rejected the Matica's legitimate demand to speak for the Slovaks abroad, insisting that this was the task of the Czechoslovak Foreign Institute (*Československý ústav zahraničný*). After some minutes, he became loud, accused Paška of 'bourgeois nationalism' and left the meeting, threatening that the CC KSČ would investigate this 'affair', Sikora, "Dubček kontra Novotný", 143–144.

1960 Czechoslovak constitution, that is, independence of Slovak institutions, add JB]."[185]

It was therefore no miracle that during the autumn of 1967 to January 1968, the majority of the KSČ members thought about the Party's future – and who should be at its helm. Novotný was not only president and First Secretary KSČ, but also Chairman of the NF, supreme commander of the Czechoslovak army and the People's militia and also had a significant say in the Party's finances.[186] In his speech to the meeting of the CC KSČ on 30 to 31 October 1967, Dubček spoke of "a new phase of Socialism [*novú etapu socializmu*]" and criticized "the disproportionate accumulation of functions [*neúmernou kumuláciou funkcií*]".[187] Although he did not mention Novotný's name, it was crystal clear to all Party members whose accumulation of power the First Secretary KSS was referring to.

What the historically informed reader might not know about yet are two events that were related to the army and the Soviets and had a crucial influence on the Party members siding with Dubček and his faction in the voting in January 1968: first, the repeated rumour of Brezhnev's allegedly saying '*Eto vaše delo* [That's your matter]', and second, Novotný planning to hold onto power by means of a putsch, using the army and the StB to arrest members of the reform-oriented faction. Such activity would have been equivalent to a Stalinist purge, an inner-Party *čistka*.

After his recovery from a cold he had acquired at the Moscow celebrations of the Russian Revolution in November 1967, Novotný asked Brezhnev to come to Prague – basically

---

[185] ŠTEFANSKÝ, M.: Postavenie SNR v rokoch 1948–1967, in: Slovenské národné rady, Bratislava 1998, s. 160, quoted from Sikora, "Dubček kontra Novotný", 144, footnote 432.
[186] Sikora, "Dubček kontra Novotný", 145.
[187] Sikora, "Dubček kontra Novotný", 145.

expecting that the Soviet General Secretary would dictate to Party members how to vote, that is, in his favour. Brezhnev did come to Prague on 8 December and stayed for a day, the official occasion was an invitation to attend a hunt; but he refused to support Novotný, most probably a sweet little revenge for Novotný's refusal to accept the stationing of Soviet troops in Czechoslovakia back in February 1967.[188] Brezhnev did not say *'Eto vaše delo'*, but something similar:

> "I did not come to Prague to help you find a solution to your problems. We [meaning: the almighty Soviet Union that had won WWII, add. JB] don't do things like that. You are certainly capable of finding a solution on your own [*Nepříjel jsem, abych se zůčastnil řešení vašich otázek. Neděláme to, a vy si je jístě sami dokážete vyřešit.*]."[189]

This was a clear sign that the Soviet Union was not interested in the details of Czechoslovakia's domestic affairs. As long as the country was a loyal bloc member, their internal affairs were their own business. The negotiations of the CC KSČ from 11 December 1967 ended in a pat situation: the modernizers under Dubček achieved as many votes as the conservatives, and the voting had to be postponed over Christmas until January 1968. The vote of the CC KSČ that would end on 5 January 1968 with

---

[188] Sikora, "Dubček kontra Novotný", 147. Iurii Vladimirovič Andropov (1914–1984), the head of the KGB and later General Secretary of the Soviet Communist Party who brought Gorbachev to power, had come with Brezhnev to Prague to negotiate about the stationing of Soviet troops. We can only speculate here, but if the Soviets, as early as February 1967, wanted to have their troops at Czechoslovakia's western border, this would be a further factor that made the Soviets decide in favour of invasion – killing two birds with one stone: getting rid of Dubček's 'counter-revolutionaries' and putting their feet or troops down in Czechoslovakia.

[189] Archív ÚV KSČ, signature f. A. Novotný CH, zv. 7, one copy at the Dokumentácii Ústavu pro soudobé dějiny AV ČR, quoted from Sikora, "Dubček kontra Novotný", 147, footnote 447.

Dubček gaining 100% (!) of the votes went down in the history of the CC KSČ as the longest voting procedure ever.[190]

Finally, what about Novotný's plans to use the army and the StB to go against the modernizers? According to Sikora, who studied the archive material and the commission's report about the defection of general Jan Šejna (1927–1997)[191] to the West, Novotný did toil with the idea of arresting Dubček and some of his followers, but, for some reason, plans remained plans:

> "Novotný's 'night of the long knives', planned for the days between Christmas 1967 and the first few days of the New Year 1968, did not materialize. Perhaps because of Novotný's failure to organize such an operation (he was a classic *aparátnik* and his involvement highly probable), but perhaps also because he was unsure how the Soviet Union would react: some authors say that L. I. Brezhnev forbade him from going ahead with these plans, based on information from the KGB."[192]

In his memoirs, Dubček briefly mentioned the preparations for a putsch, not going into details. The final verdict of the investigation commission confirmed that "at no point in time, had orders been issued nor army units mobilized".[193]

As we have mentioned above, the roadmap of the Czechoslovak Spring is well known: the abolition of censorship in February, the action programme of April that, besides economic reforms, opened Czechoslovakia's borders, and Vaculík's *Manifesto of 2000 Words* of June. Liberty and happiness now ruled in Czechoslovakia. At the meeting of 29 May to 1 June, the CC KSČ set the date of 9 September for the extraordinary 14th party congress, which was supposed to legalize the action programme and the reforms to economy and society.

---

[190] Sikora, "Dubček kontra Novotný", 152, 148.
[191] Šeina's obituary on https://www.nytimes.com/1997/08/30/world/jan-sejna-70-ex-czech-general-and-defector.html; accessed 30 May 2018.
[192] Sikora, "Dubček kontra Novotný", 150, footnote 432.
[193] Sikora, "Dubček kontra Novotný", 150.

From the viewpoint of the conservative members of the Warsaw Pact lead by Brezhnev, Prague was a nest of the counter-revolution: journalists of the Capitalist enemy were invading Czechoslovakia and setting up shop in Prague, Czechoslovak citizens travelling to the West and Vaculík's *Manifesto* were, to their way of thinking, the beginning of a serious problem for the bloc at its western border. Brezhnev, Zhizhkov, Ulbricht, Kádár and Gomułka met in Warsaw on 14 and 15 July; they wrote to the CC KSČ the so-called 'Letter of the Five', expressing their serious concerns that the current Czechoslovak government was preparing the ground for a counter-revolution. Upon reception of the letter from the Warsaw Five, the CC KSČ discussed the accusations at its meeting of 16 to 17 July.

Dubček gave a speech "The Proof of the wisdom and maturity of the Republic's citizens"[194] on national TV and radio on 27 July, a day before he would meet Brezhnev in the Slovak town Čierna nad Tisou. After addressing the viewers and listeners, he praised the newly found unity of the two nations, thanking the citizens for their support of the new political course and stressing that the government would keep acting in accordance with public sentiment – to continue the course of reform and strengthen the country's economy and social system. Only the citizens of Czechoslovakia had a say in how their country should be governed and what tasks its government should tackle as part of the reform course. Czechoslovakia was a member of the Socialist bloc and it would never betray the interests of the friendly brother states, neither in economic nor military terms. This statement was clearly in support of solidarity with the Warsaw Pact and COMECON. Clearly, Dubček's intention with

---

[194] Alexander Dubček, "Důkaz moudrosti a vyspělosti občanů republiky", *Rudé Právo*, no. 207, 28 July 1968, 1–2, 1.

this speech was to demonstrate to the citizens that the letter from the Warsaw Five did not affect the resolve of the government – which would continue its reform course. The speech was also a clever move against the conservatives who opposed the reforms, demonstrating that the people stood behind the reformers. The First Secretary KSČ also made it very clear where the boundaries of the liberalization were:

> "We demonstrated not only in minutes of Party meetings and papers that the KSČ will not renege on its leadership responsibilities nor relinquish its leading role: the principal question is how to translate this into practice, to find practical solutions that will benefit the working people."[195]

He finished his speech, stressing that Czechoslovakia's friendship with the Soviet Union was the working people's wish. He was full of hope: tomorrow, the CC KSČ would meet the CC KSS and clear away the misunderstandings and wrong accusations listed in the letter of the Warsaw Five.[196]

The meeting of the Czechoslovak government with leading members of the Soviet Communist Party did not bring positive results. Brezhnev and Dubček insisted on their points of view; no compromise could be found. The meeting, proposed by Brezhnev was not a manoeuvre to distract the Czechoslovak government from its vigilance, from paying attention to military issues, the preparation of the invasion; it was Moscow's last attempt to make the CC KSČ make concessions and tune down its reform course.[197]

Did Dubček and his reformers underestimate the conservatives' opposition and efforts? Yes, I think so. On 3 August, Alois Indra, Drahomír Kolder, Antonín Kapek, Oldřich Švestka

---

[195] Dubček, "Důkaz moudrosti...", 1.
[196] Dubček, "Důkaz moudrosti" ..., 2.
[197] Skilling, *Czechoslovakia's Interrupted Revolution*, 291.

and Vasil Bil'ak wrote the so-called 'letter of invitation' [*požývací list, poživací list*], which was meant to legitimate the invasion by the Warsaw Pact armies.¹⁹⁸

Like all General Secretaries of the CPs of the Soviet bloc, János Kádár, who had had his own bitter experience with the Soviet invasion of Hungary in 1956, was informed about the date of the invasion. After a bilateral meeting with Dubček in Komárno at the Slovak-Hungarian border on 17 August, Kádár, saying goodbye on the platform of the railway station, warned Dubček in a desperate tone: "Do you *really* not know the kind of people you are dealing with?"¹⁹⁹

Four days later, Warsaw Pact troops invaded Czechoslovakia – this military operation that destroyed so many hopes remains to this day a Czech, Slovak and European trauma. The invasion was not only a violation of Public International Law, the violation of Czechoslovakia's sovereignty; the invasion psychologically and politically scarred an entire generation and prompted the exodus of Czechoslovakia's most talented and gifted scientists, teachers and scholars – the elite. Those citizens, who remained at home, would soon become subject to a new regime of political oppression that in its scope and activities can be referred to as neo-Stalinist.

---

[198] *Chronológia Dejín Slovenska a Slovákov*, 881. The letter in Russian in Pauer, 196–197. The authors wrote, amongst other things, that Socialism was under threat and the government no longer capable of restoring order; the country was heading for a counter-revolution, with rightist hostile elements occupying the press, radio and television. Consequently, they asked the Soviet Union for help.

[199] Bryan Cartledge, *The Will to Survive* (London: C. Hurst & Co., 2011), 476; *Chronológia Dejín Slovenska a Slovákov*, 881; *Rok 1968 na Slovensku* ..., 9.

Alexander Dubček's birthplace in
Uhrovec, Central Slovakia,
© Josette Baer, 2017.
The building now hosts a museum in
honour of Ľudovít Štúr (1815–1856),
the father of the Slovak written language,
and Dubček. Both were born in the same house.

A bust of Dubček in the museum,
© Josette Baer, 2017.

The leaders of the KSS faction in the SNR in the months of preparation for the SNP, from left to right: Karol Šmidke, Gustáv Husák and Ladislav Novomeský, undated, SNK Martin, Slovak Republic.

Exhibition poster in Banská Bystrica shortly after the end of WWII, SNK Martin. The title of the poster: "The Only Way – the KSS at the Helm of the Resistance". The portraits of KSS members who fought in the SNP, from top left to bottom right: Július Ďuriš, Viliam Široký, Karol Bacílek, Jozef Lietavec, Ľudevít Benada and Štefan Dubček, Alexander's father.

The first female cosmonaut Valentina V. Tereshkova from the USSR on her state visit to Czechoslovakia in August 1963, © TASR, Bratislava, Slovak Republic.

Alexander Dubček's Sunday, undated, © TASR. The date is unknown, but the picture was most probably taken after his election as First Secretary of the KSS in 1963.

Alexander Dubček's Sunday, undated, © TASR. It was highly unusual for a Party leader to appear in a public swimming pool without bodyguards.

Alexander Dubček in conversation with Leonid I. Brezhnev, General Secretary of the CC of the CP of the SSSR, hero of the Soviet Union and twice recipient of the Lenin order, probably in Bratislava on 3 August 1968, SNK Martin.

Alexander Dubček laying a wreath at the grave of his older brother Július who died in January 1945 fighting the Fascists in the SNP, Uhrovec cemetery, 10 February 1969, ©TASR.

Dr G. Husák during his speech "News about the activities and tasks of the KSČ" at the XIV Party Convention of the KSČ on 25 May 1971 in Prague, SNK Martin.

Alexander Dubček casting his vote at the Communal elections in Bratislava on 24 November 1990, © TASR.

"I fully endorse Dubčeks politics. [...] I stand by him or I fall with him."[1]

"Prague 1968:

Hope is the first thing that dies. Then ideas and belief in each other's arms."[2]

"For almost four years now, I have been living under your constant surveillance. The Christmas period and New Year 1973 have prompted me to address you again about the activities of the State Security Service [...] I feel compelled to write to you about the fact that I am a human being (which obviously does not mean much to you) and a citizen of the ČSSR, who has his honour and conscience and, if I may speak plainly, a man, whose neck you are breathing down; your stepping in his way and your ever-alert ears listening in on him cannot make him fall to his knees in front of you. [...] You know, I am not concerned for myself, it's not the 1950s, albeit the methods of the past are appearing today in a different form. I am concerned about the persons who, suspecting nothing, can be persecuted at work or elsewhere simply because they are loyal towards me and my family."[3]

---

[1] VONDROVÁ-NAVRATIL, c.d., 18, s. 149; quoted from Vilém Prečan, "Gustáv Husák: iluze a skutečnost", in *Gustáv Husák,* 26–39, 34.

[2] Peter Thomas Hill, "Prague 1968", in *The Dictionary of Hidden Meaning*, work in progress, Zurich 2018. I thank the author for allowing me to use this bon mot.

[3] "1973, 6. Január, Bratislava. List ministerstvu vnútra, Hlavej správe štatnej bezpečnosti a Inšpekcii MV SSR a Krajskej správe Zboru národnej bezpečnosti Bratislava (Zaslaný doporučene generálnej prokuratúre SSR) o prenasledovaní Alexandra Dubčeka, jeho rodiny a o obmedzovaní občianskych práv a slobôd", in *Alexander Dubček: Od totality ...,* 229–233, 229, 232.

III. Oblivion? Dubček's Dissent and Return to Politics (1969–1992)

In this last chapter,[1] I shall briefly present the months following the invasion of August 1968, the piecemeal restoration of the *status quo ante* January 1968. In general, we can say that once Moscow saw that the CC KSČ did not implement the stipulations of the Protocol[2] as rapidly and effectively as expected, it removed the First Secretary KSČ from his position. Little did Dubček know that this decision would be but a first step in a process aimed at his complete removal from Czechoslovak collective memory.

The focus of this chapter is on Dubček's life after the Party relieved him of all his functions on 23 June 1970. From the 1970s until the Velvet Revolution of 1989, Dubček kept protesting against the Normalization regime with letters to the government, a fact that is not widely known among Western readers. Head of state and Party was Gustáv Husák, who was responsible for the StB monitoring and psychologically harassing Dubček and his family on a daily basis. How did Husák become Czechoslovakia's General Secretary and, after President Svoboda had stepped down in 1975 because of illness, president in personal union? Indeed, one is tempted to say: by sheer ruthless ambition. Yet that would be only half the story. The situation was not

---

[1] Some small sections of this chapter have been published in *COMENIUS. Journal of Euro-American Civilization II*, no 1 (2015): 43–52, my *Seven Czech Women*, and my *Seven Slovak Women*.

[2] An excellent analysis of the Moscow Protocol and the negotiations about the withdrawal of the Warsaw Pact troops, but not the Soviet troops (!) is Michal Štefanský, "Moskovský protokol a rokovania o rozmiestnení sovietskych vojsk", in *Rok 1968 a jeho miesto* ..., 265–276.

that simple. What happened when the Dubček government returned home on 27 August 1968?

III. 1 Soviet Salami Tactics

The Soviet leadership's main reason to invade Czechoslovakia was based on its perception that the Dubček government had lost control, and a counter-revolution was in the making, with Western imperialist forces entering and disrupting the achievements of Socialism – which was a threat to the entire bloc. The bloc's western border was no longer hermetically sealed, because Czechoslovakia was an entry gate for the Imperialist West.

According to Dubček,[3] the main reason for the invasion and occupation was the extraordinary 14th Party Congress, which the reformers had scheduled, a year early, for September 1968: the KSČ plenum, that is, all Party members, not just the CC with its presidium, were expected to vote for the *action programme* (*akční program*) that would determine the country's political course for the next five years. The 14th Party Congress would have provided the reform course with a legitimate basis, an incentive for all Communist Parties of the Soviet bloc.[4] It

---

[3] Dubček, *Hope Dies Last*, 204.
[4] Dubček's conviction that the 14th Party Congress would approve of his reform course conveys his honesty and belief in Marxism-Leninism. The Soviet Union, however, was not interested in reforming Marxism-Leninism; after the 'aberrations' in East Berlin in 1953 and Hungary in 1956, she had to defend the Socialist hegemonic sphere in her fight against the Capitalist world. The Cold War was no time for experiments. Paraphrasing Lenin's saying that you can't make an omelette without breaking eggs one could describe Brezhnev's thinking as follows: if the omelette that was cooking in the pan (Socialism) should ever achieve perfection (Communism), the cook (Brezhnev) had to chuck out the foul eggs (East Germany in 1953, Hungary in 1956 and Czechoslovakia in 1968), which the Capitalist Imperialist West and its agents in the Socialist states had thrown mischievously into the pan.

would have made the Czechoslovak Spring a role model for all Socialist states to follow, providing a legal precedent, which would have meant that, at the end of the day, Moscow's hold over its bloc would have been over very quickly. Just think of the open borders and the free press.

From a Soviet viewpoint, the 14th Party Congress thus had to be prevented from coming into session – or lose everything Soviet citizens had died for fighting the Nazis in WWII. To legitimize *ex post* the invasion[5] and occupation of a bloc member and military ally (!), the Soviet leadership adopted a perfidious but effective and rational process: salami tactics. You don't slice salami in big chunks; you take your time and cut it thinly, slice by slice. Only then does it develop its full flavour:

> "The Moscow Protocol opened the path to the creation of the conditions needed for the step-by-step annulment of the principles of the democratization process. The fact that the leading representatives of the ČSSR remained in their functions, was part of the perfidious plan of the Soviet representatives: to have the founders of 'Socialism with a Human Face' liquidate their own creation."[6]

In the first weeks after the invasion, Moscow supported the rightist conservative faction against the reformers, while a third faction, the so-called realists under Husák's leadership, was consolidating its influence.[7] The realists boycotted the

---

[5] Sergei Kovalev was the first to define the Brezhnev doctrine of limited sovereignty in the Soviet *Pravda* on 11 and 26 September 1968. Key words: collective self-defence; counter-revolution; vigilance; internationalist duty, Matthew J. Ouimet, *The Rise and Fall of the Brezhnev Doctrine in Soviet Foreign Policy* (Chapel Hill, NC, London: The University of North Carolina Press, 2003), 66–67. Kovalev's text from 26 September 1968 on http://soviethistory.msu.edu/1968-2/crisis-in-czechoslovakia/crisis-in-czechoslovakia-texts/brezhnev-doctrine/; accessed 11 June 2018.

[6] Sikora, "Legalizácia okupace", in *Od Predjaria* ..., 66–74, 68.

[7] Sikora, "Legalizácia okupace", 69–70.

Vysočany Party meeting;[8] politically, they considered themselves not traitors as they thought of the authors of the letter of invitation, that is, the conservatives around Biľak, Kolder and Indra. Yet, in their opinion, the reformers had gone too far too quickly, which had led to invasion of the Warsaw Pact troops. The realists' view was to accept the stipulations of the Moscow Protocol, since the government had signed it; their rationale was to do what was possible now in the given circumstances.

This situation put the Dubček government under duress from three sides, exposing it to international pressure from Moscow and intra-Party pressure from the conservatives and the realists in the CC KSČ. Dubček, like his government, had been a captive in Moscow. After days of refusing to cooperate, he had eventually caved in to the pressure of his comrades in the CC KSČ and signed the Moscow Protocol.

I deem it likely that Dubček's perception of the communication with the Soviets after 21 August 1968 was the same he had had prior to the invasion. From the Soviet perspective, Dubček's playing for time looked like wavering and weakness or a critical lack of efficiency; from the viewpoint of the rightist faction in the CC KSČ, Dubček's intransigence with regard to the effective implementation of the stipulations of the Moscow Protocol was a disturbing show of deliberate disobedience. Dubček on the strange way of communication:

> "Throughout the months of the Prague Spring, it had been clear to me that the Soviets' criticism aimed to force me to restrict, if not abandon, our reforms. Yet they never clearly stated, publicly or privately, how *far* they wanted me to retreat. Ambiguity was a trademark of the

---

[8] Details of the Vysočany *sjezd*, its preparation, support in the population and final resolution in *Deset pražských dnů*, 72–92. The latest and most comprehensive edition of the minutes and documents of the XIV. *sjezd* is Jiří Pelikán, *Tanky proti sjezdu. Protokoly a dokumenty XIV. (vysočanského) sjezdu KSČ* (Praha: Novela bohemica, 2018).

system. Inter-Party exchanges were often carried on in double-talk, indirect hints, and puzzling allusions to ideological precepts and events in Russian history. This made all communication difficult and agreements unclear."[9]

If Dubček had resisted Brezhnev in the months up to the invasion, he tried to save as much of the reforms as possible once he was back home on 27 August. But because he had signed the Moscow Protocol, he was between a rock and a hard place. In other words, he found himself in a catch-22[10] – either he stayed true to his reform course, breaching the Moscow Protocol and thereby disgracing the honesty and dignity of the Czechoslovak government, or he implemented the stipulations of the Protocol, thereby betraying his own politics and, as he must have thought, the Czechoslovak people.

---

[9] Dubček, *Hope Dies Last*, 176.
[10] A catch-22 is a problematic situation for which the only solution is denied by a circumstance inherent in the problem or by a rule, https://www.phrases.org.uk/meanings/catch-22.html, accessed 18 June 2018. The American author Joseph Heller (1923–1999) coined the concept of catch-22 in his famous novel of the same name: "Yossarian came to him one mission later and pleaded again, without any real expectation of success, to be grounded. [...] 'You're wasting your time', Doc Daneka was forced to tell him. 'Can't you ground someone who's crazy?' 'Oh, sure. I have to. There's a rule saying I have to ground anyone who's crazy.' [...] Yossarian looked at him soberly and tried another approach. 'Is Orr crazy?' 'He sure is,' Doc Daneka said. 'Can you ground him?' 'I sure can. But first he has to ask me to. That's part of the rule.' 'Then why doesn't he ask you to?' 'Because he's crazy', Doc Daneka said. 'He has to be crazy to keep flying combat missions after all the close calls he's had.' [...] 'You mean there's a catch?' 'Sure there's a catch,' Doc Daneka replied. 'Catch-22 [...] specified that a concern for one's own safety in the face of dangers that were real and immediate was the process of a rational mind. Orr was crazy and could be grounded. All he had to do was ask; and as soon as he did, he would no longer be crazy and would have to fly more missions. Orr would be crazy to fly more missions and sane if he didn't, but if he was sane he had to fly them. If he flew them he was crazy and didn't have to; but if he didn't want to he was sane and had to. [...] Yossarian saw it clearly in all its spinning reasonableness. There was an elliptical precision about its perfect pairs of parts that was graceful and shocking, like good modern art." Joseph Heller, *Catch-22* (New York: Vintage, 1994), 61–63.

Because the Soviets were interested in keeping the reformers in power so that they would compromise themselves in front of the citizens, they stopped supporting the conservatives, who were not re-elected to the new presidium CC KSČ on 31 October 1968: Kolder, Švestka and Rigo had to leave, but on Moscow's diktat, also the physician František Kriegel (1908–1979), a veteran of the Spanish Civil War, ardent reformer, confidant of Dubček's and the only one among the Moscow captives who had courageously refused to sign the Protocol.[11] Fifteen new members were elected to the presidium; all were reformers prior to the invasion, among them Svoboda, Mlynář and Husák. The Party's regional and local organs had rid themselves of conservatives long before the invasion. The clear majority of reformers in all Party organs, however, created a paradoxical situation: the reformers held all the power – which the Moscow Protocol and the Soviet troops were restricting:

> "Prior to 21 August 1968, the reformers could only dream of such a composition of the CC and other Party organs. Now, it [the reformers' majority in state and Party positions, add. JB] was a fact, which, however, as Dubček said, played no significant role under the conditions of the occupation."[12]

One event that would initiate the future of Czechoslovak domestic affairs is little if at all know to the Western reader: the extraordinary plenary meeting of the KSS in Bratislava. While one of the stipulations of the Moscow Protocol declared invalid the extraordinary 14th Congress of the KSČ in Vysočany on 22 August,[13] the Protocol completely ignored what was happening in the top echelons of the KSS. Ever only interested in who was in charge in Prague, the Soviets considered Slovakia a province –

---

[11] Sikora, "Legalizácia okupace", 71.
[12] Sikora, "Legalizácia okupace", 71, DUBČEK, Alexander. *Nádej zomiera posledná*, c. d., s. 227, quoted from Sikora.
[13] Sikora, "Legalizácia okupace", 67.

a principal element of the Soviet way of thinking Husák was very well aware of.

On 26 August, the KSS plenum met in Bratislava shortly before midnight at the club of the Chemical Factories Juraj Dimitrov; on the first day, the 358 delegates present condemned the invasion and expressed their full support of the final resolution of the Vysočany *sjezd,* that is, full support of Dubček's reform course and condemnation of the invasion as an act of foreign intrusion into Czechoslovakia's domestic affairs, hence military violation of Czechoslovakia's sovereignty.[14] On the second day, however, Husák, who had returned from Moscow, took charge: in a fiery speech, he managed to convince the majority of the delegates to distance themselves from the Vysočany resolution.[15] Within the wider framework of Czechoslovak politics after 1968, the extraordinary KSS plenary meeting was insignificant, save for one fact: Husák used the meeting as a launchpad for his career. This is what he said to persuade the delegates to elect him as First Secretary KSS, a position that would catapult him automatically to the CC KSČ, up to Prague:

> "I fully endorse Dubček's politics. I was there when he was developing the programme, I shall fully support him, I stand by him or I fall with

---

[14] Sikora, "Legalizácia okupace", 69. Present were 358 delegates, elected delegates were 638 – that means that 280 delegates preferred not to attend. 143 delegates from the Vysočany Party meeting attended the KSS extraordinary meeting. The two extraordinary Party meetings convey how the Party members in both KSČ and KSS tried to act on behalf of the abducted government, that is, standing in and up for the reform course. Both extraordinary meetings were legal since the majority of the delegates had attended. The extraordinary plenum of the KSS had, like the 14th KSČ plenum, been planned prior to the invasion, in May 1968. The KSS had planned to draft a policy how to negotiate at the 14th plenum, focussing on the federation and Slovak issues. I thank my colleague Jan Pešek for his unprecedented support and academic advice; e-mail conversation with Jan Pešek on 24 to 25 June 2018.

[15] Sikora, "Legalizácia okupace", 70. Husák had flown to Moscow with Svoboda on 23 August to support the government and negotiate its return.

him [*Ja stojím plne za Dubčekovou koncepciou, ja som bol pri jeji tvorbe, ja ho budem plne podporovať, alebo s ním budem stáť, alebo s ním odidem*]."[16]

The Czechoslovak people first heard the term *Normalization* in Dubček's broadcast of 27 August. The First Secretary KSČ conveyed a confusing message, trying to convince them that not all of the Czechoslovak Spring was lost, but he was visibly under duress.[17] The situation was incredibly complicated if one wanted to save some of the reforms: the government was meandering between sustaining its reform course and trying to fulfil the stipulations of the Protocol:

> "We are concerned to prevent any bloodshed, but this does not mean that we are going to passively submit to the current situation. On the contrary, we shall do everything we can – and we are convinced that we shall find the ways and means to do so – to develop and realize with all of you a policy which eventually will lead to the Normalization of the current conditions."[18]

No bloodshed, fine. But no passive submission either – would the government resist actively and how? What range of action did the Czechoslovak government have at its disposal? What did 'Normalization' exactly mean?

To the Czechoslovak citizens, in particular the older generations that had vivid memories of Masaryk's Republic and the civil liberties it had granted, Dubček's reform course had been a Normalization *par excellence*, that is, strict application of the rule of law, abolition of censorship and the opening of the borders; to their way of thinking, the conditions under Novotný's Stalinism had been abnormal and the Czechoslovak Spring only a much-needed correction of a staggeringly mistaken political

---

[16] Sikora, "Legalizácia okupace", 70, MLYNÁŘ, Zdeněk. Mraz přichází z Kremlu, c. d., s. 240, quoted from Sikora.
[17] Dubček's speech on https://www.youtube.com/watch?v=9E0F209PBts; accessed 22 June 2018.
[18] Bystrický a kol., *Rok 68,* 209–210.

course. The concept 'Normalization' turned into a word with an absurd meaning.

With regard to the definition of the Normalization, Slovak and Czech historians acknowledge pluralism of opinion. Generally, we can say that there are two views: first, the years from 1968 to 1971, with the restitution of the KSČ's full control of society and the country, and, second, the period from 1968 to 1989 with the Soviet occupation as the principal force that kept the Husák government in power.[19] Furthermore, the start of the Normalization could be dated either on Dubček's abdication on 17 April 1969 or the adoption of the constitutional law on the federation in December 1970. I find the following two explanations most convincing: first, according to Marušiak, the Normalization started in the night of 21 August with the invasion, since from then on the Dubček government was no more at liberty to act independently.[20] Second, Sikora speaks of an 'intermezzo' that lasted from August 1968 to April 1969, dating the beginning of the "hard Normalization" on Husák's election as General Secretary of the KSČ. [21] This implies that Sikora conceives of the months from August 1968 to April 1969 as a kind of 'soft' Normalization – which makes perfect sense, since the Soviet leadership in those months was treading carefully, playing for time.

There were hopes that some reforms could be saved.[22] The situation was paradoxical and confusing: the people were

---

[19] Juraj Marušiak, "Slovenská spoločnosť a normalizácia", in *Česká a slovenská společnost v období normalizace. Slovenská a česká spoločnosť v case normalizácie. Liberecký seminar 2001* (Bratislava: Veda a Ústav politických vied SAV, 2003), 109–153, 109.
[20] Marušiak, "Slovenská spoločnosť a normalizácia", 111.
[21] Sikora, *Po Jari ...*, 163.
[22] See the *The Czech Fate* (*Český úděl*) debate between Milan Kundera (*1929) and Václav Havel in January 1969. Kundera, a Party member, called for optimism and the continuing fight for the civil rights the Czechoslovaks had been enjoying after January 1968. Havel had no illusions

still engaging in resistance activities, while the Czechoslovak army was not allowed to interfere: a stipulation of the Moscow Protocol. The government was acting seemingly independently, while attempting to circumvent the directives it had signed in the Moscow Protocol.

The federation was the only reform that survived the new course, yet it was bereft of its true meaning. The federation granted Slovakia equal status with the Czech lands in the common state. On 14 March 1968, the SNR had issued constitutional law no. 143/1968 about the federation; the CC KSČ had incorporated it into the action programme, which the majority of the CC KSS members had adopted at the beginning of April.[23] The majority of the Czech reform Communists had spoken out for a wider democratization of society; they wanted to postpone the

---

about the future; he condemned Kundera's optimism and called for daily and peaceful protests; an English translation of the crucial parts of the debate in my *Preparing Liberty in Central Europe. Political Texts from the Spring of Nations 1848 to the Spring of Prague 1968* (Stuttgart: ibidem, 2006), 140–164. Kundera's optimism would prove him wrong: he lost his position and Party membership and emigrated to France in 1975. In his famous essay "The Tragedy of Central Europe", Kundera considered the Soviet occupation as an act of *de-Europeanization* of Czechoslovakia; Russia's Asian despotism excluded her from Europe and European culture, *The New York Review of Books 31*, no. 26 (1984): 33–39. The essay prompted a lively debate among Western and Central European intellectuals about the meaning of the concept 'Central Europe'; see Czesław Milosz, "Central European Attitudes", *Cross Currents 5* (1986): 101–108; György Konrád, "Is the Dream of Central Europe Still Alive?", *Cross Currents 5* (1986): 109–121; Timothy Garton Ash, "Mitteleuropa?", *Daedalus 119*, no. 1 (1990): 1–21; Jacques Rupnik, "Central Europe or Mitteleuropa?", *Daedalus 119*, no. 1 (1990): 249–278, and Vladimír Goněc, "Z exilových diskusí 80. let: pojem střední Evropy", in *Česko-Slovenská historická ročenka 2012. Češi a Slováci 1993–2012* (Bratislava: Veda, 2012), 203–233.

23 Kováč, *Dejiny Slovenska*, 290. The federation was declared at the end of October 1968, which made some centralists voice the absurd thesis that the Slovaks had achieved the federation, which everybody knew was not a real one, with the help of Russian bayonets; Kováč, *Dejiny Slovenska*, 290.

federation to a later point in time. The Slovak reform Communists, however, wanted the federation first, considering the constitutional equality of the Slovaks and Czechs the very basis of the democratization process of the common state. These views are referred to in the literature with the slogan *First democratization, then federation* (*Najprv demokratizácia, potom federácia*).[24]

After the invasion, the federation was also subject to Normalization: it existed only on paper. Although institutions of self-government were established in Bratislava, the directives came from Prague, and positions were filled with functionaries loyal to the new regime, regardless if they were Czech or Slovak.[25] *De jure*, the state was a federation, but in reality, the old centralism directed from Prague was back.

The Soviet government was in dire need of replacing Dubček, which was no easy task – whom to appoint? Oldřich Černík (1921–1994) was Brezhnev's prime candidate; Brezhnev offered the position to Černík, but Černík refused once he had realized what he was supposed to do. His conscience forbade him to implement the harsh neo-Stalinist measures the Soviets insisted on.[26] Biľak was no option, since he had been one of the conservatives who had signed the letter of invitation; to the people, he was a traitor. To appoint him First Secretary KSČ would prompt only further unrest and bloodshed – the Soviet analysts were spot on, in psychological and political terms.

This was Husák's hour: without a mandate from the KSČ, the First Secretary KSS and member of the CC KSČ took matters

---

[24] Kováč, *Dejiny Slovenska*, 290.
[25] About the legal and political details of the establishment of the federation see Jan Rychlík, "Normalizačná podoba česko-slovenské federace", in *Česká a slovenská společnost ...*, 59–92.
[26] Sikora, *Po jari ...*, 118.

into his own hands, ever the *Realpolitiker* he was. He clandestinely met Brezhnev on 13 April 1969 at the airport of Mukačevo (formerly the Soviet Republic of Ukraine, today Ukraine), shamelessly but realistically offering himself for the position.[27] The Soviet Politburo subsequently suggested Comrade Husák. The CC KSČ elected him on 17 April 1969, after it had forced Dubček to resign, because he had kept refusing to sign the so-called "truncheon law [*obuškový zakon*]", the adoption of paragraph 99 about the conditions of declaring martial law.[28] Dubček was sent off to Ankara, where he would act as Czechoslovak ambassador to Turkey.[29] Naturally, like all diplomats of the Soviet bloc, the Dubčeks had to leave their three sons behind, as assurance that they would return and not defect to the West.

A brief look at some figures illustrates the despair of the citizens after the invasion: the consumption of hard liquor, that is, drinks with an alcohol content of 40% and higher, increased dramatically. In the Czech lands, in 1965 a citizen consumed an average of 2 litres of liquor *per annum*, in 1970 it was already 4.2 litres and in 1978 6.8 litres; the equivalent statistics for a

---

[27] Sikora, *Po jari* ..., 126.
[28] Dubček, *Hope Dies Last*, 245. Vlasta Jaksicsová in our e-mail conversation from 23 June: "As chairman of the Federal Assembly, Dubček eventually had to sign the law, under pressure from Husák." That he caved in to Husák's pressure was a mistake Dubček regretted deeply and could not forgive himself for it, Dubček, *Hope Dies Last*, 246.
[29] He had been offered first the position of ambassador to Ghana, but he refused to go to Africa. Owing to financial issues, he and Anna decided to accept the position in Ankara. Because of the complications the regime imposed on him to get back to Czechoslovakia, Dubček was convinced that the government wanted to force him into exile, Dubček, *Hope Dies Last*, 252. I think Dubček was spot on: he suspected the government aimed to let his wife return to take care of their sons, but not him. The government's main rationale was to get rid of Dubček as the symbol of the Czechoslovak Spring; little did the authorities care if they split up a family.

Slovak citizen's intake of hard drinks were: 4.3 litres in 1965, 9.5 litres in 1970 and 14.1 litres in 1978.[30]

The opposition in Slovakia was not as brutally persecuted as in the Czech lands, because the protests against the Husák government in the Czech part involved many more citizens. Yet, one would be gravely mistaken to think that the majority of the Slovaks gained from the Normalization or even supported it. Slovak citizens were subject to the Party purges (*čistky*) at the beginning of the 1970s and the Normalization measures as much as the Czechs. Slovaks as much as Czechs spoke out against the regime of the so-called realists led by Husák.[31]

What the concept 'Normalization' really meant, how it would affect citizens' daily lives, became apparent in the early 1970s.

III. 2 The Politics of Normalization

The only explanation and description of the Normalization course can be found in the document the CC KSČ issued in December 1970: the infamous *Lessons Learned from the Critical Developments in Party and State Following the 13th Congress of the KSČ* (*Poučenie z krízového vývoja v strane a spoločnosti po XIII. zjazde KSČ*).[32]

The people conceived of the document as "the normalizers' simplistic catechism" and a "manifesto of neo-Stalinism" alike[33] that advocated the return to the old methods of

---

[30] Marušiak, "Slovenská spoločnosť", 136.
[31] An excellent account of the opposition to the normalization is Jaroslav Pažout, "Trestněprávní perzekuce odpůrců režimu v období tzv. Normalizace (1969–1989) – faktor stability a indikátor rozkladu komunistického režimu", in *Český a slovenský komunismus (1921–2011)* (Praha: Ústav pro stadium totalitních režimů, 2012), 174–192.
[32] Kováč, *Dejiny Slovenska*, 300.
[33] Kováč, *Dejiny Slovenska*, 300.

governing: oppression of civil rights, censorship, closed borders, Prague's dominance in Slovak matters and a centrally planned economy according to the Soviet model. Everybody in a higher position, professors, writers, doctors, academics, economists, lawyers, factory managers and teachers had to sign the official declaration that condemned the reforms of the Czechoslovak Spring as counter-revolutionary, publicly praising the invasion and occupation as the rightful political course; those who refused lost their positions.[34]

The normalizers were responsible for putting the measures into practice, that is, placing loyal party members in key positions and purging state institutions, factories, schools and academia. In its aim to demonstrate the new political course, the Party did not stop at its own gates: in the first large wave of purges from 1969 to 1970, some 70,000 members were expelled (*vyloučený*), and 400,000 suspended (*vyškrtnut*); those suspended got a second chance to prove their loyalty in a special hearing for which they had to apply.[35]

Generally, we can say that from 1969 to 1989, Czechoslovak society consisted of three socio-political strata: first, the dissidents (*disidenti*) were a small group of approximately 200 to 300 citizens who obeyed the law, but refused to accept the political norms of the Normalization, which resulted in their persecution. They founded the *samizdat* in the mid-1970s and *Charter 77* in 1977.[36] Second, the grey zone (*šedá zona*)

---

[34] Kováč, *Dejiny Slovenska*, 300. One of the most touching novels about the normalization I know is Ivan Klíma's *Soudce z milosti* (Praha: Rozmluvy, 1991), the English version is *Judge on Trial* (London: Vintage, 2002).

[35] Jan Měchýř, "O lidech v čase normalizace", in *Česká a slovenská společnost* ... 93–108, 96.

[36] See a collection of *Charter 77* documents in *Charta 77. 1977–1989. Od morální k demokratické revoluci. Dokumentace* (Bratislava: Archa, Čs. středisko nezávislé literatury, Scheinfeld-Schwarzenberg, 1990). The

consisted of citizens who refused Party membership but trod carefully in order not to lose their positions in the administration and academia.[37] Third, the bystanders-citizens (*obyvatelé a občané*) were the largest group with approximately ten million citizens who found a *modus vivendi* under the regime, trying to lead a normal life and securing their offspring's chances of higher education. They were careful not to draw the attention of the authorities to themselves.[38]

To illustrate the mechanisms of the Normalization, I shall present two accounts: first, the purges at the Faculty of Philosophy at Charles University in Prague,[39] and, second, the legal restrictions regulating foreign currency and travel.[40]

III. 2. 1 The Purges at Charles University (1969)

František Černý (1926–2010) was Professor of Drama Studies (*teatrologie*) and a renowned specialist in Czech theatre; after the Velvet Revolution of 1989 he would be appointed Dean of the Faculty of Philosophy. Černý's memoirs about the Normalization at the Faculty of Philosophy provide us with a rare and personal insight.

The invasion happened in the summer holidays; many students did not bother to return to the university at the beginning of the winter term of 1968/69.[41] Those who did show up

---

latest publication is the exhibition catalogue *Charta Story. Příběhy Charty 77. The Story of Charter 77* (Praha: Národní galerie v Praze, 2017).
[37] Měchýř, 100. A prominent member of the grey zone was Václav Klaus, who worked at the Institute of Prognostics as an economist; he was a principal figure of the OF in November 1989 and later founded the ODS.
[38] Měchýř, 99–100.
[39] František Černý, *Normalizace na Pražské Filosofické fakultě (1968–1989). Vzpomínky* (Praha: Mnemosyne, Filosofická Fakulta Univerzity Karlova, 2009).
[40] Jan Rychlík, *Devisové přisliby a cestování do zahraničí v období normalizace* (Praha: Ústav pro soudobé dějiny AV ČR, 2012).
[41] Černý, 8.

were united in protest: the last free meeting at the faculty took place from 21 to 23 April 1969, a few days after Dubček's abdication.[42] The students' academic council secretly convened and announced a strike. The result of the meeting was the manifesto of the Prague students that called for the re-establishment of civil rights, re-establishment of the state's sovereignty and the academic freedom of research and teaching. The inviolability of the premises of the university should be guaranteed, and the academic functionaries democratically elected; the academic community should be granted self-organization and self-government without interference from Party and state.[43] The StB called Deputy Dean Černý for interrogation at the infamous Bartolomejšská 4, having him sit there for a couple of hours. They did not interrogate him, which was just a first measure of humiliation and intimidation.

The authorities began to pressure the Faculty's governing body into obedience: academics who accepted the new course, among them persons without an international reputation who had not even published one book got 'elected' into the faculty's key positions. Persons who did not even have the *maturita* but excelled in their Marxist beliefs were catapulted into the highest academic positions.[44] Although the elections were conducted in secret, political pressure exerted beforehand made selection of certain candidates a foregone conclusion; the members of the voting plenum were already intimidated and, fearing for their jobs, voted for the candidate they knew the authorities wanted. Some of the younger faculty members and hitherto unsuccessful academics saw their window of opportunity to achieve power, position and the concomitant rise in salary,

---

[42] Černý, 10–11.
[43] Černý, 10.
[44] Černý, 28.

social prestige and political reputation. Naturally, the quality of research and teaching immediately plummeted. Envy and ruthless ambition replaced academic excellence and scholarly talent.

Some of the best teachers and researchers were expelled, among them the famous literary scholar Václav Černý (1905–1987) and the philosopher Jan Patočka (1907–1977), who would become the intellectual father of *Charter 77* and one of its first signatories. The philologist and expert in Russian linguistics Vladimír Barnet (1924–1983) committed suicide.[45] Others were offered a special arrangement: if they agreed to publicly declare that they had taken early retirement, they would receive a better reference,[46] keeping their pension. This way, their leave from the faculty looked like their personal decision, and nobody would see what was actually going on.

A small number of distinguished academics stayed on, and astonishingly few emigrated. Černý thinks that the main reason for their staying in the country was the academics' distinct sense of responsibility; they were committed to their students and did not want to leave in these difficult years.[47] Once retired, the scholars were no longer a threat to the regime – or so the authorities must have thought. But they were still around, and the phenomenon of the 'black university' emerged: those interested in studying themes and topics that had been deleted from the universities' curricula used to gather in a flat to listen to a 'normalized' professor's lectures. The 'black university' was an element of the *parallel polis*,[48] an independent

---

[45] Černý, 25.
[46] Černý, 25–26.
[47] Černý, 23.
[48] The philosopher Václav Bělohradský (*1944) coined the concept of 'parallel polis' to describe the dissidents' own confined space on the fringes of society in his *Krize eschatology neosobnosti* (London: Rozmluvy, 1983).

space, an area of civil society the authorities had no control over, a vanishing point. Eda Kriseová (*1940), a writer and close friend of the Havels, remembered how Professor Patočka's lectures impressed the listeners:

> "He was my professor, I attended his lectures on phenomenology. [...] To him, Plato and Aristotle were not theoreticians in the modern sense, [...] but individuals occupied with the basic human need to enquire about the meaning of life, [...] nobody can relieve us of that responsibility. [...] Not only students, but also teachers of the faculty came. These lectures were events, happenings. He never sat down, he used to walk through the room, gesticulating. [...] When they expelled him from the Faculty of Philosophy, it was as if they had expelled Kant from Philosophy; some courageous citizens let him use their flats for the so-called black university. [...] Ten to fifteen persons attended his lectures, sitting on the floor, side by side. [...] After his lecture, Professor Patočka went to collect signatures [for *Charter 77*, add. JB] with his old friend Zdeněk Urbánek, who drove them. Allegedly, when he came back down breathless from a flat on the fifth floor, he used to say: 'He did not sign, he will end up in hell too.' Many friends disappointed him."[49]

The guiding principle of the purges was *divide et impera*. The normalizers separated those who still stubbornly supported Dubček's reform politics from the realists, who understood the terms of the trade and the fickle tides of political power in Central Europe. The authorities concentrated on forming a new academic body, pressuring the undecided into obedience with promises and threats. Naturally, the government could not sack the entire faculty, since the students needed teachers to educate the next generation of scientists and researchers.

Largely, personal animosities and affinities influenced the arbitrary regime of employment that was quite effective:

---

[49] Eda Kriseová, *Václav Havel. Životopis* (Praha: Atlantis, 1991), 72, 74. Zdeněk Urbánek (1917–2008) was a writer and translator and a member of *Charter 77*. In Poland, the phenomenon of the 'black university' was called 'the flying university', because the students and professors kept moving between flats, evading the surveillance of the State Security.

arbitrary decisions were spreading fear and insecurity among those who still had a job. One was advised to behave, to have good relations with the offices of the dean and the rector. But arbitrary rule, as is its nature, also prompted unexpected results:

> "I have no explanation for the fact that I survived the purges at the Faculty of Philosophy. To this day, I do not understand it, since I was vice-dean from 1966 to 1969 and acting dean during the eventful days of Jan Palach's death, replacing the dean, who was on sick leave. The sad days after Palach's suicide brought me into the public eye; I spoke on TV and the broadcast the night before his funeral. Also, I had published quite extensively in the 1960s. [...] From the archives of the StB that were opened in the 1990s it transpires that the StB considered me a person hostile to the regime for my activities as deputy dean."[50]

If we believe Černý's account, and I think that he was truthful in his memoirs, there are two reasons that can explain why he was spared: first, there was nobody younger who wanted his job, and second, the StB's tactics, which Havel so aptly described in 1979:

> "You know much better than anybody else that the decision whether to arrest Gruša or Vaculík has absolutely nothing to do with the risk each of them took, but everything to do with the regime's cold and cynical calculations. In terms of tactics, it is sometimes more advisable to arrest Gruša to intimidate Vaculík; sometimes it is better to arrest Vaculík to intimidate Gruša."[51]

With the goal of positioning normalizers in key faculty positions achieved, the strategy of the StB was to gain full control over the

---

[50] Černý, 45–46. About Jan Palach's self-immolation see http://www.radio.cz/en/section/archives/the-last-days-of-jan-palach-1; accessed 1 July 2018.

[51] Václav Havel, "Milý pane Ludvíku (25 leden 1979)", in *O lidskou identitu. Úvahy, fejetony, protesty, polemiky, prohlášení a rozhovory z let 1969–1979* (Praha: Rozmluvy, 1990), 204–206, 204. In his letter to Vaculík, Havel criticised Vaculík's suggestion to publish the dissidents' texts anonymously, which would have broken the principle of legality and personal responsibility the Chartists adhered to.

smooth functioning of the personnel. Certainly, Havel's quote refers to dissident colleagues who had made their decision to speak out. Yet, I think that specific tactical calculations of the StB can explain why Professor Černý was able to keep his position.

We cannot possibly find out why the authorities spared Černý, but I deem it possible that they had considered the following, which is, of course, speculation. I think that a clever party functionary familiar with the situation at the faculty and responsible for the purges and future personnel situation would reason as follows: "Now, leave that František Černý alone, for the time being. We have the faculty under control; we have sacked the most notorious members of the reaction. Theatre and drama studies are not politically sensitive areas such as the notoriously rebellious institutes of philosophy and history. We need to keep some of our experts as an alibi to demonstrate to the citizens and the West that we are not persecuting scholars for political reasons. If Černý behaves, fine. If he does not, we can always offer him early retirement, and if he won't accept that, we can still sack him for his counter-revolutionary activities back in 1968. It's entirely up to him."

Finally, a brief word about a concept prominently used in historical research about the Normalization: alibism [*alibismus*].[52] Alibism consists in trying to evade personal responsibility, or the politics of behaving two-facedly. Two examples: "I signed the anti-Charta only because everybody else at my workplace did." Or: "I accepted the directorship of this factory only for the workers' sake, that nobody worse would get it." Worse in the sense of adapting to the Normalization course. It was a

---

[52] For a definition of alibism see https://slovnik-cizich-slov.abz.cz/web.php/slovo/alibizmus-alibismus; accessed 6 July 2018.

way to get by under the harsh conditions, safeguard one's offspring's chances of higher education and, simply, keep a well-paid position.

III. 2. 2 Travel Restrictions

To us in the 21st century, going on a trip with family or friends, booking a flight or hotel and hiring a car is very easy; thanks to the Internet and the credit card system, holidays and trips can be arranged within minutes.

To a Czechoslovak citizen in the 1970s and 1980s, who wanted to visit relatives in the West or make a trip to the countries of the Socialist bloc, tourism involved a nerve-racking endeavour that required time, patience, personal relations with the authorities and, above all, money. The Normalization regime did not conceive of mobility, the freedom of movement, as a human right; mobility was a privilege bestowed on those who behaved, who were reliable in political terms.[53]

On 21 December 1970, the government issued a new bill of law (č. 142/1970 Sb) on foreign currency: citizens wanting to travel to the West and Yugoslavia as tourists, hence not on a business trip, had to apply for a foreign currency exchange permit (*devisový příslib*).[54] With the permit granted by the authorities, they then had to apply for a special exit permit (*výjezdní doložka*) that was attached to the passport one had to apply for first. The maximum permitted length of stay abroad was 20 days. The citizen had to exchange Czechoslovak crowns for foreign currency at a branch of the ČSNB (Czechoslovak State Bank) and could leave the country only with a valid exit permit. This system was based on political and economic considerations: the government held the monopoly of foreign currency,

---

[53] Rychlík, *Devisové přisliby*..., 30.
[54] Rychlík, *Devisové přisliby*..., 19.

imposing restrictions on citizens wanting to travel to the West and Yugoslavia – from where they could easily get to the countries of Western Europe. To the Czechoslovaks, Yugoslavia, a member of NAM, was the way out: once one had arrived on Yugoslav territory, one did not require an exit permit and could leave freely to Western Europe.

Every year in January, the Czechoslovak State Bank issued a limited number of foreign currency exchange permits. To apply for one, a citizen needed the stamp of his employer. Every citizen had the opportunity, not the constitutional right (!), to apply[55] for a foreign currency exchange permit, but this did not mean that he or she would automatically receive one. The system was riddled with corruption and nepotism; some citizens received permits for several trips to the West in one year, while others, who had no personal contacts at the offices issuing the permits, never received one.

A special commission investigating the activities of the Brno branch of the ČSNB found the following:

> "The branch issued foreign currency exchange permits to 340 applicants who went on private trips to the West in the years from 1977 to 1979. 243 of these applicants neither lived in Brno nor worked there. [...] 38 functionaries of the CC KSČ went to Vienna on 12 April 1980, where they met members of the Austrian Communist Party. [...] The director of the bank's local branch got off with a disciplinary warning."[56]

The Czechoslovak crown was not freely convertible, which also made trips to the brotherly countries of the Socialist bloc very difficult. Citizens wanting to visit Bulgaria, the GDR, Hungary, Mongolia, Poland, Romania or the Soviet Union did not have to apply for an exit permit but needed an invitation from a citizen

---

[55] Rychlík, *Devisové přisliby*..., 23.
[56] Rychlík, *Devisové přisliby*..., 32.

of the state they wanted to visit as well as the foreign currency exchange permit.

Given these restrictions, it is no wonder that an ordinary Czechoslovak citizen did not even try to travel – why bother? It was just too much of a hassle. On Friday afternoons, citizens left Prague and Bratislava, their cities and towns, and drove to their *chalupas* and *chaťas* in the countryside.

III. 3 Everyday Life in Czechoslovakia

III. 3. 1 Fear

According to the psychologist and former dissident Jindřich Kabát, fear dominated citizens' lives under the Normalization: fear was everywhere, making everyone's life complicated, if not an endless stream of misery.

Kabát distinguished two kinds of fear:[57] the *primary, acute and physical fear* that originated in the experience and stories told by one's relatives and friends from the war and the terror of the Stalinist regime of the 1950s. Everybody had been afraid, feared arrest and deportation to a labour camp or prison, not only for themselves, but also for their family and friends. The *secondary fear* was less acute, subtler, since it originated in one's imagination: what will happen if I do this or not do that? One no longer feared for one's life but had to expect serious difficulties for one's family and friends. This secondary fear was omnipresent and stopped only when the regime collapsed.

The citizens were anxious all the time: in contact with the authorities, at the post, in the shops, when one found a letter with an unknown sender in one's post-box, in the hospital, and so on. Kabát described a normal day for a normal citizen, let's

---

[57] Jindřich Kabát, *Psychologie komunismu* (Praha: Práh, 2011), 12–13.

say, he is employed in a Prague administrative office. Note the *non-existent room for independent decision-making* – the citizen had no choice if he wanted to avoid drawing the attention of the StB to him and his family:

> "In the morning, you wake up in a relatively good mood. So as not to spoil it, you do not switch on the radio. But your neighbour has the radio on so loudly that you are forced to listen to it; they are broadcasting a feature about Socialist economic competition. You are thinking that he is doing this deliberately; you want him to switch off the radio, but then, you tell yourself that you are off to work very soon. [...] You get dressed and walk to the bus station. Somebody is standing in your way, distributing flyers for a *brigada*, a temporary working place. You don't want the flyer, but you have to take it. [...] At the bus station, your neighbour is waving at you, shouting: 'We have a Soviet flag for you, I noticed that you don't have one, you have only our Czechoslovak flag – I can sell you one for only 50 crowns.' You don't know what to say, and the idea of hanging up a Soviet flag is terrible. Even more terrifying to you is to visit your neighbour and spend 50 crowns [...] You do not react, but the neighbour is close to you on the bus, riding for eight stops. You cannot say nothing, so you lean towards him and tell him 'yeah, sure'. [...] You reach your place of work and find on your desk an invitation for an event. You immediately know: this is bad. Everybody is sitting at their desks and the Party member of your collective is not only your boss, but also a former co-student. He failed classes at school twice; you were happy that he had to leave your class, because he had physically attacked his co-students. A bully. He did not accomplish his vocational training as a mineworker, but the Party had saved him from his continuous brawls. Now, he is addressing you: you are being asked to lead a discussion about the theme of *Socialist economic competition*. You remember what you heard in the morning on your neighbour's radio: you repeat it and after the tenth sentence, you notice that you are speaking in phrases. You are explaining what the Party needs and what the working class is expecting from your collective. Your enemy from school is praising you and declares you to be a role mode; he starts to test others. You are ashamed – you would like to shrivel up. You know that from today on, you are a positive hero of the Party, connected to and affiliated with the Party and its propaganda. Finally, you can start working. Your colleagues are silent. Three of them are decent people, whom you have now lost. You know that the fourth one is a snitch informing to the StB. You want to say something, to apologize, but the only thing that comes to your mind is to say

that you have only repeated the radio broadcast of that morning. The colleagues are silent, and the snitch is closely monitoring you – you drop the idea of apologizing. At lunch you try to whisper to a colleague that you are sorry and ashamed. The colleagues show understanding and also praise, which encourages you to do something special. The working day is finished and you, full of courage, decide NOT to sign up for the festivities of the army that is celebrating friendship with the Soviet comrades. You make a decision: I won't attend! On your way down to the janitor you hear your name over the loudspeaker; you are told to return to your working place. You are wondering what you might have forgotten and are rushing back. Upstairs, a *troika* is awaiting you: your boss, the collective's Party delegate and an agitator: 'Comrade, you are the only one who has not yet signed up for the festivities of the army. You cannot leave it on the table. By tomorrow morning, we need all invitations signed.' You are relieved that this is only about the invitation. But then you know that you don't want to make another decision today – and automatically, you sign. You go home humiliated and tired. At home, your son gives you a letter from the teacher, who complains about his lack of interest in the pioneer youth organisation. The teacher demands that you should 'stand up for his interests'. By now, you are at the end of your tether: you write a long and civilized letter, explaining that children should be able to choose themselves what organisation they want to join. The parents should not force them. Now, you feel relieved. You discuss the letter with your wife, who is crying because her boss has criticized her for not participating in a voluntary trip to the monuments of the working class. Both of you are terribly tired. You finish the discussion and you feel a bit better. And then, the reproaches: you start to think that your letter is helping you, but not at all your son. He might reproach you about it – it's his future, after all. Finally, you decide with your wife to delete the letter and sign the demand of the teacher. You go to bed, but you can't sleep. You decide not to let yourself be terrorized by the neighbour's radio. But the next morning, you wake up to begin an absolutely identical day."[58]

---

[58] Kabát, 64–66.

III. 3. 2 The Weekend, Socialization and Humour

Every minute of the weekend[59] was precious to the citizens: on Thursday nights, children and parents used to pack their bags and food for the weekend so they could leave for the *chata* after school and work early on Friday afternoon. Once arrived at the weekend house, the citizens used to indulge themselves in barbecues and drinking with the neighbours to dilute the stress accumulated over the week. On Saturday mornings, one was working on the *chata*, doing installations and other technical work, like the water supply. On late Sunday afternoon, the family returned to the city – and everybody was tired on Monday morning at school and at work. But these weekends in the countryside were well worth it, since the citizens had the authentic feeling of being at home, of evading the stress of work in the city.[60]

What did socialization under the Normalization look like? According to Kabát, socialization posed a real problem in totalitarian states, because the children were being socialized in a political environment that did not acknowledge individualism, tolerance and respect for the law, that is, trust in the rule-of-law state. Everything was political; any activity with its potentially negative consequences had to be analysed in seconds. The chart below[61] presents the differences in socialization and the consequences of socialization in a democratic and a post-totalitarian Soviet-type system respectively:

---

[59] An interesting study about the main activities of Czechoslovak citizens in their spare time from 1957 to 1967 – culture; the weekend house; hiking; camping; pioneer camps; stamp collecting and model making – is Martin Franc a Jiří Knapík, *Volný čas v českých zemích 1957–1967* (Praha: Academia, 2013).
[60] Kabát, 420–421.
[61] Kabát, 359–361.

Democracy	Post-Totalitarian State
Easy lifestyle; I have no reason to get involved in situations that do not concern me.	Continuous sense of insecurity and anticipation of stress; any situation has the potential to become a danger to me.
Low level of concentration and alertness, which is only necessary to orientate myself in a new environment.	Conscious control and search for security. You do not join a group of unknown persons in the streets. You avoid dark places and watch out for police cars.
Certainty about how a particular situation is going to develop is possible and normal. I do not expect a conflict with the shop assistant when shopping.	Inclination to look on the negative side of a situation. For example, queuing in front of a shop I think that most probably the goods for which I am queuing are going to be sold out before it's my turn.
Tendency to spontaneous communication, but also tendency to respect the privacy of others. Trust is no problem.	Low tendency to spontaneous communication; continuous self-control: communication that is banal or projects an image; testing others out. Systematic mistrust of others, born of fear, is a means of survival.

Westerners could be sure that any activity, shopping, picking up items at the dry cleaners etc., would be done in minutes. Not so the Czechoslovak citizen, who had to invest hours in the most banal and minor activities. My Slovak and Czech friends told me that the Christmas days were particularly stressful for the women and mothers: after an eight-hour shift, they had to go to the shops to buy the traditional Christmas carp, the spices for the Christmas dishes, the Christmas tree, gifts for the children – and all this in an economic system that was acutely short of consumer goods. If one managed to purchase a carp, for which one had to have contacts, one put the fish in the bathtub, where it swam until Christmas Eve, with the result that the whole family could not wash for days.

In the early 1980s, friends from Komárno on the Danube went to Hungary to buy detergent, because the Hungarian products were cheaper and better. As soon as they were back in Czechoslovakia, the customs officers confiscated the detergents and threw them into the Danube – which was literally foaming. The regime was not interested in environmental protection. If one refused to participate in the 'elections', one could be sure to have the StB knocking at the door: 'Comrade, you have not yet cast your vote for the KSČ.' If one kept refusing to cast one's vote for the Party, one risked one's place at the university.

The principal currency of economic survival were personal relations; in an economic system that was based on bureaucrats planning what the people needed, a shortage of consumer goods prevailed. To get by on a daily basis, citizens had to be inventive, help each other out: I know someone who works at a vegetable shop, who is going to put a kilo of oranges aside for me at Christmas. Therefore, I give him the telephone number of a car mechanic, who can help him with his car, and so on. The Socialist planned economy enforced exactly what Marx and Lenin wanted to get rid of: the sense of Capitalism, embodied in human nature that for centuries had been functioning according to the simple arithmetic of supply and demand and mankind's urge for survival. To buy goods means survival; the drive to buy as much as possible enhances one's chances of survival – and those of one's offspring. Not surprisingly, the black market functioned well in each bloc state. The regimes never succeeded in completely rooting it out.

A further factor was, according to Kabát, the micro-traumas[62] of everyday life: the shops were empty and often, the shop assistants, since they were in a position of power,

---

[62] Kabát, 281–282.

humiliated the clients, in order to feel powerful and in charge. However, friends who grew up in Communist families told me that they had been quite happy with the Husák regime: they had known nothing else and been grateful for the social security, the medical care, the security of their workplace and the university education for their children.

Many chose humour as a strategy to rid themselves of psychological stress, anxiety and anger. The famous Radio Erewan jokes[63] from the Cold War made superb fun of the absurd conditions under Socialism. Furthermore, there was no political correctness, no interest in so-called *gender* issues. Why? Because citizens just did not feel they should have to obey to yet another political command; as everybody was oppressed in the Husák regime, complaints by women about sexual discrimination just did not wash – and I think the majority of women simply did not have the time or energy to complain about sexist jokes or remarks. The citizens had to let steam off, and they used jokes, also those considered to be sexist today, to get rid of their every day frustration. Here are my three favourite jokes:

> "What was there before Communism? – Everything."[64]

> "The first international meeting of the Soviets and the Americans takes place in the Soviet Union. The Soviets, eager to please the Americans, open up the first strip club in Moscow. But no Americans are going there. Khrushchev calls the Party functionary responsible for the strip club: 'Is this a good club?' – 'Yes, of course, only the best, we hired American architects!' – 'Ok, what drinks can one get there?' – 'Only the best, malt whisky, gin, all the drinks are first class. – 'Hmm ... and the girls? – 'The best ones, of course, all cleared by the KGB, all Party members before 1918!'"[65]

---

[63] Radio Erewan jokes on http://www.armeniapedia.org/index.php?title=Radio_Yerevan_Jokes; accessed 6 May 2018.
[64] Kabát, 433.
[65] Kabát, 408.

"What are the three biggest sexual perversions?

Pedophilia, zoophilia and love of the Soviet Union."[66]

III. 3. 3 The Underground

Above, we have mentioned the socio-political composition of Czechoslovak society under the Normalization, introducing the dissidents,[67] the grey zone and the vast majority of the citizens who found, or rather had to find, a *modus vivendi* under the regime. Connected to the dissidents was the underground, a most interesting but complicated theme in recent Czech historiography.[68] Let me briefly present the salient facts.

The Czech underground was a social phenomenon that did not exist in the Slovak part of the country; the political opposition in Slovakia consisted mainly of religious persons who were trying to defend their Churches' rights and therefore were persecuted, having to stand trial in the 1970s and 1980s.[69] The Slovak dissidents Jan Čarnogurský (*1944), Miroslav Kusý (*1931), Milan Šimečka (1930–1990), and Hana Ponická (1922–2007), to name but the most prominent, had to endure the same humiliating persecution as their Czech colleagues.

---

[66] I thank MuDr. Milan Novák, Czech Republic, for providing me with this joke from Czechoslovak psychiatrists of the 1970s.

[67] An interesting new study about Czechoslovak dissidents is Jiří Suk, Michal Kopeček, Kristina Andělová, Tomáš Vilímek, Tomáš Hermann a Tomáš Zahradníček, *Šest kapitol o disentu* (Praha: Ústav pro soudobé dějiny, 2017). See Francis D. Raska's review in *COMENIUS. Journal of Euro-American Civilization V*, no. 1 (2018): 126–128. Further, I recommend Jiří Lederer's collection of interviews with prominent Czech and Slovak dissidents, *České rozhovory* (Praha: Československý spisovatel, 1991) and Jiří Brabec, Jan Lopatka, Jiří Gruša, Petr Kabeš a Igor Hájek, *Slovník zakázaných autorů 1948–1980* (Praha: Státní pedagogické nakladatelství, 1991).

[68] Ladislav Kudrna, ed., *Reflexe Undergroundu* (Praha: Ústav pro studium totalitních režimů, 2016).

[69] Norbert Kmeť, "Slovenská opozícia za normalizácie", in *Česká a slovenská společnost …*, 185–207, 192.

To this day, we have no concise historical study that covers all aspects of the underground, for example, the role of prominent persons, similarity to Western counter-culture movements such as the Weathermen in the USA, the 1968 student movement in Western Europe, the hippy movement in the sixties or the beatniks in the fifties. Nor is there a study of the role of StB agents and informers in the underground.[70]

The Czech underground was an alternative way of living, a subculture and a social network; its members, mainly young people, followed other moral values than the Socialist ones, used a different language than the establishment and engaged sometimes, but not exclusively, in oppositional activities. Some underground members did have contacts with prominent members of *Charter 77*, but it would be a mistake to assume that the majority of underground members automatically supported the political activities of the Chartists, who were intellectuals and from a different generation, having experienced the Czechoslovak Spring and the 1968 invasion.

A friend born in the early 1980s told me that after the *maturita* and his two years of compulsory military service – he had been 20 years old and was not allowed to study at university – he had planned a life in the underground, basically reading and keeping himself afloat with menial jobs, forgoing Socialist society, living on the edges of society. The Velvet Revolution of November 1989 came, and he received a scholarship to study in the USA. Today, he is a member of the Czech diplomatic service. Mirek Vodražka on the significant difference between the underground and the Chartists:

> "[...] to the underground, it was important not to acknowledge the representatives of power as a realistic partner for a dialogue [...] life in the

---

[70] Jan Cholinský, "České undergroundové hnutí optikou historiografie – mýty a realita", in *Reflexe Undergroundu*, 34–74, 37–38.

underground was absolutely based on the lack of loyalty towards the regime [...] while the speakers of *Charter 77* proclaimed openly that the Chartists considered themselves loyal citizens of this state, not pursuing political change."[71]

Cholinský stated that the majority of the young underground members in the 1980s were not interested in cooperating with *Charter 77*: the young people did not want to get involved with those in politics, be it the regime or the dissidents[72] – they preferred to live their lives outside society, that is, a life in complete denial of regime and society.

Cholinský defines three main aspects and phases of underground civic resistance against the totalitarian regime: first, the underground and its links to *Charter 77* in the late 1970s and early 1980s; second, the 1980s with the rock band *Plastic People of the Universe* and the samizdat publication *Revolver Revue*; third, the end of the *Plastic People* and the separation of its members into those who opted for co-operation with the regime and those who refused to make any compromise.[73]

In March 1976, the regime arrested the members of *Plastic People of the Universe* for "hooliganism" and "vulgar texts".[74] 'Magor' (Ivan Martin Jirous, 1944–2011) and Milan 'Mejla' Hlavsa (1951–2001) were the frontmen of the rock band; their persecution and trial would lead to the foundation of *Charter*

---

[71] VODRAŽKA, Mirek: Antisystémová queer politika undergroundu a prosystémová politika Charty. *Paměť a dějiny*, 2012, č. 1, s. 121–130, quoted from Cholinský, 57. To be precise here: the Chartists adhered to the principles of legality and non-violence, but under the given circumstances, any real dialogue with the regime was utopian – and they knew it. But they insisted on the principle of legality because their aim was to demonstrate that the Husák government was violating human rights although the ČSSR had signed the CSCE Act of Helsinki. Indirectly, the Chartists did pursue political change, but in the 1970s and 1980s, such change was highly unlikely to happen.
[72] Cholinský, 57.
[73] Cholinský, 55–73.
[74] Kriseová, 67.

77.⁷⁵ Before they met, Jirous thought of Havel as a representative of the political opposition that the regime somehow tolerated, while Havel had heard wild rumours about Jirous and the underground music scene. Let us finish this subchapter with a quote from Havel, who explains to perfection the difference between the underground and the future dissidents of *Charter 77*:

> "Jirous' explanations quickly dispelled my mistrust [...], I felt that the truth was on their side, even though they were using vulgar words, and their hair reached to the floor. [...] This was no longer about the regime settling a score with political enemies, who, to some extent, had to know what they were up to, [...] it was something worse: they were just young people who wanted to live their lives as they chose, play the music they liked."[76]

III. 4 Dissent and Return to Politics (1970–1989)

III. 4. 1 Dubček's Protest Letters

The two letters[77] I have selected for the first subchapter demonstrate how courageously, directly and honestly Dubček communicated with those who did everything to make his life miserable to the maximum. Dubček was the first Czechoslovak citizen

---

[75] Baer, *Politik als* ..., 125–128, https://www.rollingstone.com/music/news/how-a-revolutionary-czech-rock-band-inspired-vaclav-havel-20111219; accessed 30 June 2018. See Ivan Jirous, *magorovy labutí písně* (Praha: Rozmluvy, 1989), and Mejla Hlavsa a Jan Pelc, *Bez ohňu je underground* (Praha: BFS, 1992). Very detailed about the normalization is also the famous actor and *Charter 77* member Pavel Landovský (1936–2014), *Soukromá vzpoura. Rozhovor s Karlem Hvížďalou* (Praha: Mlada Fronta, 1990).

[76] Václav Havel, *Fernverhör. Ein Gespräch mit Karel Hvížďala* (Hamburg: rororo, 1990), 164, 156.

[77] Dubček's letters to various government and federal institutions, his interview with the newspaper of the Italian Communists *L'Unita*, his speech at Bologna University of 1988, his reaction to the German *Spiegel*, which had published an interview with Vasil Biľak in 1985, and his telegram to Willi Brandt, sent after his accident from his Prague hospital in September 1992 in *Alexander Dubček: Od totality* ..., 224–506.

who drew attention to the regime's oppression and consistent violation of civil rights, before the bloc states signed the Helsinki Act of 1975 and before the foundation of *Charter 77* in December 1976.[78]

The first letter is dated 6 January 1973 and addressed to various government bodies; the second is addressed to Miroslav Štěpán (1945–2014), member of the presidium CC KSČ, and dated 16 October 1989.[79] When he wrote to Štěpán, little did Dubček know that within a month and a day, the people would rid itself of the Normalization regime in mass demonstrations and a general strike that even the hitherto loyal Czech and Slovak television would support. They stopped broadcasting.

In the second part of this subchapter, I present documents I have found at the archives of the State Security Service in Prague. The documents demonstrate not only the lengths the regime was prepared to go to in order to efface Dubček from Czechoslovak collective memory, but also that the StB was quite successful in placing its agents within the leadership of *Charter 77*. The StB even knew the identity of the candidates for spokesmen prior to the elections at secret *Charter 77* meetings.

In the last subchapter, I will briefly summarize Dubček's return to politics in November 1989 and his personal change of political paradigms: the once fiercely believing Marxist-Leninist who had fought in the illegal KSS during the SNP, made a stellar career in the Stalinist 1950s and initiated liberalization in the 1960s, turned into a Western-type Social Democrat in the last years of his life.

---

[78] Alexander Dubček, *Od Totality* ..., 234.
[79] "1989, 16. Október, Bratislava, Otvorený list Miroslavovi Štěpanovi, členovi predsednictva ÚV KSČ", in *Alexander Dubček: Od totality* ..., 311–313.

Fired from all Party and State functions, Dubček had to look for a job, since his eldest son Pavol was studying medicine and his younger sons Peter and Milan were at high school. Anna was ill thus unfit for full-time work. They lived on their scant savings, and Mother Paulína, who lived with them in Mišíkova Street in Bratislava, helped with her meagre pension. From June to the end of October 1970, that is, for five months (!) the regime deliberately put the Dubčeks under financial duress, a particularly cruel way of treating the former first secretary. Back then in Czechoslovakia, there were no ATMs and, naturally, no credit card system. The citizens needed cash, hence a regular income, to get by on a daily basis.

I am speculating here, but I can imagine the following rationale, the way a jealous StB boss or a new member of the Presidium CC KSČ full of whipped-up hatred and eager to please those in power might have thought, justifying this kind of 'treatment': "That counter-revolutionary is living in a villa in the most beautiful part of Bratislava, on the hill, like an aristocrat or Capitalist. He had bought that villa with the salary he had earned as Party cadre from 1963 on – paid for by the workers. Now, let him experience what poverty and financial problems are. He has lived well enough for a long time."[80]

In view of the obvious fact that Dubček could not possibly know if he would find employment at all, the psychological pressure exerted on the family most probably affected Anna the

---

[80] The regime's rationale of employing dissidents in manual jobs had an immediate effect on their future pensions: the less one earned, the lower one's pension would be – a protracted revenge for not obeying. Given that dissidents' children were not allowed to embark on education that would have meant better-paid employment, we could speak of a deliberate pauperization of entire families who opposed the regime, a practice of collective punishment or kin liability (*Sippenhaft*). Oral History interview with XY, via e-mail on 6 July.

hardest. Usually, it is the women who do the shopping, cooking, washing and cleaning – they know the prices in the stores. How do you shop for your family if you do not know how long your savings are going to last – and when the next salary will come in? Can you afford to buy detergent now or should you wait another week? Dubček about these five months:

> "I looked through classified ads, and I made a list of some twenty factories and workshops looking for locksmiths, welders, and lathe workers. [...] It did not take long to find out that 'they' had built an invisible wall around me. For me, there was no job anywhere. [...] In the next few weeks, they offered me at least three jobs that I refused, mainly because the workplaces were too far from the city and I would have to spend, in one case, three hours commuting to work. In the end they offered me a position as a mechanic in the local Forest Administration in Krasnany, just outside the city limits of Bratislava. This offer I accepted, and I started to work there in December 1970."[81]

In Dubček's protest letters, we can find six main topics: first, protest against the StB surveillance and the continuous violation of his civil rights; second, defence of his reform politics; third, putting straight the false records, comments and campaigns of current Party members about his reform politics and their justification of the invasion and occupation; fourth, defence of persons wrongly accused and campaigned against in the media, e.g. former Foreign Minister Jiří Hájek; fifth, criticism of current politics with special consideration for Gorbachev's *perestroika* and *glasnost'*, and sixth, thoughts about the future of leftist politics in Czechoslovakia and Western Europe.

When he came to power in March 1985, the reformer Gorbachev raised hope among the Slovaks and Czechs that he would condemn the invasion and occupation as a grave mistake – which he did not. Gorbachev did apologize to Dubček personally in May 1990 in Moscow, when a Czechoslovak delegation

---

[81] Dubček, *Hope Dies Last*, 254, 256.

was negotiating about the withdrawal of the Soviet troops, expressing the new government's wish to leave the Warsaw Pact, but he did not publicly condemn Brezhnev's decision of 1968.[82]

A concise presentation and summary of all the themes of Dubček's letters would make a book in its own right. Having read all the letters, I can say that Dubček's thoughts and way of expressing himself changed significantly from 1986 to 1987, when he saw that the KSČ was doing nothing to follow Gorbachev's new course. But, I think, Dubček was also motivated by the wish to get back into the ring, into politics – which makes perfect sense in psychological terms. If one has been publicly shunned and psychologically terrorized for twenty years, one wants to set the record straight. I am not talking about revenge here; I think Dubček just wanted the regime to acknowledge that his reform course had been the right way to go – and certainly no counter-revolution. In this sense, he was emotionally and intellectually still close to the KSČ. What motivated him to address the Czechoslovak Ministry of the Interior, the Slovak Main Department of the State Security Service and Inspectorate, the Ministry of the Interior and the Public Prosecutor's Office in Bratislava in January 1973?[83]

Many protest letters reached the *samizdat*, and Dubček's letter of 6 January 1973 was an independent source of information, informing those who were active in the *samizdat* what was happening to him. The core argument of his letter was the protest against the surveillance of the StB, and how it affected his nerves. He listed five cases with detailed descriptions of how

---

[82] *Alexander Dubček: Od totality ...*, 278.
[83] "1973, 6. Január, Bratislava, List ministerstvu vnútra, Hlavej správe štatnej bezpečnosti a Inšpekcii MV SSR a Krajskej správe Zboru národnej bezpečnosti Bratislava (Zaslaný doporučene generálnej prokuratúre SSR) o prenasledovaní Alexandra Dubčeka, jeho rodiny a o obmedzovaní občianskych práv a slobôd", in *Alexander Dubček: Od totality ...*, 229–233.

StB agents followed him on foot and in cars. The most impressive case[84] involved a typical Central European way of behaving and admirable humanity in an inhuman situation:

> "I got dressed and together with my cautious friend walked along Mišíkova street up to the Slavín. [...] While walking, I noticed a familiar car with state number plates and in it two service men in civilian clothes. It was not difficult for them to recognize me since they had the gate of our house well covered. I asked them: 'Are you not cold if you so rarely start the engine?' 'We are', said one of them, but it's bearable.' 'If you like, I can get you a thermos with tea and rum.' 'We don't need it, we have our own.' Then, I returned back home and went straight to bed. I don't know if you can imagine how badly I slept?"[85]

Dubček continued his letter with further descriptions of the surveillance: being followed, so he wrote, was not new to him, since his family had been monitored all their lives. Because they were Communists, the Czechoslovak State Security Service of the First Republic had had its eyes on the Dubček family when they returned from Soviet Kirgizia; the Fascist Slovak state had persecuted them too. He had had a hard life and was certainly capable of noticing the current surveillance. I cannot help but think that Dubček still tried to convince the authorities that he did not deserve such treatment, but it was certainly also his intention to expose the unlawful activities of both government and StB. Did he hope that his letter would prompt any action, or did he just write it for reasons of psychological health, that is, getting rid of stress, anger and frustration?

> "When the Inspectorate of the Interior Ministry investigates the case, they should consider this letter a protest against the illicit surveillance. [...] This letter's main reason is to protest against the violation of Socialist law and civil rights [*proti porušovaniu socialistickej zákonnosti a občianskych práv*]."[86]

---

[84] "1973, 6. Január, Bratislava ...", 230–231.
[85] "1973, 6. Január, Bratislava ...", 231.
[86] "1973, 6. Január, Bratislava ...", 232–231.

In his letter to Miroslav Štěpán, a KSČ hardliner eager to suffocate society's increasing protests in 1988 and 1989, Dubček defended his former Foreign Minister Jiří Hájek against false accusations by K. Mazurov.[87] On 15 September 1989, the Soviet newspaper *Izvestiia* had published an article by Mazurov, in which he accused the Dubček government and Hájek of having planned to leave the Warsaw Pact in 1968, thereby justifying the invasion and occupation. Mazurov, under a different name back then, had been a member of the CC KPSS under Brezhnev and organized the occupation. Dubček wrote that it had not been the ČSSR that broke the Warsaw Pact Treaty and its obligations, but the five invading armies and their respective governments. Neither Foreign Minister Hájek nor his government had done anything that justified Mazurov's untrue statements twenty-one years on.

One did not have to be a politician to notice that protest and anger were beginning to boil up in Czechoslovak society: in June 1989, the Chartists published a petition *Několík vět* (*A Few Sentences*),[88] which demanded the immediate release of political prisoners, freedom of the press and an open discussion of the events of 1968. The Party hardliners reacted with drastic measures, arresting dissidents and mounting defamation campaigns against prominent critics of the regime. Dubček reproached the government that it had lost its sense of time and history:

> "One has to look critically at the senseless purge in the Party, organized by the presidium of the CC KSČ in 1970, and the 'politics of Normalization', which plunged the KSČ, the economy and society as a whole into a deep crisis. [...] Listen to the people who have experienced the truth about 1968 and disagree with you. If you are not capable of

---

[87] "1989, 16. Október, Bratislava, Otvorený list ...", 311.
[88] The petition *Několík vět* on http://www.totalita.cz/vysvetlivky/nvet.php; accessed 8 July 2018

doing this, why then does the government sign international treaties (Helsinki, Vienna), which it refuses to integrate into our legislation and comply with?"[89]

To summarize, we can say that Dubček acted like a dissident, but did not consider himself to be one; he signed no *Charter 77* documents and kept to himself until the events of 1989 unfolded, for example, the trial of the Bratislava Five, which he attended out of solidarity for the unlawfully accused.[90] For twenty years, he withstood surveillance, false accusations, the smearing of his name and politics in press campaigns. He continuously protested against the violation of his civil rights.

Why did the regime not arrest him and put him on trial? Havel, for example, was arrested on 19 January 1989 and sentenced to nine months imprisonment for his participation in a demonstration.[91] I think there are two explanations that make sense in this context. The first is domestic affairs, the second one is the relations with Moscow, thus with the bloc as a whole. Since the Husák regime had been trying for twenty years to efface Dubček and his reform politics from Czechoslovak collective memory, it would have been completely counter-productive and absolutely irrational to arrest him and put him on trial. News about his arrest and trial would not only have catapulted him back into public consciousness, but would quite certainly have prompted a protest wave in the Western media, possibly

---

[89] "1989, 16. Október, Bratislava, Otvorený list ...", 313. Dubček referred to the Helsinki Treaty of 1975 and the UN Vienna Convention of 1969. The Vienna Convention on https://treaties.un.org/doc/publication/unts/volume%201155/volume-1155-i-18232-english.pdf: accessed 10 July 2018. The Helsinki Final Act on https://history.state.gov/milestones/1969-1976/helsinki; accessed 10 July 2018.

[90] Juraj Marušiak, "Bratislavská päťka. Prejav agónie komunistického režimu", in *Storočie procesov. Súdy, politika a spoločnosť v moderných dejinách Slovenska* (Bratislava: Veda, 2013), 241–258.

[91] Baer, *Politik als ...*, 137.

also diplomatic problems. Furthermore, I think that the fact that Dubček had been a pensioner since 1980 played no role in the regime's way of reasoning; the authorities had interrogated Professor Patočka, who was seventy years old, for 12 (!) hours in March 1977. Patočka died of a heart attack at the infamous Prague Bartolomejšska 4 during the interrogation.

Second, Gorbachev's politics did have some impact on the Husák government; news that the ČSSR authorities had arrested the 68-year-old pensioner and father of the Czechoslovak Spring for a couple of protest letters would have probably jeopardized the Soviet-US negotiations about nuclear disarmament Gorbachev was eager to sign with US President Ronald Reagan. This reasoning was most probably behind the government's decision to allow Dubček to travel to Italy to receive the honorary doctorate of Bologna University. From a Western perspective and also in the eyes of Czechoslovak citizens, the decision made the Husák government look generous, seemingly following Gorbachev's reform course – and one thing was sure: Dubček would not ask for political asylum in Italy, he would come back home to his family. Thus, this was a win-win situation for the government, at home and abroad.

III. 4. 2 The StB's Psychological Terror

According to former StB agent Karol Urban, the primary reason for monitoring Dubček, his family and, sometimes, also his near neighbours, was to make their lives miserable[92] – an operation that lasted twenty years! When he joined the StB as a young man in the early 1970s, Urban believed in the regime and was convinced that the Czechoslovak Spring had been a counter-

---

[92] Urban, 44. When Urban was in service in the 1970s and 1980s, the StB had almost 11,000 employees, Urban, 88.

revolution; yet, the older he got and the longer he had to observe Dubček's every move, the more doubts he had.

In a conversation with one of his bosses, Urban asked if it was really necessary to monitor Anna Dubčeková as well; what had they done to deserve such attention? So many agents, cars and hours spent – everybody on Mišíkova Street already knew that they were StB agents. Were the Dubčeks spies? No, his boss replied. Eser, Dubček's codename, would never go against the Party and state; they were monitoring him for different reasons.[93]

The StB had Dubček completely covered; they opened his letters, installed devices in his house to listen in on the family and followed him to the weekend *chalupa* in Senec, with bathing trunks in their cars, because Dubček loved water sports. The former first secretary about the surveillance:

> "Naturally, many people recognized me and greeted me. Often strangers came up to me, inquired after my well-being, and tried to express their sympathy. Soon I noticed that anyone who had greeted me was followed by one of the agents as soon as he or she stepped off the car. Then I learned from some of those who had received this attention that they were stopped, had to show their IDs, and a few days later were called for interrogation. Some were threatened with the loss of their jobs if they talked to me again."[94]

When Anna left the house and walked down to Štefaníková Street, where she used to buy groceries, two agents followed her. A young agent, who had still a human heart, once helped her carry her heavy bags up to the house.[95]

To me, three operations are particularly telling evidence of the StB's continuous psychological terror exerted on the

---

[93] Urban, 44–45.
[94] Dubček, *Hope Dies Last*, 257.
[95] Urban, 178.

family: first, the incident at the Bratislava theatre, and second and third, Peter and Pavol Dubček's trips to Prague.

In 1988, the Dubčeks attended the theatre play *Na provazku* (*On the Rope*), presented by a Moravian group in Bratislava.[96] The actors were unable to finish the play, because the StB intervened: StB agents stopped the play and escorted the Dubčeks out of the theatre. The rationale was clear: social isolation.

When Pavol Dubček, codename Pavel, the eldest son, went to Prague on 5 November 1977 to attend an international karate tournament, he was followed. The StB files were usually entitled "Contents of the written documents" and structured as follows: personal files of the expenses; overview of the pictures and negatives; suggestion of how to carry through the surveillance; organization of the surveillance; summary of the object's movements; final assessment of the operation; envelope with photo documentation.[97] Five agents and two cars followed Pavol in Prague.[98] Agent Liptáková wore a green coat, brown boots and a green handbag; she paid for three admission tickets to the sports hall costing KČS 38. Agent Šroub wore a black jacket, grey trousers and brown boots. The final assessment of the operation was dated 22 December 1977, that is, approximately five weeks after the operation of 5 and 6 November:

> "Visits: ∅ Contacts: ∅ Places the object frequented: ∅ Walking tours the object repeated: ∅ Important places where the object was not under surveillance: ∅ Public transport and cars the object used: bus SPZ PH 60-26; further tram no. 5, bus ČSA. Places visited: sports hall IPS, Slávie Praha. ČSA-ul. Revoluční. Demeanour of the object: the object's

---

[96] ABS ÚSTRČR, 812702-MV-72-78-0047-1.jpg, 0047-2.jpg.
[97] ABS ÚSTRČR, SL_5140_MV_Pavel_2_001_0002.jpg.
[98] ABS ÚSTRČR, SL_5140_MV_Pavel_2_001_0010.jpg.

behaviour is quiet; he is unaware of the surveillance. Contacts not identified and places where the object was lost: ∅."[99]

Another operation was called Katalyzátor 1: the surveillance of Peter Dubček, the second son and an ingenieur by training, from 22 to 23 March 1976. The reason for the operation was the danger that Katalyzátor 1 could contact "rightist exponents [*styky s pravycovými exponenti*]", among them Jiří Hájek and Zdeněk Mlynář.[100] Thirteen agents and four cars monitored Peter upon arrival at the airport in Prague. He was with a woman and a man; they took the bus to the city centre, then, the little group split up. The woman, code name Eva, stayed at the Hotel Tatran. Unlike his elder brother, Peter Dubček was aware of the StB following him, because he often turned around, and his walks were quite confusing, entering shops and not buying anything. He also stayed at the Hotel Tatran. On the second day, 23 March 1976, he was also followed; I think that Peter was on a business trip, because he visited a factory making automated machines in Prague 5 and Pragoexport, a government institution for international trade.[101]

Who was Eva? The StB identified her as Mrs Livia Herzová from Bratislava, born 1928; I think she was a colleague from work who accompanied Peter to Prague. Interesting in this case is that Peter obviously tried to shake off his followers, vanishing into department stores and shops without buying anything. Operation Katalyzátor 1 lasted until 3 December 1988, when Peter stayed in Prague on a business trip.[102] One cannot possibly imagine the costs of these operations, funded by taxpayers.

---

[99] ABS ÚSTRČR, SL_5140_MV_Pavel_2_001_0017.jpg.
[100] ABS ÚSTRČR, SL_3110_MV_KATALYZATOR_1_001_0005.jpg
[101] ABS ÚSTRČR, ABS USTRČR, SL_3110_MV_KATALYZATOR_1_001_0020.jpg
[102] ABS ÚSTRČR, ABS USTRČR, SL_3110_MV_KATALYZATOR_1_001_0042.jpg

The StB also had prominent members of *Charter 77* under surveillance. On 13 November 1986, the chartist Anna Marvanová told the source about the candidates for the position of next year's *Charter 77* speakers.[103] To authenticate their documents, the Chartists used to elect three speakers, who naturally were immediately arrested and imprisoned, but sometimes only interrogated. Marvanová had no clue that the person she was talking to was an informant for the StB. On 9 December 1986, Marvanová told the source that the meeting of the Chartists had been chaotic; furthermore, Petr Uhl (*1941) had had a long conversation with Václav Havel and reproached him for creating a cult of personality, thereby pushing *Charter 77* as a group into the shadows. Havel had been very angry.[104]

Finally, to the StB, Dubček was an internal enemy, an enemy within the state. We cannot possibly imagine, how the constant surveillance affected his and Anna's psychological condition. The StB had monitored them already in the months he was ambassador to Turkey.[105] On the day of the beginning of the end of the regime, on 17 November 1989, Dubček was in Prague, naturally, under StB surveillance. He met his friend Václav Slavík and Luigi Coleani, a delegate of the Italian Communist Party PCI.[106]

Karol Urban, whom we have to thank for the information about how the StB's operations were planned and realized, left

---

[103] ABS ÚSTRČR, 812702-MV_72_78_0007-1.jpg
[104] ABS ÚSTRČR, 812702-MV_72_78_0007-2.jpg
[105] ABS ÚSTRČR, carton 80410_300; his code name in Turkey had been Bukanýr. For a definition of buccaneer see https://en.oxforddictionaries.com/definition/buccaneer; accessed 12 July 2018.
[106] ABS ÚSTRČR, X_008_0041.jpg. For a history of the PCI see https://www.marxist.com/the-dissolution-of-the-italian-communist-party-1991.htm; accessed 12 July 2018.

the StB after the Velvet Revolution. He had the decency to end his book with the words "I apologize [*Ospravedlňujem sa*]".[107]

III. 4. 3 November 1989 and the Transition to Democracy

"A politician became a statesman."[108]

In this last chapter, I present three speeches Dubček held in public during and after the Velvet Revolution; I consider them telling evidence of his leftist political reasoning, and correctness in democratic and legal issues. I have selected first, his speech to the people on 23 November 1989 in Bratislava;[109] second, his speech to the people of 25 May 1990 before the first free elections scheduled for July;[110] and third, his interview with ČSTK about the attacks of members of ODS, who wanted him to resign as chairman of the Federal Assembly.[111]

After twenty years, people saw their former leader again; he could speak freely, and the StB no longer followed him. The psychological terror was over, and euphoria, hope and goodwill ruled in the country. The chronology of the Velvet Revolution[112] is well known, also the events that led to the Velvet Divorce in the summer of 1992, which came into effect on 1 January 1993. Dubček spent the last two years of his life in the centre of politics; after the umbrella organisations OF and VPN had pressed

---

[107] Urban, 240.
[108] Laluha, *Alexander Dubček* ..., 25.
[109] "1989, 23. November, Bratislava, Prejav na zhromaždení občanov na Námestí Slovenského národného povstania v Bratislave", in *Alexander Dubček: Od Totality* ..., 320–321.
[110] "1990, 25. Máj, Bratislava, Príhovor k voličom pred prvými slobodnými voľbami", in *Alexander Dubček: Od Totality* ..., 403–404.
[111] "1991, 29. Júl, Bratislava–Praha, Rozhovor pre ČSTK pod názvom ‚Neprezliekam kabát' – o útokoch českej pravice (ODS) na jeho osobu, o podpore federálnej vláde a o odmietnutí zriadenia domobrany", in *Alexander Dubček: Od Totality* ..., 425–426.
[112] The Velvet Revolution on https://www.bbc.com/news/world-europe-30 059011; accessed 12 July 2018.

the Normalization regime to abdicate, the political scene began to change in both parts of the country.

OF and VPN dissolved owing to the foundation of new political parties that were preparing for the parliamentary elections scheduled for July 1992 – this phenomenon was common to all post-Communist states of the bloc. ODS under Klaus won in the Czech part, and Mečiar's HZDS in Slovakia. Both prime ministers would dissolve Czechoslovakia,[113] a decision, which was illegal according to Dubček and also Czechoslovak President Václav Havel, who stepped down in protest.

Dubček held two important political positions: on 28 November, for VPN, the people elected him chairman of the Federal Assembly (FZ), and in July 1992 he was elected delegate to the FZ as a member of the newly founded Social Democratic Party of Slovakia (SDSS).

Let us now have a look at his first speech in public after twenty years in silence. He addressed the people in an old-fashioned way, how he had spoken in the 1960, but with new content. Revitalizing socialism and linking it to democracy had been a movement that had begun in 1968. The consolidation of the "neo-Stalinism of Brezhnev and Suslov [*upevnenia brežnevovsko-suslovského neostalinizmu*]" had stopped the democratic process of 1968 with military force, while the twenty years of the harsh, morally intimidating politics of Normalization could not lead the country out of the economic and social crisis.[114] What was happening now was the direct

---

[113] Very interesting are the memoirs of Ivan Laluha, *O ceste k slovenskej štátnosti v rokoch 1990–1992. Čriepky z poslaneckých lavíc* (Bratislava: Vydavateľstvo Pozsony-Pressburg-Bratislava – Peter Rašla, 2015).

[114] "1989, 23. November, Bratislava, Prejav …", 320. Michail Andreevič Suslov (1902–1982) was considered second most important man after Brezhnev and unofficial chief Party ideologue. Suslov on https://www.britannica.com/biography/Mikhail-Andreyevich-Suslov; accessed 27 August 2018.

consequence of the abolished reform course of 1968 – a new movement had emerged:

> "One of many civic initiatives is Public Against Violence VPN. I want to inform this convention that the initiative of former members of the KSČ, the party of those excluded by the CC KSČ, is also part of the many civic initiatives. I am turning to the CC KSS, all Party members, those excluded, to the workers, farmers, the working intelligentsia and the People's army, the ZNB and the People's militia with an urgent challenge: the renaissance of our society requires practical steps."[115]

He was interested in a wide dialogue with other civic initiatives and asked the citizens to avoid provoking violence with extreme slogans. Nothing would be worse for the "new rebirth [*pre novú obrodu*]"; the citizens should not ignore the call for peaceful conduct issued by Prime Minister Ladislav Adamec.[116]

The second speech was a classic pre-election speech: Dubček was a candidate for VPN and chairman of the Federal Assembly. Many members of VPN were former reform Communists and KSS members. New parties were just emerging, the Christian Democrats, the Slovak National Party, while the KSS transformed itself into a modern leftist party. These were the months of transition to a pluralist political system and the emerging of a new party landscape in both parts of the country. Dubček on the past and the future:

> "After all these years, you are going to attend free elections on 8 and 9 June. You are going to decide not only about your future, but also about the future of your children, the nation and the republic. [...] We are just at the beginning of a difficult path, which demands all our commitment and sacrifices in politics and economics. If you give me your vote, if I am elected delegate to the Federal Assembly, I shall work for our republic in such a way that it receives an honourable place among the

---

[115] "1989, 23. November, Bratislava, Prejav ...", 321.
[116] "1989, 23. November, Bratislava, Prejav ...", 321. Ladislav Adamec (1926–2007) acted as the last KSČ Premier.

world's nations, that our republic shall be integrated into Europe and contribute to the development of civilization and freedom."[117]

I think he hinted at his plan to use his good reputation and international contacts to advance the young republic's integration into Western political stuctures; Dubček stressed at the end of his speech what he would do for the nation in domestic affairs. His politics were, of course, still leftist, but his goals were clearly social democratic ones. Above all, he would be committed to the rule-of-law state, true equality of citizens, social justice and the protection of civil rights in a democratic society. In economics, he would dedicate all his efforts to helping create a prosperous and modern economy.[118] He mentioned also the environment that had suffered under the previous regime: the beautiful countryside was inherited from their ancestors and they had the duty to hand it over to the next generation in a better, restored and unpolluted condition.

What he did not mention is also interesting: Dubček had never been a nationalist. In his way of thinking, the common state was the only form in which Czechs and Slovaks could live together. Now, it was about the transition to democracy. He did not foresee that Mečiar and Klaus would dissolve the federation and the state.

The third speech dealt with a most interesting aspect of the transition to democracy and was, with hindsight, the first probing into a process that would lead to the dissolution of the state within a year. The Czech rightist-conservative ODS attacked Dubček on 23 July 1991, demanding that he resign from

---

[117] "1990, 25. Máj, Bratislava, Príhovor ...", 403–404.
[118] "1990, 25. Máj, Bratislava, Príhovor ...", 404. He did not mention the key word 'market economy', neither the key word 'economic transformation of the system'. It was thus not clear, what kind of economic system he would support: his 1968 reform of the planned economy or a market economy.

the chairmanship of the FZ because he was still a member of VPN, which, in the meantime, had dissolved.[119] It was a simple attempt to replace Dubček with a conservative Slovak who shared their political views. Also, as a member of a non-existent party, he was no longer independent – or so the ODS members must have thought. When VPN was dissolved, several new parties approached Dubček to join them; in March 1992, he eventually joined the new Social Democratic Party of Slovakia. But in July 1991, he was an independent, a fact ODS members were well aware of. Dubček reacted in an interview with the Czechoslovak Press Chancellery ČSTK, setting the record straight:

> "On 23 July 1991 I received a letter from the club of ODS parliamentarians. They wrote, amongst other things: 'We share the opinion, that your leaving the government coalition and your support for the opposition are not in keeping with the function of chairman of the Federal Assembly.' [...] My activities in parliament do not serve the opposition but support the federal government; they are in tune with the constructive work of the Federal Assembly. [...] Is it not strange that ODS aligns me now with the opposition, placing me outside the government coalition, just because I am no longer a member of VPN, while the foundation of ODS was realized with members who left the coalition partner OF? [...] In what direction is this new party going, judging others? [...] Did they not leave the government coalition, when they left OF and joined ODS?"[120]

ODS politicians reproached Dubček with what they themselves were guilty of doing – leaving the government coalition of OF and VPN, risking the unity of the state in those difficult transitional months. The attempts of ODS politicians, as Dubček said, to position themselves for the elections of July 1992 were signs that particular interests were winning over the interests of the common good. I think it possible that ODS politicians were already beginning to think about dividing the state; without the

---

[119] "1991, 29. Júl, Bratislava–Praha, Rozhovor pre ČSTK ...", 425.
[120] "1991, 29. Júl, Bratislava–Praha, Rozhovor pre ČSTK ...", 428.

large state factories in Slovakia difficult to privatize, the Czech transition to market economy could be realized faster and more efficiently. Also, they knew that Dubček was an ardent defender of the federation; if he were re-elected chairman of the Federal Assembly, it would be difficult to push the separation through.

The last text in the collection is a telegram Dubček sent from hospital following a road accident. It was dictated to Hubert Maxa (*1925), a friend and biographer, who forwarded it to Willy Brandt in September 1992. Dubček thanked Brandt for his telegram with good wishes for a speedy recovery.

Alexander Dubček died on 7 November 1992, shortly after 9 pm; his wife Anna had died in 1991. He was buried at Anna's side at the Slávičie údolie cemetery in Bratislava.

Conclusion

Let me now answer the research questions I listed in the introduction to this biography.

1. Democratization and liberalization of the Stalinist regime: Dubček grew up in a Communist environment. What were the intellectual origins of his reform course?

Until 1963, when he was elected First Secretary, Dubček kept a low profile; he was a loyal member of the KSS and in line with the KSČ's Stalinist course under Novotný. In 1959, he still adhered to the official Party line that Husák and Novomeský had been 'Slovak bourgeois nationalists' and deserved their long prison sentences. I think Khrushchev's liberalization – which the Hungarians who survived 1956 would certainly not call liberalization – was a first glimpse of the possibility of reforming the Stalinist system. The Barák and Kolder Commissions and their refusal to reveal the full truth about the Stalinist trials of the 1950s demonstrated to him that change was pressing, in legal, political and economic terms. Also, Dubček was in Moscow at the Higher Party School, when Khrushchev was in power. He was able to observe the new Soviet political course at first hand.

Dubček was no intellectual like Gustáv Husák, a doctor of law, or Zdeněk Mlynář, a political scientist and academic teacher, but he was a practically thinking man who observed the economic stagnation of the early 1960s. As a member of the Barnabite Commission, he insisted that justice had to be done, the victims fully rehabilitated, which meant the public renewal of their Party membership and an apology and financial compensation for the years in prison. This was only possible in 1968 when he would successfully replace Novotný as First Secretary KSČ. In Dubček's way of thinking, men made mistakes; to admit mistakes, correct them and then moving on to build Socialism was the right way to go.

Dubček did not care about the fate of the imprisoned non-Communists, the Catholic priests and centre-right Czech and Slovak politicians. They were simply not in the focus of his attention. This was a way of thinking and political approach he shared with Vladimír Clementis, Husák and Slovak and Czech Communists of the pre-war generation. The Communists thought that the unlawful persecution of the 1950s had happened only to them, a particular form of tunnel vision.

Elected first secretary KSS in 1963, Dubček wanted to develop the Slovak economy to be more independent from the Czech economy, which could only strengthen the common state's economic development. His engagement for Slovakia's economy was not born from nationalism, but from economic considerations; first and foremost, Dubček's political identity was Czechoslovak and his national one Slovak – but national identity was never an important issue to him.

He was no theoretician, but highly intelligent, an accomplished strategist and tactician, pragmatic and a truthful and decent person, but after 21 August 1968 he committed, I think, one big mistake – which is very easy to say with hindsight and from a Western European perspective: he signed the Moscow Protocol, signalling to the people that he still believed he could save some of the reforms – thereby putting himself in a catch-22 situation. Had he resigned in protest and left the Party for good, his life would not have become easier, but quite different. But this is speculation, and a psychological one at that. I think that Dubček simply could not believe that the Soviets would establish a neo-Stalinist system, having undergone political socialization under the reformer Khrushchev.

The KSS had been his home and family, since he had joined the illegal KSS in 1939 as a teenager. His father had been sent to Mauthausen for his KSS leadership in the Slovak state. The belief in Marxism-Leninism was almost genetically inherited in the Dubček family, which was from a working-class background; both his parents were Communists. Marxism-Leninism's moral goals were Dubček's moral goals: workers' rule; a classless society; end of Capitalist exploitation and the building of a new world according to the principle of democratic centralism. That the Soviet Union, which had liberated the Slavic nations from Nazi terror, governed her political hemisphere in Central and Eastern Europe was only just and right; millions of Soviet citizens had given their lives for the liberation of their Slavic brothers.

Dubček was no cold-war warrior; the competition of the Soviet bloc with the Imperialist and Capitalist West did not interest him. He was focussed on reforming Socialism at home, in Czechoslovakia, another factor that prevented him from understanding Brezhnev's big picture. Important in this regard is also Dubček's childhood and youth: he felt at home in the Soviet Union and spoke Russian fluently. I think this was a factor that prevented him from seeing clearly what Brezhnev wanted with the Moscow Protocol. We could say that he was the victim of a paradox: because of his familiarity with the Russian language and Soviet politics, Dubček was too close to the Soviet leadership to understand what was going on after Khrushchev had been removed. He thought he knew the Soviets' reasoning. Dubček was not capable of thinking outside the Marxist-Leninist box: from August 1968 to April 1969, he concentrated on saving details of his reform programme.

Gorbachev's election to General Secretary of the KPSS in March 1985 must have raised his hopes that, finally after twenty years, the Husák government would see the rightfulness of his 1968 reform course – and follow Gorbachev's *perestroika* and *glasnosť*. He was disappointed; his action programme was of no interest to the new Soviet leader. To the Soviets, the Czechoslovak Spring was a thing of the past. Gorbachev was only interested in signing a nuclear disarmamament deal with the Americans to stop the arms race and liberate funds to finance the much-needed reforms in the Soviet economy and state, to save Communism at least in the Soviet Union, for which he was even ready to sacrifice the bloc.

Observing that the politics of Normalization did not change, on the contrary, the regime arranged for a trial of the Bratislava Five in the summer of 1989, when East Germans were fleeing en masse to the West German embassy in Prague, Dubček understood that Socialism in Europe could only be saved with a Western pluralist approach: Western European Social Democracy, a market economy and a rule-of-law state.

Even before the Helsinki Act of 1975 that led to the foundation of *Charter 77* in December 1976, Dubček had protested against the regime's continuous violation of his civil rights, against the lawlessness of the Husák regime. He was therefore the first Czechoslovak dissident, in the truest sense of the word: a former believer who stopped believing, who was critical of the catechism he had believed in. Intellectually, he had in common with Havel the demand for civil rights – so, why did he not join *Charter 77*?

I think that, unlike the Slovak and Czech *Charter 77* members Havel, Uhl, Kantůrková, Kusý, Ponická and Šimečka, Dubček just could not bring himself to go against the Party, cutting all emotional and psychological ties with his past. The Party had removed him from politics; once he learned that his KSČ and KSS memberships were cancelled, he was deeply hurt. By contrast, Havel had never been a member of the Communist Party, while Kusý and Ponická had been reform communists in 1968. To Dubček, signing *Charter 77* documents would have meant acknowledging that his reform course of 1968 had been a grave mistake, that Socialism could not be reformed – a complete break with everything he had believed in since 1939. Also, membership of *Charter 77* would have meant to him admitting that his life's work, the *akční program*, had been an error. He certainly kept writing protest letters, but still considered himself an authority of the Party, albeit a persecuted and psychologically terrorized one.

2. Constitutional status of Slovakia within Czechoslovakia: what constitutional arrangement did Dubček pursue for Slovakia? Was the projected constitutional arrangement the principal driving force of his reform course or a minor, collateral issue on his political agenda? What came first in his political thought: democratization, then federalization of Czechoslovakia? Or, first federalization, then democratization?

Clearly, the federalization of Czechoslovakia was a minor issue of Dubček's action programme in 1968. The government's focus in January 1968 was on the economy and democratization of Socialist society. Naturally, the constitutional status of the Slovaks and Czechs had to be re-arranged to be truly fair, but in Dubček's view, the federalization could wait. Much more pressing was the economy and the country's democratization within Socialist law.

Lastly, a question, which I consider of crucial importance for understanding the post-1989 political development of Czechoslovakia: why did the parliament elect Václav Havel as

Czechoslovak president and not Dubček? When the people had gathered in November 1989 at the Letná stadion, they had shouted '*Dubček na hrad* (Dubček to the Castle)', meaning that they wanted Dubček as Czechoslovak president. Yet, to many dissidents and new politicians and parliamentarians, Dubček seeemed still too much involved with the KSČ.

It had been the Party, which had abrogated his membership; had he decided in 1968 not to sign the Moscow Protocol and left the Party in protest, that is, clearly demonstrating that he was against the invasion and occupation, I think he would have been elected president. Also, in the early 1990s, the newly elected Czech, Slovak and Czechoslovak parliaments had to consider their democratic future in the context of international relations: first and foremost, they wanted to integrate to Western political institutions, the European Community and NATO.

As the symbol of the Czechoslovak Spring, Dubček was certainly respected in the West, but Communism and Reform Communism was a thing of the past, and new beginnings were best made with new persons – or so the parliamentarians must have thought. To elect Dubček Czechoslovak president, even if he deserved it, would have signalled to the West that the democratic Czechoslovak government was not capable of cutting its ties with the Socialist past – it would have possibly protracted the country's integration into Western political structures.

Havel had an absolutely clean record in political terms; he had been an outsider since the 'victorious February 1948', fought the Communist regime since 1969 and gone to prison for long years, which had almost cost him his life. He was the perfect candidate for the Czechoslovak presidency, because Western politicians trusted him. Dubček ran as a candidate in the presidential elections; the parliamentarian's preference for Havel must have deeply disappointed him. According to Jozef

Banáš,[1] a further factor in favour of Havel winning the presidency was an unwritten law in the federation that prescribed that the presidency had to be shared: since the last president had been the Slovak Husák, the next one had to be a Czech – thus Havel.

In his last two years after the Velvet Revolution, Dubček, ever modest, sincere and disciplined, slaved on as delegate to the Federal Assembly for the newly founded Social Democratic Party of Slovakia. Much like Havel, Dubček was very critical of the political events that would finally lead to the Velvet Divorce of 1993, but he could do nothing to prevent the dissolution of Czechoslovakia. On his way to Prague for a meeting of the Federal Assembly in September 1992, his driver caused an accident.

Alexander Dubček, an icon of Slovak, Czechoslovak and European history, a politician whom the Czechoslovak citizens loved, died on 7 November 1992 in a Prague hospital.

Let us never forget him.

---

[1] Jozef Banáš, "Prečo sa Dubček nie dostal na hrad", https://www.youtube.com/watch?v=zX4_NgELub8; accessed 15 July 2018.

Oral History Interview with Pavol Dubček, MD

Bratislava, 20 July 2018, 4 pm to 5.30 pm. The interview was conducted in Slovak, English translation by me.

JB: Dear Dr Dubček, it is an honour to meet you. You are Alexander Dubček's eldest son. You studied and practised medicine. Why this professional choice?

PD: I was always interested in natural sciences, but also in culture and art. I wanted to become a sculptor. Both the art school and the medical faculty, on Sasínková Street in Bratislava, offered me a place to study. My father told me to study medicine. Artists had a hard life, but a doctor was never out of work, even in politically bad times. A doctor would always have money for bread and an onion.

    I started to study medicine in 1965. My father was hard headed; he knew what he wanted and followed his goals – his ideal was a decent life for all citizens. I studied medicine for six years and I was good at it. I had good professors, who exerted no political pressure on me.

    When I graduated, there was no job for me in a Bratislava hospital, in the capital. For some months, I worked as a nightwatchman on Mytná Street; I wanted to go to the West. My mother sensed it; she did not want me to leave and said that our family needed a physician. Finally, I got a position in Záhorie, at the Slovak Moravian border, a military zone, where I worked until 1989.

JB: If it's not too personal a question: what is your worst memory from the eight months, January to August 1968, when your father was Czechoslovakia's most powerful politician?

PD: After the invasion of 21 August 1968, we feared for our father's life. We did not know where he was. The Soviets abducted him. Was he still alive or already executed? Would we all be executed? What was our fate? Two-thirds of my former schoolmates emigrated. They scattered to countries all over the world. After 1989, I had the possibility of visiting them.

JB: At the Archives of the State Security Services in Prague I found a file about you, dated November 1977: you went for two days to Prague to attend an international karate competition. The StB had you followed with two cars and five agents. How do you remember the years of the Normalization? How did you and your parents and brothers cope with being continuously watched by the StB?

PD: Really? I didn't know about that. I attended that karate competition as a spectator, I did not participate in the competition. Our mother Anna and our grandmother Pavlina kept us together, protecting my father. They took care of us three brothers. Both of them were ill, but they did the best they could. We knew, of course, that the StB was following us. When the regime was coming apart, in the latter years of the 1980s, some of the StB agents complained to us about the regime. They thought their work was pointless. When I bought a new TV set, the man who had to put in the bugging device told me openly about it. My boss at the hospital, the *primator*, told me that he had to report my every move to the StB: with whom Dr Pavol Dubček went on holidays, whom he met, whom he talked to, since Dr Dubček was an enemy of the Socialist state.

JB: Why is your father so popular in Italy?

PD: I think it's because European Social Democracy was a movement my father admired. He met Willy Brandt and Olof Palme; they shared their experiences in politics.

JB: Why did you, as the son of Alexander Dubček, not go into politics?

PD: I am not important. Politics? Father took great risks, but somebody has to make the first step. He taught us a lot: he took us to other countries so that we could see how people lived, for example, to Kirghizstan and Africa. He taught us discipline and a sense for responsibility. We visited Tito in Brioni in the 1960s; I remember that the path to the Mediterranean was covered with carpets. I was a small boy and asked father: "Is Tito, a former partisan, afraid of stones?" Father told me: "Look, he is old; when he dies, there will be Civil War in Yugoslavia." Father admired Gandhi and kept to Gandhi's principle: what I think, I say, what I say, I do.

JB: My last question: what do you think about current Slovak politics?

PD: The citizens expected something completely different after 1989, from democracy. It is always easier to tear something down than to build something new.

JB: Dear Dr Dubček, I thank you very much for your time.

Oral History Interview with Professor Ivan Laluha

Bratislava, 21 July 2018, 1 pm to 3 pm. The interview was conducted in Slovak, English translation by me.

JB: Dear Professor Laluha, you have extensively published about Dubček and reform communism in Slovakia and Czechoslovakia. In 1968, you were a member of the KSS reform communists. Looking back to 1968 from today's perspective, were Dubček's reforms realistic in economic and political terms in the political context of the 1960s?

IL: We thought yes, because Stalinism, that is, the remainders of Stalinism in our country were blocking economic development. Our reforms provoked great interest also in other Socialist states, which quickly became a problem. For example, there was a saying in Poland: "Cała Polska czeka na swego Dubczeka (All Poland is waiting for its Dubček)." We saw also that our reforms were internationalizing, that the political process was going against the Kremlin's interests, but the situation was developing so fast, because the citizens were actively participating and we could not and did not want to stop them. Andrei P. Kirilenko, secretary of the Soviet Communist Party, said: the Czechoslovak action programme is the Czechoslovak virus. The USA was neutral, respecting Europe's partition, that is, the borders fixed after the end of WWII, which had determined our existence in the Soviet sphere. International relations and dependencies determined that our future fate would not be favourable for us.

We were quite naïve, we believed in the good of mankind and thought that if Czechoslovakia was doing well, other countries would see that reforms were the way to go. To him who is pure, everything is pure. Professor Kočtuch, who was against the occupation, used to reply to the question why the tanks came: "The reason is that in Czechoslovakia the sun was rising, while deep night ruled in the East."

Our reforms also awoke those citizens who had lost property in the collectivization and nationalization of the 1950s, that is, citizens with experience of private economy in their background. We had planned that, by 1972, the accomplishment of the first phase of the action programme, we could build a new constitution that would grant pluralism in society and politics, correcting the mistakes of the past. Brezhnev's argument was that we would open the doors to Capitalism. But it was not that simple. In eight months, you cannot predict everything. Our goal was the first phase of the action programme, to renew and build a democratic society. In a survey of 1968, 80% of the citizens preferred our Dubček Socialism to Capitalism.

JB: If it's not too personal a question: when the borders were open in 1968 and 1969, you had the possibility of emigrating to the West, like so many Czechs and Slovaks did. You are a historian and sociologist, thus an academically trained expert. What kept you in Czechoslovakia?

IL: You see, my wife, a dentist, and I are from Central Slovakia, from the Kremnica district. We were patriots, not nationalists, and we could not leave our country. My wife got an offer to join an elderly colleague who left for Switzerland; he wanted her to emigrate with him and join the practice he would open. She asked him what I, a professor of philosophy, would do in Switzerland. He told her that she would earn so much that I could stay at home with the children. Czechoslovakia was our home; we simply could not and would not leave.

JB: From one of your biographical texts about Dubček, I learned about the group or association *obroda (renaissance)*, founded in 1989 by former reform communists. I did not mention *obroda* in my text, because I considered it a detail of history that had no consequences for Slovakia's political development in the early 1990s. Could you explain to our readers the goals of *obroda*?

IL: *Obroda* was the association of former Party members who had been evicted in the Normalization years. And what united them was the wish to come back into politics. Our problem was that many members who had been humiliated for twenty years, wanted financial recompense and social rehabilitation. Their average age was 59. Also, the VPN's pressure on Dubček to found a political party was immense; but in the parliamentary elections of 1990, Dubček and I ran as candidates for VPN, since *obroda* was the VPN's smaller coalition partner.

Before 1989, Dubček and I used to meet in Horský Park on the outskirts of Bratislava. The bench we used to sit on now has a plate in memory of Dubček. Sitting on that bench, we drafted his speech to the University of Bologna. And he often told me: "Vanja (the Russian diminutive for Ivan, add. JB), the Social Democrats were right," (referring to the schism in the Russian Socialist Party in 1903 into Mensheviki and Bolsheviki; add. JB). In the spring of 1992, Dubček joined the Slovak Social Democrats and was the party's chairman until his tragic accident in September 1992.

Some Czech parliamentarians were speaking about *obroda* as a Fascist organisation that wanted to bring back Clerical Fascism to Slovakia. These persons wanted to spread fear among the citizens for their own political reasons and goals.

JB: You were very close to Alexander Dubček. The Party kicked both of you out – how did you deal with being a *persona non grata* for the Party, and how did Dubček deal with it? Was it a psychological problem for you, for Dubček?

IL: No, not for me. I thought if the Party does not want our reform course, then I have nothing in common with them any longer. We were beginning to think about Social Democracy. We did have problems in our lives after the Party had evicted us: the regime decided what school our children could go to. My children were allowed only to the economic university. They were not allowed to study international relations. We lived a simple life, but I was relieved; I had the distinct sense of a purified soul. I did not change my political opinion.

Dubček did not take the eviction as lightly as I did, because he had that distinct sense of responsibility and he had been at the top of our Czechoslovak reform politics; the loss of his Party membership was a personal trauma in the years after April 1969. But they did not break him.

To this day, I think that Dubček was a visionary: he foresaw that Socialism had to rid itself of dilettantism. Economics and politics should be separated, and only experts should steer the economy, not some Party functionaries who had neither education nor imagination. Thus, the origin of Dubček's reform course was not only his fight against Novotný, but much more: he wanted to make life better for all Czechoslovak citizens.

JB: My last question: what do you think about current Slovak politics?

IL: Today, it is clear to me that we wanted to find a third way, a new form of government that would unite the best aspects of Western Democracy and Eastern Socialism. This would mean:

parliamentary democracy and a state-guided economy, social security, a welfare state that allowed entrepreneurship and private economic activity. And many problems Slovakia has to deal with today are imported; their origins are not in Slovakia. The political problems of today are not new, they only appear to be new; basically they are old problems in a new design. Current Slovak politics thus are not original. They are a compromise between what we can do and what we have to do and that which is feasible in international relations. Current Slovak politics clearly lack a codex of political morality and persons embodying and realizing these values.

Dubček said in 1992 that "once the struggle of the East against the West is over (the end of the Cold War, add. JB), the struggle of the rich North against the poor South will begin. But we have to protect our blue planet". He was a decent person; he lived the way he thought. He anticipated the political problems of the 21st century.

JB: Dear Professor Laluha, thank you very much for your time.

Oral History Interview with Mr Miloslav Liška

Prague, 28 July 2018, 1 pm to 3 pm. The interview was conducted in Czech, English translation by me.

JB: Dear Miloslav, for many years you played rugby for Sparta Prague. Can you tell our readers why you engaged in sport?

ML: My decision to play sports had nothing to do with the political regime. I was young; all young people love sports. In Czechoslovakia, we had the idols Emil Zátopek, Jiří Skobla and Vladimír Zábrodský. I started to play ice hockey for Sparta Prague. When I was 16 or 17, I noticed that my talent was not sufficient to take me to the top, to the first league or the Czechoslovak national ice hockey team. In those years, in the late 1950s, we sportsmen used to have a second sport; in March, the ice hockey season was finished; so, in the summer, we played tennis or football. And 50% of Sparta's ice hockey players used to train in the summer with the Sparta Rugby team. Why change sports with the seasons? In 1961, we had only two ice hockey halls with a roof, in Štvanice and Holešovice, two districts of Prague.

    I did not want to do military service in the normal army, at the age of 19, so I joined the army sports team. Many Czechoslovak sportsmen tried to get into the army team *Dukla* or the police team *Ruda Hvězda* (Red Star), because these teams had excellent training facilities – and no drill like in the regular army. The outfits and gear were excellent, and we had two or three training sessions daily, for example: one session in the morning, one in the afternoon, and the third in the late afternoon, for example, strength training at a gym. In winter, we did cross-country skiing, and in summer, we went to recreation camps and lakes.

Those hockey players and athletes who were members of the army and police teams received financial support, which was not understood as salary, but as *odměna*, a kind of premium or bonus for a competition. The best players, the playmakers, also received financial bonuses for food, the so-called *kalorné odměna*. Since many citizens went to see football and ice hockey games, the organizers had money. The bonuses were, of course, never as high as in professional sports in the West, but in those years the bonuses were very nice to have and motivational.

JB: What were the training sessions like, let's say before an international tournament – how did you prepare with your team?

ML: We trained the entire week and went to competitions at the weekend. Two or three weeks before Olympic games, all sports teams underwent intensive training at the Nymburk sports centre; it had swimming baths, a sauna, good food and medical services. For the normal citizen, it was very complicated to get to the West, but sportsmen saw a different world and culture. We could buy nice gifts, dresses for the wife or jeans. Sportsmen bought foreign currency from the *vekslaki*, which was forbidden; some hid the *valuta* in their hockey sticks. If the border control found out, the team member was sent home immediately and kicked out of the team. When we passed the border to the West, we shouted hooray, we made it! To pass the Iron Curtain was a small sporting success and the dream of every young sportsman.

JB: How did you travel and with whom in the team? The Soviet teams always had a *politruk* (*političeskii rukovoditeľ*, political supervisor) with them, the Czechoslovak team too?

ML: We called that person the sharp little eye (*bystré očko*); of course, we knew that person's task. They were usually friendly and equally happy to get to the West. The Czechoslovak Association for Sports and Physical Education was a big organization; their functionaries or administrators were referred to as technical advisors. Their task was to monitor the sportsmen's behaviour abroad, making sure they did not get drunk or criticize the regime. The relatives of those sportsmen who stayed in the West faced problems. For example, the brother of ice hockey player František Tykal emigrated to Australia in 1948; Tykal was a playmaker. He was so good that they had to let him play in the West. A playmaker was a VIP.

JB: What changed in sports when Dubček became first secretary of the KSČ in January 1968?

ML: Nothing.

JB: Did the manifesto of the normalizers *Lessons learnt ...* of December 1970 affect sports and, if so, how?

ML: Some sportsmen emigrated; nobody expected that the occupation would last that long. Moscow decided about everything; the regime strangled all civil rights, took away our passports, dismissed professors at the universities and closed down newspapers and revues. If one co-operated and collaborated, one had advantages. Fear ruled in the country.

JB: How did Czechoslovak sport change after November 1989?

ML: This is not easy to answer. First, the borders opened, and many successful sportsmen and sportswomen emigrated, for example, ice hockey players, soccer players and athletes whom the Western coaches had scouted. They started to play for Western teams. The Canadian NHL was very methodical; they knew our players from the competitions and were very interested in signing contracts with them – and our players were of course happy – finally big money! Later, there was a problem, since the army and police clubs *Dukla* and *Rudá Hvězda* closed: the general level of sporting performance went down. This can be observed right up to the present day. In general, we can say that the majority of citizens and sportsmen and -women hoped the regime would end, because it was lawless, pseudo-Communist and inhuman, full of harassment.

Sportproprag was a large association that organized the Spartakiades and children's sports competitions. It was linked with the Institute of Prognostics; for example, President Zeman worked there. This association protected the intelligent people, the brains. They came up with major campaigns, for example Keep Fit! to keep the people under control.

JB: Dear Miloslav, thank you very much for your time.

Appendix

Dubček in Data

Education	Trained as metal worker (1938–1944)
	Studied Law in a writing course at Comenius University evening school, Bratislava (1952–1955), did not graduate
	Higher Political School of the Soviet Communist Party, Moscow (1955–1958)
Books, journalism, broadcasts	See bibliography in the appendix
Political Thought	Czechoslovak state theory (political Czechoslovakism)
	Marxism-Leninism; economic and social reform of Marxism-Leninism
	Western-type Social Democracy
Political regimes	Soviet Marxism-Leninism, 1925–1938
	Clerical Fascism in the Slovak State, 1939–1945
	Second Czechoslovak Republic, limited by the NF, 1945–1948
	Stalinist Czechoslovakia, 1948–1968
	Reform Communism, 1968
	Neo-Stalinism under the Normalization, 1969–1989
	Democratic Czechoslovakia, 1989–1992
Political Parties	Slovak Communist Party KSS: 1939–1969

	Czechoslovak Communist Party KSČ, 1968–1969
Political positions	Minister of Industry KSČ (1960–1962)
	First Secretary CC KSS (1963–1968)
	First Secretary CC KSČ (January 1968 – April 1969)
	Chairman of the Federal Assembly (April – December 1969)
	Czechoslovak ambassador to Turkey (December 1969– June 1970)
	Chairman of the ČSFR Federal Assembly for VPN (December 1990–June 1992)
	Delegate for the Slovak Social Democratic Party in the Federal Assembly (July – September 1992)
Wars, armed conflicts	WWII, 1939–1945, resistance activities as member of the illegal KSS in the SNP
Punishment for political activities	Expulsion from the KSČ (23 June 1970); from then on under constant surveillance by the StB until November 1989
Confession	Baptised Slovak Lutheran, atheist Marxist-Leninist

Chronology

1918, 28 October — The Slovak physician Vavro Šrobár (1867–1950), a member of the Agrarian Party, signs the Czechoslovak Declaration of Independence as representative of the SNR.

30 October — The Declaration of Martin, signed by all prominent Slovak politicians of the SNR, expresses the free will of the Slovaks to live in a common state with the Czechs, thereby announcing Slovak secession from the Hungarian Kingdom.

1919, 18 January — Šrobár declares Pressburg/Poszony the seat of the Czechoslovak government in Slovakia, the Slovak capital.

27 March — Pressburg/Poszony renamed Bratislava.

1921, 30 Oct–4 Nov — Foundation of the Czechoslovak Communist Party KSČ in Prague. Klement Gottwald (1896–1953) was Chairman, and Rudolf Slánský (1901–1952) First Secretary until his arrest in 1951.

27 November — Alexander Dubček born in Uhrovec, Central Slovakia, to Štefan Dubček (1891–1969) and Paulína Dubčeková, née Kobidová (1897–1972). Elder brother Július (1919–1944) was born in Chicago, IL, USA. Štefan, a carpenter, had emigrated to the USA in 1912, and Paulína, a cook and housemaid, in 1909. In early 1921, they returned to Czechoslovakia. Little Šaňo was born in a house that belonged to the Protestant Parish; Ľudovít Štúr (1815–

	1856), the father of the Slovak literary language, had been born there. His parents named their second son after the vicar Alexander Trancík, who had moved out to make room for the young family.
1924, 21 January	Death of Lenin (Vladimir Iliič Uľianov).
1925, 29 March	With the Socialist co-operative INTERHELPO, some 300 Czechoslovak citizens, among them the Dubčeks, leave for Pishpek, the capital of Soviet Kyrgyzia that would become the Soviet Republic of Kyrgyzstan in 1936.
24 April	The Dubčeks arrive with the first INTERHELPO group in Pishpek. Five more groups, in total 1078 persons, would arrive from 1925 to 1928. Among them, the Ondris family; little Sasha meets little Anna Ondrisová, whom he would marry in 1945.
1926	Pishpek renamed Frunze, after the commander of the Reed Army and hero of the Civil War Mikhail Vasilievich Frunze (1895–1925).
1929	Sasha begins his compulsory education (primary school) at the co-operative's own school in Frunze.
1930	Beginning of collectivization in Kyrgyzia.
1933	The Dubček family moves to Gorki (Nižnii Novgorod), where Alexander goes to high school. Father Štefan works in the Gorkiovski Avtozavod GAZ, an automobile plant that adopts the Ford Company's new industrial assembly line.

1935	Brother Július and mother Paulína return to Czechoslovakia and stay with relatives in Trenčín, because they anticipate difficulties with the Soviet authorities after Július hurts a boy in a street fight. Sasha and his father stay in Gorki.
18 December	Edvard Beneš (1884–1948) elected Czechoslovak president. The KSČ vote for him, forfeiting their usual opposition because of the threat of German National Socialism in the Sudetenland.
1936, 24 April	Antisemitic student rally in Bratislava, incited by radicals of the HSĽS. Catholic students protest against the film *Golem* and plunder Jewish shops.
1937, 14 September	Death of President Tomáš Garrigue Masaryk (1850–1937) in Lany Castle.
1938, 16 August	Death of Andrej Hlinka (1864–1938).
30 September	Munich agreement. ČSR loses the Sudetenland and Silesia to Germany. In October, President Beneš and the Czechoslovak government leave for London, where they establish the government in exile. Milan Hodža (1878–1944), Prime Minister from 1935 to 1938, leaves for France and later joins Beneš in London. Gottwald and Slánský leave for exile to Moscow.
6 October	Declaration of Slovakia's autonomy. HSĽS and the Hlinka Guards in power.
2 November	German-orchestrated Vienna Arbitrage (*Viedenská arbitráž*); ČSR loses territory in the south to Hungary.

	Alexander and his father return to Slovakia. Alexander finds employment as a metal worker in Dubnica nad Váhom in northwestern Slovakia.
1939, 9–10 March	Czechoslovak President Emil Hácha (1872–1945) orders the occupation of Slovakia, referred to as the Homola putsch (*Homolov puč*).
13 March	Slovak President Jozef Tiso (1887–1947) in Berlin; pressed into declaring Slovakia's sovereignty.
14 March	Tiso declares Slovakia's sovereignty in the Bratislava Parliament. Foundation of the KSS; after the Tiso government declares the Communist Party illegal, its members have to operate in the underground. All ties with the Czech Communists severed.
15 March	Hácha signs the Czech capitulation. German troops occupy the Czech lands, referred to as the protectorate (*Reichsprotektorat Böhmen und Mähren*).
18 March	Beginning of the expulsion of Czechs and their families from Slovakia.
23 March	In the Small War (*malá vojna*), Slovakia loses more territory in the southeast to Hungary.
29 March	The Tiso regime begins to deport oppositional Slovak citizens to Ilava prison in north-central Slovakia.
May	Alexander joins the newly founded, illegal KSS; together with his brother and mother engages in underground activities for the resistance. Father Štefan, a member of the

	KSS leadership, goes into hiding; end of the marriage to Paulína.
23 August	German-Soviet Non-Aggression Pact.
1 September	Beginning of WWII with the German attack on Poland.
1940, 22 June	German occupation of northern France. The Czechoslovak exile army in France is transferred to Great Britain.
Summer	Alexander and Anna meet again in Velcice, north east of Nitra and south of Trenčín. The Ondris and Dubček families renew their friendship dating from the years in Pishpek. The Ondris parents hide Alexander's father.
1941, 21 June	Operation Barbarossa: Nazi Germany attacks the Soviet Union.
9 September	Adoption of the 'Jewish Codex' in the Slovak constitution, infringing the Jews' civil and religious rights.
7 December	Japanese attack on Pearl Harbor. US President Franklin Delano Roosevelt (1882–1945) declares war on Japan and Germany.
1942, 15 May	Adoption of the constitutional law that deprives the Jews of their Slovak citizenship and legitimates their deportation to concentration camps in Poland and Germany. By October 1942, 60,000 Slovak Jews have been deported.
4 June	Czechoslovak officers Jozef Gabčik (1912–1942) and Jan Kubiš (1913–1942) shoot *Reichsprotektor* Reinhard Heydrich in Prague. The Germans take cruel revenge

	with the destruction of the villages Lidice and Ležaky.
1943, 12 December	Stalin (Josip Visarionovič Džugašvili, 1858–1953) and Beneš sign the Soviet-Czechoslovak Treaty of Alliance in Moscow. Christmas Agreement of the Slovak political parties and resistance groups, followed by the foundation of the SNR.
1944, 6 June	Allied landings in Normandy.
20 July	Failed attempt on Hitler's life by Wehrmacht officers.
29 August	German occupation of Slovakia, called in by the Tiso government. Start of the Slovak National Uprising (SNP) in Banská Bystrica. The Dubček brothers join partisan units; Július is killed, Alexander wounded twice.
27 October	Fall of Banská Bystrica, end of the uprising. Resistance activities of partisans in the mountains continue, awaiting the arrival of the Red Army.
1945, 20 January	Armistice Treaty of the Allies with Hungary.
February	The authorities of the Slovak state hand Štefan Dubček and other Slovak Communists over to the Germans; Štefan deported to the Mauthausen concentration camp. Alexander works in a factory that produces yeast in Trenčín.
4–11 February	Yalta Conference on Crimea. Roosevelt, Stalin and Churchill discuss the progress of the war and the post-war reconstruction of Europe.

22–29 March	Moscow negotiations, which led to the Košice Agreement (*Košický vládny program*). The negotiating parties are the members of the London exile government, Czech centre-right parties (*občiansky blok*), the SNR and the Communist exiles in Moscow, represented by Gottwald and Slánský. No direct intervention by Beneš and the Soviets.
5 April	Declaration of the Košice Agreement and the National Front (NF) as its executive on Czechoslovak liberate territory in Košice in eastern Slovakia.
8 May	Victory in Europe: Germany signs unconditional surrender.
9 May	Liberation of Prague by the Red Army.
10 May	Czechoslovak government moves to Prague.
2 June	First Agreement of Prague (*prvá Pražská dohoda*). The Slovaks' attempt to establish equal status with the Czechs in the common state fails.
26 June	Inaugural UN conference in San Francisco, USA; adoption of the UN Charter.
17–18 July	At the Party meeting in Prague, the KSČ and KSS formally united; the KSS is now subjected to the command of the KSČ, executing the KSČ's policy in Slovakia with no independent scope for decision-making. The KSS loses the autonomy it had during WWII. The Slovak Communists stand behind Gottwald, as the Party's main long-term goal is to assume power.

17 July–2 August	Potsdam conference of the Big Three (USA, GB and SSSR). They agree to create the Interallied Council that will coordinate the administration of the four occupation zones. The International War Crimes Tribunal is to organize the Nuremberg trials.
2 August	President Beneš issues constitutional decree no. 33/1945 about the abolition of Czechoslovak citizenship of Germans and Magyars, giving the *odsun* (expulsion) of both minorities legal validity.
15 September	Alexander Dubček and Anna Ondrisová marry at the Protestant church in Velcice. Dubček's best man is Alexander Trančík, his godfather.
1946, 27 February	ČSR and Hungary sign the Treaty on the Transfer of Population (*Dohoda medzi ČSR a Maďarskom o výmene obyvateľstva*) in Budapest. Hungary tries to prevent the transfer with various interventions at the UN, protracting the population exchange until 1949.
11 April	Second Agreement of Prague. Slovaks again unsuccessful.
26 May	First post-war parliamentary elections to the Constitutional Assembly. In Slovakia, DS wins 62% of the vote, KSS 30% and SSl 3.73%. In the Czech part, the KSČ wins a majority with 41% of the vote.
2 July	President Beneš appoints Gottwald Prime Minister.

27 July	Third Agreement of Prague. Slovak failure.
29 July – 5 October	Peace Conference in Paris, which leads to the peace treaties signed on 5 February 1947.
20 November	Start of the Nuremberg trials.
1947, 10 February	Twelve states, including Czechoslovakia, sign a peace treaty with Hungary in Paris. The Vienna Arbitrage is declared invalid and the borders restored to the *status quo ante*.
25 February	Great Britain turns the Palestine issue over to the UN. The General Assembly adopt resolution 181 III that leads to the partition of Palestine into an independent Jewish state and an independent Arab state.
5 June	US Secretary of State George C. Marshall (1880–1959) announces his plan for Europe's economic recovery and US humanitarian assistance in his speech at Harvard University.
4 July	ČSR receives an official invitation to the conference on the Marshall Plan.
7 July	Foreign Minister Jan Masaryk (1886–1948) instructs the Czechoslovak ambassador in Paris to attend the preparations for the conference on the Marshall Plan.
9 July	Foreign Minister Masaryk, Premier Gottwald and Prokop Drtina (1900–1980), a centre-right politician, negotiate with Stalin in Moscow about Czechoslovakia's participation in the Marshall Plan. Stalin

	presses them into revoking their delegation in Paris.
22–27 September	Delegates of the Communist Parties from the Soviet Union, Eastern Europe, France and Italy found the Cominform (Communist Information Bureau, *Informbyro*) in Belgrade, Yugoslavia, an organization whose objective is to coordinate the Communist Parties in Europe.
17–18 November	Dress rehearsal for the coup d'état: the pressure of the KSS in Slovakia forces three DS *poverénici* (government trustees with executive power) to resign. Gustáv Husák (1913–1991) establishes KSS control in Slovakia.
1948, 10 February	Yugoslav-Soviet negotiations in Moscow, followed by the expulsion of Yugoslavia from the Cominform on 29 June, which provides the pretext for the show trials of the 1950s in the bloc states.
25 February	President Beneš dissolves the democratically elected government and appoints a new government according to Gottwald's suggestions. The KSČ in control of the country, referred to in Marxist-Leninist literature as the 'victorious 25 February'.
10 March	Mysterious death of Jan Masaryk, found dead in the courtyard of the Czernín Palace, the building of the Foreign Ministry in the Prague Castle district.
14 May	Declaration of Independence of the State of Israel; David Ben-Gurion (1886–1973) elected Israel's first Prime Minister. On

	the next day, Arab armies from Egypt, Iraq, Jordan, Lebanon and Syria invade, as the British mandate ends; beginning of the War of Independence, which Israel wins thanks to the Czechoslovak-Jewish arms deals (1946–1948). Because of the international boycott, none of the victorious allies had been able to sell weapons to the Jishuv prior to the foundation of Israel. Stalin had thus commanded Czechoslovakia to act as proxy: Foreign Minister Masaryk and Assistant Secretary of State Clementis concluded arms deals with the Jewish Agency, selling aircraft, weapons and ammunition to the Jewish part of Palestine.
24 June	Berlin Airlift as reaction of the Western Allies to the Soviet Union's blockade of Berlin. Until the end of 1949, the USA, GB and France fly supplies into West Berlin, demonstrating that they would not give up on the Western zone of the divided city.
3 September	Edvard Beneš dies in Sezimovo Ústi; state funeral in Prague on 8 September.
31 December	Formal end of the population transfer between ČSR and Hungary.
1949	Start of Dubček's career in the Party.
5–8 January	Foundation of the COMECON (RVHP) in Moscow.
4 April	Foundation of NATO in Washington, DC.
16 April	ČSR and Hungary signs a Treaty on Friendship, Co-operation and Mutual Assistance in Budapest. The treaty signals

	the Normalization of relations between the two states.
11 May	Israel becomes a member of the UN after her victory in the War of Independence.
24 September	The People's Court in Budapest condemns former Foreign Minister László Rajk to death for Titoism, high treason and conspiracy with the Imperialist West.
15 October	László Rajk executed in Budapest.
16 December	Traicho Kostov executed for Titoism and espionage in Sofia, Bulgaria.
1950	Yugoslavia elected a non-permanent member of the UN Security Council
31 May–8 June	First Stalinist show trial of Milada Horáková (1901–1950) and co-accused in Prague. The four centre-right politicians are sentenced to death for espionage, conspiracy with the Imperialist West and high treason; they are executed on 27 June.
1951	Dubček elected delegate for the KSS to the National Assembly in Prague.
1952, 20 Nov	Show trial of Slánský, Clementis and co-accused starts. They are accused of Titoism, Zionism, conspiracy against the state and collaboration with Western Imperialism. The trial concludes on 27 November. President Gottwald confirms the death sentences on 2 December.
3 December	Eleven accused, among them Slánský and Clementis, are executed by hanging. Their bodies are burnt and the ashes dispersed in the countryside close to Ruzyně prison.
1953, 5 March	Death of Stalin.

14 March	Gottwald follows; he dies of a cold caught at Stalin's funeral in Moscow. The CC KSČ elect Viliam Široký (1902–1971) Prime Minister and Antonín Zápotocký (1884–1957) President.
1954, 17 April	Lucrețiu Pătrășcanu executed in Bucarest.
21–24 April	Trial of the 'Slovak bourgeois nationalists' in Bratislava. Husák, Daniel Okali, Laco Holdoš and Ivan Horváth receive long prison sentences.
1955	Dubček in the sixth semester of external law studies at Comenius University in Bratislava; he does not finish his studies. The Party send him to the Higher Political School in Moscow.
14 May	Foundation of the Warsaw Pact in Warsaw, Poland.
1956, 14–25 Feb	At the 20th Congress of the Soviet Communist Party in Moscow, Khrushchev reveals Stalin's crimes and criticizes the personality cult. Beginning of the Thaw.
1958	Dubček graduates from the Higher Political School in Moscow and returns to Slovakia.
16–18 May	At the KSS meeting chaired by Karol Bacílek (1896–1974), Dubček is appointed candidate for the bureau of the CC KSS.
1960, 9 May	On the occasion of the 15th anniversary of Czechoslovakia's liberation, President Novotný announces a general amnesty. 5601 prisoners are released, among them Husák and Novomeský. Dubček is re-elected KSS delegate to the National

	Assembly in Prague. The CC KSČ appoints him Secretary for Industry.
1961, 28 April	Soviet cosmonaut Iurii A. Gagarin (1934–1968), the first man in space, visits Czechoslovakia.
31 May	On his way to meet US President John F. Kennedy (1917–1963) in Vienna, Krushhcev passes through Slovakia by train. The citizens give him an enthusiastic welcome.
1962, 1 June	CC KSS and CC KSČ rename the highest mountain in the High Tatra; Stalin's Shield (*Stalinový štít*) becomes Gerlach Shield (*Gerlachov štít*), a sign of late de-Stalinization.
24–25 November	Dubček elected member of the CC KSS.
1963, January	The Slovak weekly *Život* (*Life*) publishes the first part of Aleksandr Isaievič Solženicin's (1918–2008) *One Day in the Life of Ivan Denisovič* (1962) in Slovak translation. The novel addresses the horrors of the Soviet Gulag.
March	Party member and Slovak historian Miloš Gosiorovský (1920–1978) sends his study about the relations between Slovaks and Czechs to top Party members and institutions. The official political institutions sharply reject his study, which proposes the creation of a federation.
8 April	The CC KSS elect Alexander Dubček First Secretary.
22 April	At the Third Congress of the Slovak Writers' Union, Novomeský and others

	criticize the findings of the Kolder Commission for not fully rehabilitating former Foreign Minister Clementis and the comrades imprisoned for 'Slovak bourgeois nationalism'.
1 May	Open letter from Husák to the CC KSS, demanding full political rehabilitation and renewal of Party membership. The letter circulates in *samizdat*, informing the citizens what the accused 'bourgeois nationalists' had to endure in the interrogations and in prison. It also reveals the half-hearted rehabilitation based on the findings of the Kolder commission. Husák's letter prompts a second commission, the Barnabite Commission, of which Dubček is a member.
29–30 May	At the meeting of the CC KSČ, new views about the country's economic policy emerge. Start of the planning of the economic reforms, headed by professor of economics Ota Šik (1919–2004).
19 August	Soviet cosmonaut Valentina V. Tereshkova (*1937), the first woman in space, visits Bratislava.
18–19 December	At the meeting of the CC KSČ, the Slovaks Clementis, Holdoš, Husák, Novomeský and Šmidke, accused of 'bourgeois nationalism' are rehabilitated as citizens, but not in political terms. The Barnabite Commission admits that the accusation was contrived, but the political future of the accused, their return to the Party, remains unclear.

1964

14–15 March	At the Bratislava Party meeting, Husák sharply criticizes the KSS for not seeking justice for the persecuted in the 1950s. His speech preserves his Party membership and enables him to relaunch his political career.
14 October	Leonid I. Brezhnev (1906–1982) elected new General Secretary of the Soviet Communist Party; the CC KSSS dismisses Khrushchev for his 'liberalism'.
1965, 24 January	Death of Sir Winston Churchill in London.
1966, 19 February	Havel's play *Vyrozumění* (*Notification*) premiered at the Bratislava state theatre Malá scéna.
28 March	The Czechoslovak film *Obchod na korze* (*The Shop on Main Street*) by director Ján Kadár and screenwriter Elmar Klos wins the Oscar for best foreign film.
1967, 4–6 February	On their state visit to Prague, Brezhnev and KGB boss Iurii V. Andropov (1914–1984) suggest to President Novotný that two Soviet divisions be stationed at the Czechoslovak-German border. Novotný declines.
26–27 June	At the Prague meeting of the Czechoslovak Writers' Union (*Svaz československých spisovatelů*), Czech authors harshly criticize the government for its failure to initiate reforms. The young Václav Havel criticizes the Writers' Union for its political meekness.

26–27 August	President Novotný's infamous visit to Martin: he offends the CC KSS and the Slovak nation during what should have been festivities in honour of the 100th anniversary of the foundation of the first Slovak high school.
26–27 September, 30–31 October	Dubček attacks Novotný at two meetings of the CC KSČ, reproaching him for his intransigence in questions of economic and social reforms.
8–9 December	After repeated invitations, Soviet General Secretary Brezhnev comes to Prague, but refuses to meddle in the KSČ's internal affairs, for which Novotný had hoped to gain his support against Dubček and the modernists.
1968, 5 January	After months of struggling against Novotný and his conservative adherents, the reform-minded majority of the CC KSČ elect Dubček First Secretary. Beginning of the Czechoslovak Spring.
10 August	The KSČ publishes its plans for the federalization of the Party: the KSČ is to rule in the Czech lands, the KSS in Slovakia. Both Parties would be independent and have their own institutions and executive and legislative powers.
21 August	Invasion of Warsaw Pact armies; the troops of the GDR, Soviet Union, Hungary, Bulgaria and Poland occupy strategically important cities and towns in Czechoslovakia. After six months, all troops save for

	the Soviet troops, leave; Czechoslovakia remains a country under Soviet occupation until 1990.
1969, 17 April	Dubček forced to step down. 'Elected' Chairman of the Federal Assembly.
16 Dec–24 June	Dubček appointed acting Czechoslovak ambassador to Turkey.
1970, 25–26 June	The KSČ relieve Dubček of all his Party and state functions. Banned from political life, Dubček finds work as a mechanic at the Western Slovak state forestry service. Start of his open resistance and criticism of the Normalization.
December	Publication of the document that renders the Normalization legitimate: *Lessons Learned from the Critical Developments in Party and State Following the 13th Congress of the KSČ* (*Poučenie z krízového vývoja v strane a spoločnosti po XIII. zjazde KSČ*).
1981	Dubček retires from his post at the state forestry service. From 1970 to 1989, he writes some twenty protest letters to the government and political institutions. The StB keep him and his family under close surveillance.
1988, 13 November	The University of Bologna, Italy, awards him an honorary doctorate (*doctor honoris causa*). He is allowed to travel to Bologna to receive the doctorate.
1989, January	After Václav Havel's arrest and imprisonment, Dubček writes a letter of protest to

	General Secretary Miloš Jakeš and President Gustáv Husák.
April	He visits Havel, released in April, at his home in Prague.
August	Signs a letter of protest in support of the Bratislava Five and attends their trial.
17 November	Dubček participates in the mass demonstration in Prague that brings down the Communist government.
28 November	Elected chairman of the Federal Assembly.
1990–1991	Awarded honorary doctorates by Comenius University, Bratislava; Universidad Complutense de Madrid; The American University, Washington; Université Libre de Bruxelles; University of Dublin, Trinity College.
1992	Elected chairman of the newly founded Slovak Social Democratic Party.
1 September	Car accident while on his way to Prague.
7 November	Dubček dies in a Prague hospital of the consequences of the car accident. Rumours circulate that he has been murdered because he was an ardent opponent of the division of Czechoslovakia.
14 November	State funeral at the Slávičie údoli cemetery in Bratislava.

Bibliography

Archival sources

ABS ÚSTRČR, 812702-MV_72_78_0007-1.jpg
ABS ÚSTRČR, 812702-MV_72_78_0007-2.jpg
ABS ÚSTRČR, 812702-MV-72-78-0047-1.jpg, 0047-2.jpg
ABS ÚSTRČR, SL_3110_MV_KATALYZATOR_1_001_0020.jpg
ABS ÚSTRČR, SL_3110_MV_KATALYZATOR_1_001_0042.jpg
ABS ÚSTRČR, carton 80410_300
ABS ÚSTRČR, SL_3110_MV_KATALYZATOR_1_001_0005.jpg
ABS ÚSTRČR, SL_5140_MV_Pavel_2_001_0002.jpg
ABS ÚSTRČR, SL_5140_MV_Pavel_2_001_0010.jpg
ABS ÚSTRČR, SL_5140_MV_Pavel_2_001_0017.jpg
ABS ÚSTRČR, X_008_0041.jpg
AMSNP. "Spomienky Š. Dubčeka", Fond XII, 16 pages, typewritten, undated.
SNA Bratislava, Fond ÚV KSS, tájomniki 1963–1968, A. Dubček, carton 2395, file 113, typewritten, 51 pages.
"Individuálny posudok". SNA, Fond ÚV KSS, tájomniki 1963–1968, A. Dubček, carton 2395, file 113", typewritten, 1 page, dated 10 July 1953.
"Informácia". SNA, Fond ÚV KSS, tájomniki 1963–1968, A. Dubček, carton 2380, typewritten, 3 pages.
"Letter from Alexander Dubček to Ladislav Novák". SNA, Fond ÚV KSS, tájomniki 1963–1968, A. Dubček, carton 2393, typewritten, 2 pages.
"Lukáč Vincent, Bratislava, Ružová dolina č. 22". SNA, Fond ÚV KSS, tájomniki 1963–1968, A. Dubček, carton 2395, file 113, typewritten, 2 pages.
"Mikuláš Rudolf, Topoľčany". SNA, Fond ÚV KSS, tájomniki 1963–1968, A. Dubček, carton 2395, file 113, typewritten, 2 pages, dated 8 October 1965, signed by Rudolf Mikuláš.
"Odpis". SNA Bratislava, Fond ÚV KSS, tájomniki 1963–1968, A. Dubček, carton 2393, typewritten, 3 pages, dated 24 May 1966, signed by Boďa.

"Opis!" SNA Bratislava, Fond ÚV KSS, tájomniki 1963-1968, A. Dubček, carton 2393, typewritten, 2 pages.

"Opis". SNA, Fond ÚV KSS, tájomniki 1963-1968, A. Dubček, carton 2395, file 113, typewritten, 5 pages, dated 14 March 1966.

"Pervomu sekretariu TSK KPS tov. A. Dubčeku". SNA, Fond ÚV KSS, tájomniki 1963-1968, A. Dubček, carton 2393, typewritten, 1 page, dated 21 June 1963, in Russian Cyrillic, signed by Soviet General Consul I. Šuľgin.

"Příspěvek do diskuse na teze k XIII. sjezdu KSČ". SNA, Fond ÚV KSS, tájomniki 1963-1968, A. Dubček, carton 2391, typewritten, 10 pages.

"Sudruh Novotný". SNA, Fond ÚV KSS, tájomniki 1963-1968, A. Dubček, carton 2395, file 113, typewritten, 1 page, dated 28 February 1966.

"Usnesení 33. schůze předsednictva ÚV KSČ ze dne 13. srpna 1963". SNA, Fond ÚV KSS, tájomniki 1963-1968, A. Dubček, carton 2380, typewritten, 9 pages.

"Usnesení 39. schůze sekretariátu ÚV KSČ ze dne 19. února 1964, k bodu: 11) Články s. dr. Vladimíra Maňáka, CSc. (s. J. Valenta)". SNA, Fond ÚV KSS tájomniki 1963-1968, A. Dubček, carton 2384, typewritten, 4 pages.

"Usnesení 44. schůze sekretariátu ÚV KSČ ze dne 20. května 1964, k bodu: 3) Usnesení sekretariátu ÚV KSČ k posílení a prohloubení ideologické jednoty strany (s. J. Hes)". SNA, Fond ÚV KSS, tájomniki 1963-1968, A. Dubček, 1963-1968, carton 2384, typewritten, 13 pages.

"Usnesení sekretariátu ÚV KSČ, schválené per rollam dne 16. 11. 1964, k bodu: Uspořádání XI. mezinárodního zimního setkani novinářů v Československé socialistické republice (s. J. Hes, s. O. Kaderka)". SNA, Fond ÚV KSS, tájomniki, A. Dubček, 1963-1968, carton 2384, typewritten, 3 pages, dated 16 November 1964.

"Usnesení sekretariátu UV KSČ, schválené per rollam dne 29. října 1964, k bodu: Zajištění publicity volby presidenta Československé socialistické republiky (s. J. Hes)". SNA, Fond ÚV KSS, tájomniki 1963-1968, A. Dubček, carton 2384, typewritten, 3 pages, dated 3 November 1964.

"Vážený Generálny konzulát SSSR, Bratislava". SNA, Fond ÚV KSS, tájomniki 1963-1968, A. Dubček, carton 2393, typewritten, 1 page, dated 18 June 1963, signed by V. M. and R. K.

"Vážený súdruh prezidente!" SNA, Fond ÚV KSS, tájomniki 1963-1968, A. Dubček, carton 2393, typewritten, 2 pages, dated 18 June 1963.

"Vyjadrenie k šetreniu okolo s. Dubčeka a s. Dubčekovej". SNA, Fond ÚV KSS, tájomniki 1963-1968, A. Dubček, carton 2395, file 113, typewritten, 6 pages, signature not readable, dated 12 March 1966.

"Zpráva o výsledcích šetřenístižnosti soudruha Alexandra DUBČEKA, prvního tajemníka ÚV KSS a člena předsednictva ústředního výboru KSČ". SNA Bratislava, Fond ÚV KSS, tájomniki 1963-1968, A. Dubček, carton 2395, file 113, typewritten, 5 pages, dated 4 January 1967.

Texts by Alexander Dubček

"1963, 8. Apríl, Bratislava, Prejav Alexandra Dubčeka na zasadaní ÚV KSS o výsledkoch činnosti tzv. Kolderovej rehabilitačnej komisie". In *Alexander Dubček: Od totality k demokracii. Prejavy, články a rozhovory. Výber 1963-1992*. Bratislava: Veda, 2002.

"1973, 6. Január, Bratislava, List ministerstvu vnútra, Hlavej správe štatnej bezpečnosti a Inšpekcii MV SSR a Krajskej správe Zboru národnej bezpečnosti Bratislava (Zaslaný doporučene generálnej prokuratúre SSR) o prenasledovaní Alexandra Dubčeka, jeho rodiny a o obmedzovaní občianskych práv a slobôd". In *Alexander Dubček: Od totality k demokracii. Prejavy, články a rozhovory. Výber 1963-1992*. Bratislava: Veda, 2002.

"1989, 16. Október, Bratislava, Otvorený list Miroslavovi Štěpanovi, členovi predsednictva ÚV KSČ". In *Alexander Dubček: Od totality k demokracii. Prejavy, články a rozhovory. Výber 1963-1992*. Bratislava: Veda, 2002.

"1989, 23. November, Bratislava, Prejav na zhromaždení občanov na Námestí Slovenského národného povstania v Bratislave". In *Alexander Dubček: Od totality k demokracii. Prejavy, články a rozhovory. Výber 1963-1992*. Bratislava: Veda, 2002.

"1990, 25. Máj, Bratislava, Príhovor k voličom pred prvými slobodnými voľbami". In *Alexander Dubček: Od totality k demokracii. Prejavy, články a rozhovory. Výber 1963-1992*. Bratislava: Veda, 2002.

"1991, 29. Júl, Bratislava-Praha, Rozhovor pre ČSTK pod názvom 'Neprezliekam kabát' – o útokoch českej pravice (ODS) na jeho osobu, o podpore federálnej vláde a o odmietnutí zriadenia domobrany".

In *Alexander Dubček: Od totality k demokracii. Prejavy, články a rozhovory. Výber 1963–1992.* Bratislava: Veda, 2002.

"Důkaz moudrosti a vyspělosti občanů republiky". *Rudé Právo*, no. 207, 28 July 1968, 1.

"Zostaneme verní". *Hlas ľudu VI*, no. 34, 26 August 1959, 1–2.

Hope Dies Last. The Autobiography of Alexander Dubcek. London: HarperCollins, 1993.

Leben für die Freiheit. München: Bertelsmann, 1993.

Dubček's Blueprint for Freedom. His Documents on Czechoslovakia Leading to the Soviet Invasion. London: William Kimber, 1969.

Scholarly literature

1948. Únor 1948 v Československu: Nástup komunistické totality a proměny společnosti. Praha: Ústav pro soudobé dějiny AV ČR, v.v.i., 2011.

Ash, Timothy, Garton. "Mitteleuropa?" *Daedalus 119*, no. 1 (1990): 1–21.

Baer, Josette. *'Spirits that I've cited?' Vladimír Clementis (1902–1952). The Political Biography of a Czechoslovak Communist.* Stuttgart, New York: ibidem, Columbia University Press, 2017.

Baer, Josette. "A Man Motivated by Power". *New Eastern Europe 4*, no. 5 (2014): 156–160.

Baer, Josette. "Chaviva Reiková (1914–1944) – a Jewish resistance fighter." In S*even Slovak Women*. Stuttgart, New York: ibidem, Columbia University Press, 2015.

Baer, Josette. "*The Czech Fate (Český úděl)* debate". In *Preparing Liberty in Central Europe. Political Texts from the Spring of Nations 1848 to the Spring of Prague 1968*. Stuttgart: ibidem, 2006.

Baer, Josette. "The Genesis of Czechoslovakism. An Interdisciplinary Inquiry into the Influence of Rousseau's Réligion Civile". In *East European Faces of Law and Society: Values and Practices.* Leiden: Brill Nijhoff, 2014.

Baer, Josette. "Thomas G. Masaryk and Svetozár Hurban Vajanský. A Czecho-Slovak friendship?" *KOSMAS. Czechoslovak and Central European Journal 26*, no. 2 (2013): 50–62.

Baer, Josette. "Vertrauen ist nichts, Macht ist alles. Gustáv Husák (1913–1991) und die tschechoslowakische Normalisierung.

Versuch eines politischen Psychogramms". In *Vertrauen*. Basel: Schwabe, 2015.

Baer, Josette. *A Life Dedicated to the Republic. Vavro Šrobár's Slovak Czechoslovakism*. Stuttgart, New York: ibidem, Columbia University Press, 2014.

Baer, Josette. *Politik als praktizierte Sittlichkeit. Zum Demokratiebegriff von Thomas G. Masaryk und Václav Havel*. Sinzheim: Pro Universitate, 1998.

Baer, Josette. *Revolution, Modus Vivendy or Sovereignty? The Political Thought of the Slovak National Movement from 1861 to 1914*. Stuttgart: ibidem, 2010.

Baer, Josette. *Seven Czech Women. Portraits of Courage, Humanism and Enlightenment*. Stuttgart, New York: ibidem, Columbia University Press, 2015.

Baer, Josette. *Slavic Thinkers or The Creation of Polities. Intellectual History and Political Thought in Central Europe and the Balkans in the 19th Century*. Stuttgart: ibidem, 2007.

Banáš, Jozef. *Zastavte Dubčeka! Príbeh človeka, ktorý prekážal mocným*. Bratislava: Ikar, 2009.

Bárta, Milan, Jiří Bašta, Jan Kalous, Jan Pešek, Branislav Kinčok, a Jiří Pernes. Contributions to the chapter "Na cestě k moci a ovládnutí státu". In *Český a slovenský komunismus (1921–2011)*. Praha: Ústav pro stadium totalitních režimů, 2012.

Bartlová, Alena. "Posledné parlamentné voľby v máj 1935". In *V medzivojnovom Československu 1918–1939*. Bratislava: Veda, 2012.

Batscha, Zwi. *Eine Philosophie der Demokratie. Thomas G. Masaryks Begründung einer neuzeitlichen Demokratie*. Frankfurt a. Main: Suhrkamp, 1994.

Bažantová, Ilona. "Zapomenutý ekonom Karel Havlíček Borovský". *Politická Ekonomie 5*, no. 2 (1999): 621–629.

Bělohradský, Václav. *Krize eschatology neosobnosti*. London: Rozmluvy, 1983.

Beneš, Edvard. *Paměti II. Od Mnichova k nové válce a k novému vítězství*. Praha: Academia, 2008.

Berlin, Isaiah. *Karl Marx*. Princeton, NJ: Princeton University Press, 2013 (5).

Borák, Mečislav. *České stopy v gulagu*. Opava: Slezské zemské muzeum, 2003.

Brabec, Jiří, Jan Lopatka, Jiří Gruša, Petr Kabeš a Igor Hájek. *Slovník zakázaných autorů 1948–1980*. Praha: Státní pedagogické nakladatelství, 1991.

Březina, Miloš. *Interhelpo. Pomoc Československých dělníků při modernizaci Sovětského Kyrgyzstánu*. Pardubice: Univerzita Pardubice, 2008.

Bystrický, Valerián, a kol. *Rok 1968 na Slovensku a v Československu*. Bratislava: HÚ SAV, 2008.

Bystrický, Valerián, Miroslav Michela, Michal Schwarc a kol. *Rozbitie alebo rozpad? Historické reflexive zániku Česko-Slovenska*. Bratislava: VEDA, 2010.

Bystrický, Valerián, Jaroslava Roguľová a kol. *Storočie procesov. Súdy, politika a spoločnosť v moderných dejinách Slovenska*. Bratislava: Veda, 2013.

Bystrický, Valerián, a Jaroslava Roguľová, eds. *Storočie škandálov. Aféry v moderných dejinách Slovenska*. Bratislava: Spoločnosť Pro Historia, HÚ SAV, 2008.

Cartledge, Bryan. *The Will to Survive*. London: C. Hurst & Co, 2011.

Černý, František. *Normalizace na Pražské Filosofické fakultě (1968–1989). Vzpomínky*. Praha: Mnemosyne, Filosofická Fakulta Univerzity Karlova, 2009.

Charta 77. 1977–1989. Od morální k demokratické revoluci. Dokumentace. Bratislava: Archa, Čs. středisko nezávislé literatury, Scheinfeld-Schwarzenberg, 1990.

Charta Story. Přiběhy Charty 77. The Story of Charter 77. Praha: Národní galerie v Praze, 2017.

Cholinský, Jan. "České undergroundové hnutí optikou historiografie – mýty a realita". In *Reflexe Undergroundu*. Praha: Ústav pro stadium totalitních režimů, 2016.

Conversations with Gorbachev. On perestroika, socialism, the Prague Spring and the crossroads of socialism. New York: Columbia University Press, 2002.

Courtois, Stéphane, Nicolas Werth, Jean-Louis Panné, Andrzej Paczkowski, Karel Bartošek and Jean-Louis Margolin. *The Black Book of Communism. Crimes. Terror. Repression*. Cambridge, MA, London: Harvard University Press, 1999.

Cséfalvay, František, a Ľubica Kázmerová. *Slovenská republika 1939–1945. Chronológia najdôležitejších udalosti*. Bratislava: HÚ SAV, 2007.

Dalos, György. *Der Gast aus der Zukunft. Anna Achmatova und Sir Isaiah Berlin. Eine Liebesgeschichte*. Hamburg: Europäische Verlagsanstalt, 1997 (2).

Dangl, Vojtech, Valerián Bystrický a kol. *Chronológia Dejín Slovenska a Slovákov. Od najstarších čias po súčasnosť. Dejiny v dátumoch, dátumy v dejinách, vol I a II*. Bratislava: Veda, 2014.

Dubova, Alice. "War experiences with Slovakian partisans (1958)". Yad Vashem Archives, Israel, Wiener Library Collection, record group 0.2, file no. 668, 14 pages.

Fano, Š. "Internacionálna pomoc československého proletariátu mladému sovietskemu štátu pri obnove národného hospodárstva". *Slovanské štúdie 1*, (1983): 56–70.

Franc, Martin, a Jiří Knapík. *Volný čas v českých zemích 1957–1967*. Praha: Academia, 2013.

Funda, Otakar. *Thomas Garrigue Masaryk. Sein philosophisches, religiöses und politisches Denken*. Bern: Peter Lang, 1978.

Furet, François. *The Passing of an Illusion. The Idea of Communism in the Twentieth Century*. Chicago, London: The University of Chicago Press, 1999.

Galandauer, Jan. *Vznik Československé Republiky 1918*. Praha: Svoboda, 1988.

Getty, J., Arch, and Oleg V. Naumov, with the assistance of Nadezhda V. Muraveva. *Yezhov. The Rise of Stalin's "Iron Fist"*. New Haven, London: Yale University Press, 2008.

Goněc, Vladimír. "Z exilových diskusi 80. let: pojem střední Evropy". In *Česko-Slovenská historická ročenka 2012. Češi a Slováci 1993–2012*. Bratislava: Veda, 2012.

Gorbačov, Michail, a Zdeněk Mlynář. *Reformátoři nebývají šťastni. Dialog o „perestrojce", Pražském jaru a socialism*. Praha: Victoria Publishing, 1994.

Grigar, Michail. *Žizň dlja radosti*. Moskva: Gosudarstvenoie izdatelstvo političeskoi literatury, 1962.

Guelton, Fréderic, Emanuelle Braud a Michal Kšiňan. *Milan Rastislav Štefánik v archívnich dokumentov Historickej služby francúzskeho ministerstva obrany*. Paris, Bratislava: service historique de la Défense, Vojenský historický ústav, Ministerstvo obrany SR, 2008, 2009.

Halaj, Dušan, ed., *Fašistické represálie na Slovensku*. Bratislava, 1990.

Hain, Radan. *Staatstheorie und Staatsrecht in T. G. Masaryks Ideenwelt*. Zürich: Schulthess, 1999.

Hanák, Harry, ed. *T. G. Masaryk (1850–1937). Statesman and Cultural Force*. Basingstoke: MacMillan, SSEES, University of London, 1990.

Harding, Neil. *Leninism*. London: MacMillan, 1996.

Havel, Václav. *Fernverhör. Ein Gespräch mit Karel Hvížďala*. Hamburg: rororo, 1990.

Havel, Václav. "Milý pane Ludvíku (25 leden 1979)". In *O lidskou identitu. Úvahy, fejetony, protesty, polemiky, prohlášení a rozhovory z let 1969–1979*. Praha: Rozmluvy, 1990.

Heller, Joseph. *Catch-22*. New York: Vintage, 1994.

Hill, Peter, Thomas. "Prague 1968". In *The Dictionary of Hidden Meaning*. Work in progress, Zurich 2018.

Hlaváčková, Konstantína. *Móda za železnou oponou. Společnost, oděvy a lidé v Československu 1948–1989*. Praha: Grada Publishing, Uměleckoprůmyslové museum v Praze, 2016.

Hlavsa, Mejla, a Jan Pelc. *Bez ohňu je underground*. Praha: BFS, 1992

Hoensch, Jörg, K. *Geschichte der Tschechoslowakei*. Stuttgart, Berlin, Köln: Kohlhammer, 1992 (3).

Hoffmann, Roland, J. *Thomas G. Masaryk und die tschechische Frage*. München: Oldenbourg, 1988.

Holubec, Stanislav. "Léta 1948–1949". In *Ještě nejsme za vodou. Obrazy druhých a historická paměť v období postkomunistické transformace*. Praha: Scriptorium, 2015.

Hronský, Márian, a Miroslav Pekník. *Martinská deklarácia. Cesta slovenskej politiky k vzniku Česko-Slovenska*. Bratislava: Veda, 2008.

Hubenák, Ladislav. *U pramenů přátelství: k 60. výročí Interhelpa*. Praha: Lidové nakladatelství, 1984.

Husák, Gustáv. "Barnabitky a čo im predchádzalo". *Nové slovo*, 20 June 1968, no. 5, p. 16.

Jablonický, Jozef. *Z ilegality do povstania. Kapitoly z občianskeho odboja*. Banská Bystrica: Muzeum SNP, 2009 (2).

Jaksicsová, Vlasta. "Spor o Dubčeka". In *DUBČEK*. Bratislava: Veda, 2018.

Jirous, Ivan, Martin. *Magorovy labutí písně*. Praha: Rozmluvy, 1989.

Judt, Tony, with Timothy Snyder. *Thinking The Twentieth Century*. New York: Penguin, 2012.

Kabát, Jindřich. *Psychologie komunismu*. Praha: Práh, 2011.

Kalous, Jan, a Jiří Kocian, eds. *Český a slovenský komunismus (1921– 2011)*. Praha: Ústav pro studium totalitních režimů, 2012.

Kalous, Jan. "KSČ jako iniciátor a vykonavatel politických čistek a procesů". In *Český a slovenský komunismus (1921–2011)*. Praha: Ústav pro studium totalitních režimů, 2012.

Kamenec, Ivan. "Novohlasistická skupina a Robotnická academia na Slovensku v rokoch 1933–1937". In *Slovensko v labyrinte moderných europských dejín. Pocta historikov Milanovi Zemkovi*. Bratislava: HÚ SAV, 2014.

Kamenec, Ivan. *Tragédia politika, kňaza a človeka. Dr. Jozef Tiso, 1887– 1947*. Bratislava: Premedia, 2013.

Kaplan, Karel. *Protistátní Bezpečnost 1945–1948. Historie vzniku a působení StB jako mocenského nástroje KSČ*. Praha: Plus, 2015.

Kaplan, Karel. *Report on the Murder of the General Secretary*. Columbus: Ohio State University Press, 1990.

Kaplan, Karel. *The Short March. The Communist Takeover in Czechoslovakia 1945–1948*. London: Hurst & Co, 1987.

Kershaw, Ian. "Biography and the Historian". In *Biography between structure and agency. Central European lives in international historiography*. New York: Berghahn, 2008.

Kershaw, Ian. *Hitler*. London: Penguin, 2008.

Klíma, Ivan. *Judge on Trial*. London: Vintage, 2002.

Klíma, Ivan. *Soudce z milosti*. Praha: Rozmluvy, 1991.

Kmeť, Norbert. "Slovenská opozícia za normalizácie". In *Česká a slovenská společnost v období normalizace. Slovenská a česká spoločnosť v case normalizácie. Liberecký seminar 2001*. Bratislava: Veda a Ústav politických vied SAV, 2003.

Kokaisl, Petr, a Petr Usmanov. *Amirbek. Dějiny Kyrgyzstánu očima pamětníků. 1917–1938*. Praha: Nostalgie, 2012.

Kołakowski, Leszek. *Main Currents of Marxism. The Founders. The Golden Age. The Breakdown*. New York, London: Norton, 2005.

Konrád, György. "Is the Dream of Central Europe Still Alive?" *Cross Currents 5* (1986): 109–121.

Kořalka, Jiří. "Nationsbildung und nationale Identität der Deutschen, Österreicher, Tschechen und Slowaken um die Mitte des 19. Jahrhunderts". In *Ungleiche Nachbarn. Demokratische und nationale*

Emanzipation bei Deutschen, Tschechen und Slovaken (1815–1914). Essen: Klartext, 1993.

Kosta, Jiří. "Systemwandel in der Tschechoslowakei. Ökonomische und politische Aspekte". In *Osteuropa 41*, no. 9 (1990): 802–818.

Kováč, Dušan. *Dejiny Slovenska*. Praha: Lidové Noviny, 2007 (2).

Kováč, Dušan. *Slováci. Česi. Dejiny*. Bratislava: AEP, 1997.

Kováčiková, Terézia. "Ženy v národnooslobodzovacom zápase (1939–1945)". In *Zborník múzea Slovenského Národného povstania 7*. Martin, Múzeum SNP v Banskej Bystrici: Osveta, 1982.

Kozák, Jan, B. *T. G. Masaryk a vznik Washingtonské deklarace v říjnu 1918*. Praha: Melantrich, 1968.

Kriseová, Eda. *Václav Havel. Životopis*. Praha: Atlantis, 1991.

Kudrna, Ladislav, ed. *Reflexe Undergroundu*. Praha: Ústav pro stadium totalitních režimů, 2016.

Kundera, Milan. "The Tragedy of Central Europe". *The New York Review of Books 31*, no. 26 (1984): 33–39.

Laluha, Ivan. "Alexander Dubček. 1921–1992". In *Alexander Dubček: Od totality k demokracii. Prejavy, články a rozhovory. Výber 1963–1992*. Bratislava: Veda, 2002.

Laluha, Ivan. *O ceste k Slovenskej štátnosti v rokoch 1990–1992. Čriepky z poslaneckých lavíc*. Bratislava: Vydavateľstvo Pozsony-Pressburg-Bratislava – Peter Rašla, 2015.

Landovský, Pavel. *Soukromá vzpoura. Rozhovor s Karlem Hvižďalou*. Praha: Mlada Fronta, 1990.

Langer, Jo. *Convictions. My Life with a Good Communist*. London: Granta, 2011.

Langerová, Jo. *Môj život s Oscarom L*. Bratislava: Marenčin PT, 2007.

Lässig, Simone. "Introduction: Biography in Modern History – Modern Historiography in Biography". In *Biography between structure and agency. Central European lives in international historiography*. New York: Berghahn, 2008.

Lederer, Jiří. *České rozhovory*. Praha: Československý spisovatel, 1991.

Londák, Miroslav, Slavomír Michálek, Peter Weiss et al. *Slovakia. A European Story*. Bratislava: Veda, 2016.

Londák, Miroslav, Stanislav Sikora a Elena Londáková. *Od predjaria k normalizácii. Slovensko v Československu na rozhraní 60. a 70. rokov 20. Storočia*. Bratislava: Veda, 2016.

Londák, Miroslav, Stanislav Sikora a Elena Londáková. *Predjarie. Politický, ekonomický a kultúrny vývoj na Slovensku v rokoch 1960–1967.* Bratislava: VEDA, 2002.

Londák, Miroslav, Stanislav Sikora a kol. *Rok 1968 a jeho miesto v našich dejinách.* Bratislava: Veda, 2009.

Londák, Miroslav. "Príčiny peňažnej (menovej) reformy z jari 1953 v Československu so zreteľom na vojenské súvislosti". *Vojenská história 19*, no. 2 (2015): 73–82.

London, Artur. *On Trial.* London: Macdonald, 1970.

Lübbe, Hermann. *Politischer Moralismus. Der Triumph der Gesinnung über die Urteilskraft.* Berlin: WJS Corso, 1987 (2).

Macho, Peter. *Milan Rastislav Štefánik. V hlavach a v srdciach.* Bratislava: HÚ SAV a Prodama, 2011.

Marušiak, Juraj. "Bratislavská päťka. Prejav agónie komunistického režimu". In *Storočie procesov. Súdy, politika a spoločnosť v moderných dejinách Slovenska.* Bratislava: Veda, 2013.

Marušiak, Juraj. "Slovenská spoločnosť a normalizácia". In *Česká a slovenská společnost v období normalizace. Slovenská a česká spoločnosť v case normalizácie. Liberecký seminar 2001.* Bratislava: Veda a Ústav politických vied SAV, 2003.

Marzík, Tomas, D. "The Slovakophile Relationship of T. G. Masaryk and Karel Kálal prior to 1914". In *T. G. Masaryk (1850–1937). Thinker and Politician.* Basingstoke: MacMillan, SSEES, University of London, 1989.

Masaryk a myšlenka evropské jednoty. Praha: Filosofická Fakulta Univerzity Karlovy FFUK, 1992.

Masaryk, Tomáš Garrigue. "Slavjanofilství. Mesianismus pravoslavné teokracie. Slavjanofilství a Panslavismus". In *Rusko a Evropa. Studie o důchovních proudech v Rusku, vol. I.* Praha: Ústav T. G. Masaryka, 1995.

Masaryk, Tomáš, G. "Proststředky národa malého". In *Ideály humanitní.* Praha: Melantrich, 1991.

Měchýř, Jan. "O lidech v čase normalizace". In *Česká a slovenská společnost v období normalizace. Slovenská a česká spoločnosť v case normalizácie. Liberecký seminar 2001.* Bratislava: Veda a Ústav politických vied SAV, 2003.

Michálek, Slavomír, and Peter Weiss. "The Foreign Policy Context of the Break-Up of Czechoslovakia from 1989 to 1992 and the

Relations of Prague and Bratislava with Washington". In *Slovakia. A European Story*. Bratislava: Veda, 2016.

Michálek, Slavomír, Miroslav Londák a kol. *Gustáv Husák. Moc politiky. Politik moci.* Bratislava: Veda, 2013.

Michálova, Tereza, ed. *Dubček známy neznámy*. Bratislava: Prospero, 1989 (2).

Miłosz, Czesław. "Central European Attitudes". *Cross Currents* 5 (1986): 101–108.

Mlynář, Zdeněk. *Mraz přichází z Kremlu*. Köln: Index, 1979.

Neudorflová, Marie, L. "Karel Havlíček, T. G. Masaryk a demokracie". In *Spisovatelé, společnost a noviny v promínách doby*. Praha: Literární Archiv Národného Písemnictví, 2006.

Neudorflová, Marie, L., ed. *Charlotta G. Masaryková. Sborník příspěvků z konference ke 150. výročí jejího narození, konané 10. listopadu 2000*. Praha: Masarykův ústav Akademie věd ČR, 2001.

Novák, Jozef, ed. *On Masaryk. Texts in English and German*. Amsterdam: Rodopi, 1988.

Opat, Jaroslav. *Filozof a politik T. G. Masaryk, 1882–1893*. Praha: Melantrich, 1990.

Ouimet, Matthew, J. *The Rise and Fall of the Brezhnev Doctrine in Soviet Foreign Policy*. Chapel Hill, NC, London: The University of North Carolina Press, 2003.

Pacepa, Ion. *Red Horizons. The True Story of Nicolae and Elena Ceauşescus' Crimes, Lifestyle and Corruption*. Lanham, MD: Abebooks, 1990.

Pauer, Jan. *Prag 1968. Der Einmarsch des Warschauer Paktes. Hintergründe – Planung – Durchführung*. Bremen: Edition Temmen, 1995.

Pažout, Jaroslav. "Trestněprávní perzekuce odpůrců režimu v období tzv. Normalizace (1969–1989) – factor stability a indikátor rozkladu komunistického režimu". In *Český a slovenský komunismus (1921–2011)*. Praha: Ústav pro stadium totalitních režimů, 2012.

Pekník, Miroslav, ed. *Slovenské národné povstanie 1944. Súčať europskej antifašistickej rezistencie v rokoch druhej svetovej vojny*. Bratislava: Veda, 2009.

Pelikán, Jiří. *Tanky proti sjezdu. Protokoly a dokumenty XIV. (vysočanského) sjezdu KSČ*. Praha: Novela bohemica, 2018.

Peroutka, Ferdinand. "O účasti na revoluci" (1924). In *Kdo nás osvobodil?*. Praha: Náklad Svazu národního osvobození, Tisk 'Pokrok', 1927.

Pešek, Jan. "Cvikiáda. Rudolf Cvik v konflikte Antonína Novotného a Alexandra Dubčeka." In *Storočie škandálov. Aféry v moderných dejinách Slovenska*. Bratislava: Spoločnosť Pro Historia, HÚ SAV, 2008.

Pešek, Jan. "Komunistická Strana Slovenska: Od Prevratu 1948 do Pokusu o Reformu 1968 (KSČ a KSS, Členstvo, Organizácia, Stranícky Aparát, Vedenie Strany)". In *Štátna Moc a Spoločnosť na Slovensku 1945 – 1948 – 1989*. Bratislava: HÚ SAV, Prodama, 2013.

Pešek, Jan. "Najbrutálnejšie obdobie komunistického režimu (1948– 1953)". In *Štátna moc a spoločnosť na Slovensku 1945 – 1948 – 1989*. Bratislava: HÚ SAV a Prodama, 2013.

Pešek, Jan. "Nepriateľ so stráníckou legitimáciou. Proces s tzv. Slovenskými buržoáznymi nacionalistami". In *Storočie procesov. Súdy, politika a spoločnosť v moderných dejinách Slovenska*. Bratislava: Veda, 2013.

Pešek, Jan. *Centrum Moci. Aparát Ústredného výboru Komunistickej strany Slovenska 1948–1989*. Bratislava: AEP, 2006.

Pešek, Jan. *Komunistická Strana Slovenska. Dejiny politického subjektu I*. Bratislava: Veda, 2012.

Petruf, Pavol. "Vojenská intervencia krajín Varšavskej zmluvy v Československu v auguste 1968 na stránkach publikovaných francúzskych diplomatických dokumentov". In *Slovensko a Európa medzi Demokraciou a Totalitou. Kapitoly z dejín 20. Storočia k jubileu Bohumily Ferenčuhovej*. Bratislava: Veda, 2017.

Petruf, Pavol. *Československá zahraničná politika 1945–1992 (vybrané udalosti a fakty v dátumoch)*. Bratislava: Prodama, HÚ SAV, 2007.

Pollák, Pavel. "Die Auswanderung in die Sowietunion in den zwanziger Jahren". *Bohemia 10* (1969): 287–311.

Prečan, Vilém. "Gustáv Husák: iluze a skutečnost". In *Gustáv Husák. Moc politiky. Politik moci*. Bratislava: Veda, 2013.

Pynsent, Robert B., ed. *T. G. Masaryk (1850–1937). Thinker and Critic*. Basingstoke: MacMillan, SSEES, University of London, 1989, 1990.

Radzinsky, Edvard. *Stalin*. New York, Toronto: Anchor books, 1996.

Reinfeld, Barbara, K. *Karel Havlíček (1821–1856). A National Liberation Leader of the Czech Renascence*. New York, NY, Boulder, CO: Columbia University Press, 1982.

Reissner, Larissa. *Oktober. Ausgewählte Schriften.* Berlin: Universum-Bücherei für alle, 1932.

Roguľová, Jaroslava, ed. *Pramene k dejinám Slovenska a Slovákov, XIIIC: Slováci a nástup socialism.* Bratislava: Literární informačné centrum, 2017.

Roguľová, Jaroslava, ed. *Slováci a ľudovodemokratický režim.* Bratislava: Literárne informačné centrum, 2016.

Roháčková, Naďa. "Chvíľka s Pavlínou Dubčekovou",. *Slovenka 21* no. 21 (1968): 8.

Rupnik, Jacques. "Central Europe or Mitteleuropa?" *Daedalus 119*, no. 1 (1990): 249–278.

Rychlík, Jan. "Normalizačná podoba česko-slovenské federace". In *Česká a slovenská společnost v období normalizace. Slovenská a česká spoločnosť v case normalizácie. Liberecký seminar 2001.* Bratislava: Veda a Ústav politických vied SAV, 2003.

Rychlík, Jan. *Češi a Slováci ve 20. století. Česko-slovenské vztahy 1914–1945.* Bratislava, Praha: AEP, Ústav T. G. Masaryka, 1997.

Rychlík, Jan. *Češi a Slováci ve 20. století. Česko-slovenské vztahy 1945–1992.* Bratislava, Praga: AEP, ÚTGM, 1998.

Rychlík, Jan. *Devisové přisliby a cestování do zahraničí v období normalizace.* Praha: Ústav pro soudobé dějiny AV ČR, 2012.

Rychlík, Jan. *Rozdělení Česko-Slovenska, 1989–1992.* Praha: Vyšehrad, 2012.

Scholten, Jaap. *Comrade Baron. A journey through the vanishing world of the Transylvanian aristocracy.* Reno, NV: Helena History Press, 2016.

Sedm pražských dnů. 21–27. srpen 1968. Dokumentace. Praha: Academia, 1990.

Shawcross, William. *Dubcek. Revised and Updated Edition.* New York: Touchstone, 1990.

Sikora, Stanislav. "KSS a čiastočná liberalizácia režimu na Slovensku počas predjaria (1963–1967)". In *Český a slovenský komunismus (1921–2011).* Praha: Ústav pro stadium totalitních režimů, 2012.

Sikora, Stanislav. "Slovensko v predjarí – na ceste k roku 1968". In *Od predjaria k normalizácii. Slovensko v Československu na rozhrani 60. a 70. rokov 20. Storočia.* Bratislava: VEDA, 2016.

Sikora, Stanislav. *Po Jari krutá zima.* Bratislava: Veda, 2013.

Skilling, Gordon, H. *Czechoslovakia's Interrupted Revolution*. Princeton, NJ: Princeton University Press, 1976.

Skilling, Gordon, H. "The Czechoslovak Constitution of 1960 and the Transition to Communism". In *The Journal of Politics 24*, no. 1 (1962): 142–166.

Slovenská Republika 1939–1945. Bratislava: Veda, 2015.

Šolc, Jaroslav. "Smrť sa tentoraz volá Edelweiß". In *Protifašistický bojovník*, no. 1, January (1963).

Štefánek, Anton. *Masaryk a Slovensko*. Praha: Náklad spisovatelový, 1931.

Štefanský, Michal. "Moskovský protokol a rokovania o rozmiestnení sovietskych vojsk". In *Rok 1968 a jeho miesto v našich dejinách*. Bratislava: Veda, 2009.

Strategic Warning & the Role of Intelligence. Lessons learnt from the 1968 Soviet Invasion of Czechoslovakia. CreateSpace Independent Publishing Platform, 2012.

Sudoplatov, Anatolii. *Special Tasks. The Memoirs of an Unwanted Witness – A Soviet Spymaster*. London Little, Brown and Company, 1994.

Šufliarsky, Jozef. *Akcia Edelweiß*. Bratislava, 1963.

Suk, Jiří, Michal Kopeček, Kristina Andělová, Tomáš Vilímek, Tomáš Hermann a Tomáš Zahradníček. *Šest kapitol o disentu*. Praha: Ústav pro soudobé dějiny, 2017.

Šváčová, Soňa, Michela Garaiová, Anna Klimová a Blanka Snopková. *Alexander Dubček v slovenskej a českej tlači*. Banská Bystrica: Štátna vedecká knižnica, 2007.

Taubman, William. *Gorbachev. His Life and Times*. London: Simon & Schuster, 2017.

Taubman, William. *Khrushchev. The Man and His Era*. New York, London: Norton & Co., 2004.

Teich, Mikuláš, Dušan Kováč, and Martin D. Brown, eds. *Slovakia in History*. Cambridge: Cambridge University Press, 2011.

Tigrid, Pavel. *Why Dubcek Fell*. London: Macdonald, 1971.

Truhlar, Dalibor. *Thomas G. Masaryk. Philosophie der Demokratie*. Frankfurt a. Main: Peter Lang, 1994.

Urban, Karol. *Sledoval som Dubčeka. Spomienky eštebáka*. Bratislava: Trio, 2012.

Urban, Zdeněk. "K Masarykovu vztahu ke Slovensku před první světovou válkou". In *Masaryk a Slovensko (soubor statí)*. Praha: Masarykova společnost a Ústav T. G. Masaryka, 1992.

Vaksberg, Arkadi. *Stalin's Prosecutor. The Life of Andrei Vyshinsky*. New York: Grove Weidenfeld, 1990.

Veber, Václav. "O rehabilitacích a o tom, co s nimi souvisí". *Securitas Imperii 16*, no. 1 (2010): 10–29.

Viest, Rudolf, M. *General Viest's notebooks. Call to arms came in 1938*. Brainigsville, PA: JMV, 2009.

Vodička, Karel. "Wie der Koalitionsbeschluss zur Auflösung der ČSFR zustande kam". *Osteuropa 45*, no. 2 (1994): 175–186.

Williams, Kieran. *The Prague Spring and its Aftermath. Czechoslovak Politics, 1968–1970*. Cambridge, New York: Cambridge University Press, 1997.

Winters, Stanley B., ed., *T. G. Masaryk (1850–1937). Thinker and Politician*. Basingstoke: MacMillan, SSEES, University of London, 1989.

Žatkuliak, Jozef, a Ivan Laluha, eds. *Alexander Dubček: Od totality k demokracii. Prejavy, články a rozhovory. Výber 1963–1992*. Bratislava: Veda, 2002.

Žatkuliak, Jozef, and Peter Weiss. "The Slovak National Council's Role in the Constitutional Development from 1990 to 1992 and the Trouble Slovakia Encountered on Its Way towards Sovereignty". In *Slovakia. A European Story*. Bratislava: Veda, 2016.

Zemko, Milan. "Prúdisti v čase, ktorý trhol oponou". In *Kapitoly z histórie stredoeurópskeho priestoru v 19. a 20. Storočí. Pocta k 70-ročnému jubileu Dušana Kováča*. Bratislava: HÚ SAV, 2012.

On-line sources

A bear-resistant container. On http://slovakwildlife.org/en/news.

Alibism. On https://slovnik-cizich-slov.abz.cz/web.php/slovo/alibizmus-alibismus.

Banáš, Jozef. "Prečo sa Dubček nie dostal na hrad." https://www.youtube.com/watch?v=zX4_NgELub8;

Buccaneer. On https://en.oxforddictionaries.com/definition/buccaneer.

Catch-22. On https://www.phrases.org.uk/meanings/catch-22.html.

Černý, Václav. On http://www.slovnikceskeliteratury.cz/showContent.jsp?docId=357.

Cervantes' Don Quixote de la Mancha. On http://cervantes.tamu.edu /cervantes/biography/new_english_cerv_bio.html.

Cold War International History Project at the Woodrow Wilson Center. On https://www.wilsoncenter.org/program/cold-war-international-history-project.

ČT 1 documentary about INTERHELPO. On http://www.ceskatelevize.cz/porady/10123387223-interhelpo-historie-jedne-iluze/

Death of Alexander Dubček. On https://www.washingtonpost.com/archive/local/1992/11/08/czech-leader-alexander-dubcek-dies/6d214b3a-0224-4de1-b025-171d9d4fbc83/?utm_term=.8b0539ebebdc

Definition of utopia. On https://www.etymonline.com/word/utopia.

Dubček's speech on 27 August 1968. On https://www.youtube.com/watch?v=9E0F209PBts.

Goethe in Karlsbad. On https://www.karlovyvary.cz/en/bust-johann-wolfgang-von-goethe.

Golian, Jan. On http://www.muzeumsnp.sk/historia/osobnosti/general-jan-golian/.

Grand Hotel Pupp. On http://www.pupp.cz/en/section/15-history.html.

Helsinki Final Act. On https://history.state.gov/milestones/1969-1976/helsinki.

History of the PCI. On https://www.marxist.com/the-dissolution-of-the-italian-communist-party-1991.htm.

Hohenlohe hunting castle. On http://slovakia.travel/en/hunting-chateau-hohenlohe-is-now-open-to-the-public.

Idiot. Definition on https://en.oxforddictionaries.com/definition/idiot.

IMF Annual Report of 1954. On http://www.imf.org/external/pubs/ft/ar/archive/pdf/ar1954.pdf.

Kharms, Daniil. *The Dream.* On http://absurdist.obook.org/kharms/display.php?p=26.

Kovalev's Brežnev doctrine of limited sovereignty. On http://soviethistory.msu.edu/1968-2/crisis-in-czechoslovakia/crisis-in-czechoslovakia-texts/brezhnev-doctrine.

Let us sow! (Nech šije!) on https://www.sng.sk/sk/vystavy/1046_nech-sije-moda-na-slovensku-1945-1989.

Lidice. On http://www.lidice-memorial.cz/en/; http://www.holocaustresearchproject.org/nazioccupation/lidice.html.

Lukes, Igor. *Rudolf Slansky. His Trial and Trials. Cold War International History Project Working Paper no. 50* (Washington, D.C.: Woodrow Wilson Center, 2008), on http://www.wilsoncenter.org/sites/default/files/WP50IL.pdf.Slánský.

Mandel, Ernest. On https://www.ernestmandel.org/en.

Mao suit. On http://www.sacu.org/dresspolitics.html.

Mao Tse-tung on Chruščev's revisionism. On https://www.marxists.org/reference/archive/mao/works/1964/phnycom.htm.

Masaryk Institute and Archive. On http:// https://www.mua.cas.cz.

Nižňanský, Ladislav. On http://www.spiegel.de/spiegel/print/d-32060815.html.

Obchod na Korze. On http://www.imdb.com/title/tt0059527/.

Operation Anthropoid. On http://www.ww2inprague.com/operatin-anthropoid.

Palach, Jan. On http://www.radio.cz/en/section/archives/the-last-days-of-jan-palach-1.

Petition *Několík vět.* On http://www.totalita.cz/vysvetlivky/nvet.php.

Plastic People of the Universe. On https://www.rollingstone.com/music/news/how-a-revolutionary-czech-rock-band-inspired-vaclav-havel-20111219.

Radio Erewan jokes. On http://www.armeniapedia.org/index.php?title=Radio_Yerevan_Jokes.

Requiem by Anna Akhmatova. On http://www.ronnowpoetry.com/contents/akhmatova/Requiem.html.

Requiem read by Anna Akhmatova. On https://www.youtube.com/watch?v=P--7yKgBfro.

Richta, Radovan a kol. *Civilizace na rozcestí.* On http://www.sds.cz/docs/prectete/eknihy/rri_cnr.htm.

Russian bear. On http://russia-ic.com/culture_art/traditions/1074#.Wr9N9mW_1PM.

Schneider, Miroslav. *Die tschechoslowakische Auswanderung in die Sowjetunion in der Zwischenkriegszeit (1921–1939).* Inaugural-Dissertation zur Erlangung der Doktorwürde der Philosophischen Fakultät III (Geschichte, Gesellschaft und Geographie) der Universität Regensburg. Regensburg 2007. On http://epub.uni-regensburg.de/10791/1/Elektronische_Publikation_2008_pt11.pdf

Seifert, Jaroslav, Nobel Laureate. On https://www.nobelprize.org/nobel_prizes/literature/laureates/1984/seifert-poetry.html.

Seifert, Jaroslav. On https://www.nobelprize.org/nobel_prizes/literature/laureates/1984/seifert-bio.html.

Šeina, Jan. On https://www.nytimes.com/1997/08/30/world/jan-sejna-70-ex-czech-general-and-defector.html

Sub-Carpathian Ruthenia. On http://www.carpatho-rusyn.org/fame/pod.htm.

Suslov, Michail. On https://www.britannica.com/biography/Mikhail-Andreyevich-Suslov.

Stalin cult. On http://press-files.anu.edu.au/downloads/press/n2129/pdf/ch01.pdf.

Svoboda, Ludvík. On https://www.hrad.cz/en/president-of-the-cr/former-presidents/ludvik-svoboda.

SS group Edelweiss. On https://plus7dni.pluska.sk/Domov/SNP-Mali-Edelweiss-zastavit-partizani-Takto-vycinali-Niznanskeho-zlocinci; https://www.vtedy.sk/prislusnikov-oddielov-edelweiss-postavili-pred-ceskoslovensky-sud.

Swiss referendum for a granted minimal income. On https://www.admin.ch/opc/de/federal-gazette/2015/9553.pdf.

Tereshkova, Valentina. On https://www.rt.com/news/379550-tereshkova-facts-80-anniversary/; https://www.theguardian.com/global-development-professionals-network/2017/mar/29/valentina-tereshkova-first-woman-in-space-people-waste-money-on-wars.

Tatra National Park. On http://www.tanap.org/english/.

Uj Szó. On https://ujszo.com.

Velvet Revolution. On https://www.bbc.com/news/world-europe-30059011.

Vienna Convention. On https://treaties.un.org/doc/publication/unts/volume%201155/volume-1155-i-18232-english.pdf.

Viest, Rudolf. On http://www.muzeumsnp.sk/historia/osobnosti/general-rudolf-viest/.

Yezhov, Nikolai. On https://www.britannica.com/biography/Nikolay-Ivanovich-Yezhov.

Index

1
1960 constitution 101

A
Adamec, Ladislav 206
Agrarians 30, 37
Akhmatova, Anna 49
alibism 178
appeasement 28
Ausgleich 27, 33
autonomy 3, 22, 28, 29, 30, 31, 44, 235, 239

B
Bacílek, Karol 86, 87, 245
Banská Bystrica XIII, 6, 63, 66, 111, 112, 238
Barnabite Commission 61, 81, 83, 99, 104, 211, 247
Bartolomejšská 4 174
Bašťovanský, Štefan 46, 61
Bělohradský, Václav 175
Beneš, Edvard 9, 18, 23, 24, 29, 31, 32, 33, 34, 36, 41, 45, 53, 61, 81, 115, 235, 238, 239, 240, 242, 243
Bologna University 191, 199
Brandt, Willy 191, 209, 221
Brezhnev doctrine of limited sovereignty 161
Brezhnev, Leonid I. 3, 4, 105, 120, 146, 147, 148, 149, 150, 160, 161, 163, 169, 170, 197, 205, 213, 248, 249

C
Canadian NHL 230
Čarnogurský, Jan 188
catch-22 163, 212
Ceaușescu, Nicolae 13, 106
Černík, Oldřich 169
Černý, František 82, 173, 174, 175, 177, 178
Černý, Václav 82, 173, 174, 175, 177, 178
Cervantes 96, 97
Československá jednota 25
Charter 77 172, 175, 176, 189, 190, 191, 192, 198, 203, 214
Christmas Agreement 31, 238
Chudík, Michal 86, 87, 92, 111, 128
Čierna nad Tisou 149
civic resistance 190
Clementis, Vladimír 7, 44, 61, 70, 72, 212, 243, 244, 247
clerical Fascism 59, 117
Cold War XVII, 7, 10, 17, 160, 187, 226
Cold War International History Project 7, 17
COMECON XIII, 12, 149, 243
Constitutional status 47, 215
contextual biography 15
Control and Revision Commission XIV, 113, 116, 117, 122, 123
counter-revolution 147, 149, 151, 160, 161, 172, 178, 193, 195, 200
CSCE Act of Helsinki 190
ČSSR 14, 88, 108, 109, 157, 161, 190, 197, 199
Cvik, Rudolf 110, 111, 112
Czechoslovak state-building theory 18
Czechoslovak union of writers 82, 138
Czechoslovak virus 222

Czechoslovakism 14, 17, 18, 22, 23, 25, 26, 27, 32, 231

D

David, Pavol 86, 87, 92, 242
de Montaigne, Michel 138
Democratic Party XIV, XV, 3, 39, 232, 251
Devín 94
dilettantism 225
Dimitrov, Georgi 39, 165
Dior, Christian 78
dissident XVII, 11, 14, 178, 181, 198, 214
divide et impera 176
Dubček's reform programme (*akční program*) XVII
Dukla 227, 230

E

economic survival 186
Eisenhower, Dwight D. 70
Eser 200
EU 11, 75
EXPO 78
extraordinary 14th Party Congress 160

F

Federal Assembly XIV, 10, 170, 204, 205, 206, 208, 209, 217, 232, 250, 251
federation 29, 33, 37, 39, 165, 167, 168, 169, 207, 209, 217, 246
First democratization, then federation 169

G

Gandhi, Mahatma 221
Garrigue, Charlotte 21
German minority 20
Golian, Ján 65

Gorbachev, Mikhail S. 4, 16, 71, 147, 194, 199, 214
Gottwald, Klement 41, 45, 46, 67, 76, 106, 233, 235, 239, 240, 241, 244, 245
government trustees 33, 38, 40, 242
guided democracy 34

H

Habsburg monarchy 17, 19, 26
Hájek, Jiří 138, 188, 194, 197, 202
Havel, Václav 9, 11, 70, 80, 142, 167, 176, 177, 191, 198, 203, 205, 214, 215, 216, 217, 248, 251
historic rights 20
Hlasists 19, 25
Hlavsa, Milan 190, 191
Hlinka, Andrej XIV, 28, 235
Holdoš, Ladislav 72, 105, 245, 247
Horvath, Ivan 72
HSĽS XIV, 29, 30, 37, 114, 117, 235
Hungarian minority 20, 107
Husák, Gustáv XI, XVII, 7, 8, 14, 44, 61, 70, 72, 73, 83, 87, 103, 105, 106, 117, 135, 157, 159, 164, 165, 167, 170, 171, 187, 190, 198, 199, 211, 212, 214, 217, 242, 245, 247, 248, 251

I

idiot 132
INTERHELPO 52, 53, 54, 56, 57, 64, 118, 234
International Monetary Fund XIV, 76
invasion XVII, 4, 8, 12, 13, 112, 116, 141, 147, 150, 151, 159, 160, 161, 162, 163, 164, 165, 167, 169, 170, 172, 173, 189, 194, 197, 216, 220

J

Jakeš, Miloš 68, 251
Javorina 125, 126, 127, 128
Jirous, Ivan Martin 190, 191

K

K 231 83
Kádár, Janós 13, 149, 151
Katalyzátor 1 202
Kennedy, John F. 104, 246
KGB 122, 147, 148, 187, 248
Kharms, Daniil I. 57
Kim Il-sung 106
kin liability 193
Kolder Commission 61, 81, 99, 114, 135, 211, 247
Košice Agreement 33, 36, 41, 239
Kriegel, František 164
Kroner, Jozef 110
Krushchev, Nikita S. 2, 71
KSČ XI, XIII, XIV, XVI, XVII, XIX, 1, 2, 3, 6, 7, 30, 36, 37, 40, 41, 42, 43, 44, 45, 46, 47, 53, 65, 70, 72, 73, 75, 77, 78, 80, 81, 82, 83, 84, 85, 86, 87, 88, 89, 90, 91, 93, 94, 95, 97, 98, 99, 100, 101, 103, 104, 105, 106, 107, 108, 109, 110, 111, 112, 113, 115, 117, 118, 121, 122, 123, 124, 137, 138, 139, 140, 143, 144, 145, 146, 147, 148, 149, 150, 159, 160, 162, 164, 165, 166, 167, 168, 169, 171, 180, 186, 192, 193, 195, 197, 206, 212, 215, 216, 229, 232, 233, 235, 239, 240, 242, 245, 246, 247, 249, 250
KSS XI, XIII, XIV, XVI, XVII, XIX, 2, 3, 4, 5, 6, 7, 11, 33, 37, 39, 43, 44, 45, 46, 47, 61, 63, 64, 67, 71, 72, 74, 75, 85, 86, 87, 88, 92, 93, 94, 95, 99, 100, 102, 103, 104, 105, 107, 108, 109, 110, 111, 112, 113, 114, 116, 117, 118, 121, 122, 123, 124, 125, 126, 128, 129, 130, 131, 133, 134, 136, 138, 142, 144, 145, 146, 150, 164, 165, 168, 169, 192, 206, 211, 212, 213, 215, 222, 231, 232, 236, 239, 240, 242, 244, 245, 246, 247, 248, 249
Kundera, Milan 167
Kusý, Miroslav 188, 214

L

Laluha, Ivan XIX, 6, 64, 69, 129, 204, 205, 222, 226
Landovský, Pavel 191
Langer, Jo 7
legia 23, 66
Lenárt, Jozef 68, 81, 138
Limited democracy 36

M

Magyarization 25, 51, 104
Manifesto of 2000 Words 148
Mao Tse-tung 104
Marvanová, Anna 203
Marxism-Leninism XVIII, 1, 14, 16, 45, 51, 61, 67, 69, 70, 160, 213, 231
Masaryk, Tomáš Garrigue 8, 18, 19, 20, 21, 22, 23, 24, 25, 28, 41, 53, 80, 235, 241, 242, 243
Matica Slovenská 142, 143, 145
Mauthausen 64, 65, 213, 238
medicine 94, 95, 131, 193, 219
micro-traumas 186
Mlynář, Zdeněk 3, 4, 71, 164, 202, 211
Moscow Protocol 159, 161, 162, 163, 164, 168, 212, 213
Munich Agreement 2, 28, 44

N

NATO XV, 11, 12, 216, 243
natural law 18, 20

Několík vět (*A Few Sentences*)
197
neo-Stalinist 151, 169, 213
NF XV, 9, 14, 32, 34, 37, 40, 41,
146, 231, 239
Normalization regime XI, XVII,
159, 179, 192, 205
Novomeský, Laco 61, 72, 73, 211,
245, 246, 247
Novotný, Antonín 4
nuclear disarmament 199

O

obroda 224
odsun 34, 240
OF XV, 1, 173, 204, 205, 208
Okali, Daniel 72, 245
Osoha, Jan 54, 64

P

Palme, Olof 221
parallel polis 175
Patočka, Jan 175, 176, 199
perestroika and *glasnost'* 194
personality cult 61, 84, 86, 96,
98, 105, 106, 107, 135, 245
Pittsburgh Agreement 19, 22, 23,
28
Plastic People of the Universe 190
Plato 176
playmaker 229
political nation 24
politruk 228
Ponická, Hana 188, 214
post-Communist states 205
Professor Kočtuch 223
protectorate of Bohemia and
Moravia 29

R

Radio Erewan jokes 187
Reagan, Ronald 199
Red Army 31, 34, 65, 125, 238,
239

responsibility 33, 83, 95, 100,
120, 175, 176, 177, 178, 221,
225
Revolver Revue 190
Richta, Radovan 3, 79
rovný s rovným 31, 32, 42
Ruda Hvězda 227
Russian political power 124

S

Sakharov, Andreii D. 6
Šalgovič, Viliam 116, 117, 121
samizdat 172, 190, 195, 247
secret speech 2, 10, 69, 71
Seifert, Jaroslav 82
Šejna, Jan 148
Šimečka, Milan 188, 214
Slánský, Rudolf 7, 8, 42, 46, 61,
233, 235, 239, 244
Slovak National Council XV, 10,
22, 31, 128, 143
Slovak Pre-Spring (*predjarie*)
XIX, 63
SNP XV, 11, 31, 32, 37, 40, 63, 64,
65, 66, 68, 72, 103, 112, 113,
114, 115, 116, 119, 121, 124,
125, 134, 192, 232, 238
Social Democratic Party of
Slovakia XV, 205, 208, 217
Socialism with a Human Face XII,
3, 14, 161
socialization 184, 213
Soviet Kyrgyzia 2, 51, 52, 54, 234
Sovietization 41, 67, 78, 84, 107
Spanish Civil War 72, 164
Sparta Prague 227
Sportproprag 230
Šrobár, Vavro 22, 23, 24, 26, 115,
119, 233
StB XI, XV, XVII, 6, 40, 113, 114,
117, 118, 120, 121, 122, 124,
129, 132, 133, 146, 148, 159,
174, 177, 182, 186, 189, 192,
193, 194, 195, 196, 199, 200,
201, 202, 203, 204, 220, 232,
250

Štefánik, Milan Rastislav 18, 23
Štěpán, Miroslav 192, 197
Štoll, Ladislav 82
Štúr, Ľudovít 18, 52, 94, 233
Subcarpathian Ruthenia 37
Suvorov, Alexander Vasilievič 119

T

TANAP 124, 126, 127, 129, 130
Tereshkova, Valentina V. 88, 89, 90, 91, 92, 93, 247
The Big Theft 76
The Czech Fate (Český úděl) debate 167
the trial of the Bratislava Five 198
third way 225
Three Prague Agreements 30, 34
Tiso, Jozef 29, 32, 44, 59, 64, 65, 68, 115, 236, 238
Tito 69, 70, 106, 221
Titoism 46, 244
Trančík, Alexander 52, 240
transition 14, 67, 74, 100, 206, 207, 209
trauma 71, 131, 151, 225
Trianon 21, 24
truncheon law 170
Turkey XVII, 170, 203, 232, 250

U

Uhl, Petr 203, 214
Uhrovec XVIII, 51, 52, 233
Ukraine 71, 170
Ulbricht, Walter 106, 149

underground 60, 188, 189, 190, 191, 236
utopia 74

V

Velvet Divorce XIX, 10, 42, 204, 217
Velvet Revolution XIX, 1, 11, 106, 159, 173, 189, 204
victorious 25 February 1948 9, 31
Vienna Arbitration 29
Viest, Rudolf M. 63, 65
Visegrad Four 75
VPN XVI, 1, 204, 205, 206, 208, 224, 232
Vyshinsky, Andrei Y. 57

W

Warsaw Pact XI, XVII, 4, 8, 10, 12, 13, 105, 141, 149, 151, 159, 162, 195, 197, 245, 249
Weathermen 189
Werich, Jan 138
Wilson, Woodrow 7, 17

Y

Yezhov, Nikolai I. 49, 54, 55, 56, 57
Yugoslavia 13, 70, 104, 106, 179, 221, 242, 244

Z

Žilina Agreement 29, 30, 32
Zionism 46, 244